Recent explanations of changes in early modern European thought speak much of a move from orality and emphasis on language to print culture and a 'spatial' way of thinking. Timothy J. Reiss offers a more complex explanation for the massive changes that occurred. He describes how by the late fifteenth century the language arts of the trivium had come to seem useful only for communication, teaching and public debate, and how humanists turned to the mathematical arts of the quadrium – including music – to enable new means and methods of discovery. Reiss goes on to argue that the new 'mathematical' ideal formed the basis of wide sociocultural renewal; he analyzes Northern vernacular grammars, examines the work of French and Italian mathematicians, musicians and philosophers including Descartes, and censures such modern commonplaces as the supposed impact of print and 'spatial' thinking. He ends by exploring the broad impact of this 'mathematization' of the Western imagination.

Cambridge Studies in Renaissance Literature and Culture 15

Knowledge, discovery and imagination in early modern Europe

Cambridge Studies in Renaissance Literature and Culture 15

General editor
STEPHEN ORGEL
Jackson Eli Reynolds Professor of Humanities, Stanford University
Editorial board
Anne Barton, *University of Cambridge*
Jonathan Dollimore, *University of Sussex*
Marjorie Garber, *Harvard University*
Jonathan Goldberg, *Duke University*
Nancy Vickers, *University of Southern California*

The last twenty years have seen a broad and vital reinterpretation of the nature of literary texts, a move away from formalism to a sense of literature as an aspect of social, economic, political and cultural history. While the earliest New Historicist work was criticized for a narrow and anecdotal view of history, it also served as an important stimulus for post-structuralist, feminist, Marxist and psychoanalytical work, which in turn has increasingly informed and redirected it. Recent writing on the nature of representation, the historical construction of gender and the concept of identity itself, on theatre as a political and economic phenomenon and on the ideologies of art generally, reveals the breadth of the field. Cambridge Studies in Renaissance Literature and Culture is designed to offer historically oriented studies of Renaissance literature and theatre which make use of the insights afforded by theoretical perspectives. The view of history envisioned is above all a view of our own history, a reading of the Renaissance for and from our own time.

Recent titles include

Anxious masculinity in early modern England
MARK BREITENBERG

Seizures of the will in early modern English drama
FRANK WHIGHAM, University of Texas at Austin

The emergence of the English author: scripting the life of the poet in early modern England
KEVIN PASK, Concordia University

The poetics of English nationhood, 1590–1612
CLAIRE McEACHERN, University of California, Los Angeles

Textual intercourse: collaboration, authorship, and sexualities in Renaissance drama
JEFFREY MASTEN, Harvard University

A complete list of books in the series is given at the end of the volume.

Knowledge, discovery and imagination in early modern Europe

The rise of aesthetic rationalism

Timothy J. Reiss
New York University

CAMBRIDGE
UNIVERSITY PRESS

Published by the Press Syndicate of the University of Cambridge
The Pitt Building, Trumpington Street, Cambridge CB2 1RP
40 West 20th Street, New York, NY 10011–4211, USA
10 Stamford Road, Oakleigh, Melbourne 3166 Australia

© Timothy J. Reiss 1997

First published 1997

Printed in Great Britain at the University Press, Cambridge

A catalogue record for this book is available from the British Library

Library of Congress cataloguing in publication data
Reiss, Timothy J., 1942–
Knowledge, discovery, and imagination in early modern Europe:
the rise of aesthetic rationalism / Timothy J. Reiss.
    p.   cm. – (Cambridge studies in Renaissance literature and culture; 15)
Includes bibliographical references and index.
ISBN 0 521 58221 0 (hardback) – ISBN 0 521 58795 6 (paperback)
1. Language and culture – Europe – History – 16th century.
2. Europe – Intellectual life.   3. Renaissance.   I. Title.   II. Series
P35.5.E85R45   1997
940.2'32–dc20   96–24764   CIP

ISBN 0 521 58221 0 hardback
ISBN 0 521 58795 6 paperback

FE

For Matthew, Suzanna and Justin

Contents

Contents

Prologue and acknowledgements

The matter of this volume, which attempts to give part of an explanation for the vehemence of debates about 'method', the deep change in nature of the attention paid to language, and the concomitant rise in importance of mathematics as a science of discovery in the European sixteenth century, has been in my mind for many years now. My debt to friends, colleagues, commentators and opponents is considerable. In earlier books, I have discussed the process and 'meaning' of apparently dramatic changes in discourses of what was afterwards called 'literature', trying to catch something of the complexity of these changes as well as the continuities that they nevertheless maintain. This book and its companion, on the historically vexed and theoretically fraught issues of subject and self, take on two of the more controversial areas of consideration: controversial both for those who argued and fought about them in the late fifteenth century, through the sixteenth and into the seventeenth, and for intellectual historiography today.

Since Jules Michelet (*La Renaissance*, 1855), Jacob Burckhardt (*Die Zivilisation der Renaissance in Italien*, 1860), and Walter Pater (*Studies in the History of the Renaissance*, 1873), this era in European history has been defined above all in terms of three main elements, one historiographical, the second 'psychological', the third philosophical.

In the first instance, it was asserted that a transformation occurred in fifteenth- to sixteenth-century Europe that could only be seen as a *rupture*: people thought and acted differently, societies organized and understood themselves differently, indeed the 'world' itself was different afterwards from what it had been before. That some of the founding figures argued that Abelard or Dante were mysteriously two or three hundred years ahead of time or Winckelmann two hundred years behind hardly affected the wider claim, any more than did one's choice of setting its marker at 1453 with the fall of Constantinople, at 1492 with Columbus' first contact with the Americas and the final expulsion of the Moors from Spain, or at some other more or less proximate if less exact date.

In the second case, people claimed that the most dramatic sign of the change was a liberation of Man from the absolute tutelage of God and total embeddedness in a world of which he was just a part (I use the masculine generic here because not only disputants at the time, but historians until very recently, so saw the matter – and it was an essential part of the claims). Humans were newly endowed with the individual dignity and worth of agents responsible for their own thoughts and actions, and would eventually acquire that self-consciously subjective authority that alone allows us to refer to ourselves as 'human'. Simultaneously, they could grasp the world's order, change its organization, and master its nature to their own ends. This indeed was also part of what being human was all about.

In the third instance, it was argued that understanding was no longer now a matter of theological and ontological debate, but one of epistemological research and discovery. This was to be seen not only in the humanists' emphasis on finding and editing the texts of Greek and Latin antiquity (human, not divine, writings, evidence of unaided human knowledge and rational power), on translating and on making vernaculars that matched particular societies and their histories, but most dramatically in the discovery of the natural sciences and the technologies following from them. Since the first volume of Ernst Cassirer's *Das Erkenntnisproblem in der Philosophie und Wissenschaften der neueren Zeit* (1906), many have stressed the concomitant, even causal, development of mathematics. Most notable amongst these many, perhaps, were Edmund Husserl, whose clearest statement of the development and what he argued as its consequences was in *The Crisis of European Sciences* (especially 21–61), and his disloyal pupil Martin Heidegger.

Thought about these several elements has usually made them coincident, though actual historical treatments have mostly kept them well distinct. So, too, as importantly, have discussions of developments taken to have produced them. This has made serious elisions. Such a one, for instance, is the claim that the idea of the 'world' as a visual image or a spatial representation was simultaneous with the growth of explanatory mathematical models (Heidegger is actually an exception here, who, in 'Die Zeit des Weltbildes', has the latter precede the former, the one signalled notably by Galileo, the other not consolidated until the end of the eighteenth century). Another is the dictum that the 'modern subject' sprang full-fledged into being not just simultaneously with these two, but with Protestantism, the capitalist State, imperial expansion and the decay of Community. Most commentators, to be sure, acknowledge that things are more complicated than that, but to make so bald and blunt-minded a statement is still to be only mildly parodic.

In 1966, Michel Foucault's *Les mots et les choses* did not question this model in any fundamental way, although it sought to view the case as it were from outside, from a contemporary moment when 'we' (Euro-Americans) had come to realize that the thought and practice of Man as subject and centre were only but *un effet d'histoire*. This argument, too, was one that came in large part from Heidegger and a post-Hegelian tradition. Foucault's effort to dethrone the possessive individual provoked an outcry that was quite predictable if largely uncomprehending. Yet his and others' efforts to historicize the subject involved, initially anyway, an even greater stress on historical rupture (an idea he drew from Gaston Bachelard via Georges Canguilhem). So could be emphasized the thought that 'Man' was the creation of a particular society and history and the criticism that Western European history and its avatars were a world–historical aberration: no other culture having set the individual *before* community or *over* nature.

Besides its intrinsic quality, Foucault's work (not alone, no doubt, but surely principally) had the immensely fruitful effect of returning people's attention to this moment in European history that certainly did seem to have seen something unfamiliar occur. Equally importantly, the age seemed to offer some sort of model. For if one could plausibly argue that the era's debates responded to a widely felt and ever-growing sense of crisis in societies faced with vast unfamiliarities, even as they further provoked such a sense of uncertainty, one could suggest equally plausibly that the debates and struggles of the 1960s and seventies, responding to a similar sense of communal breakdowns, social injustices, new intercultural pressures and global shifts, were fully analogous phenomena. So we might take important lessons as to how cultures pass from one such time to another – better, as to how humans struggle with and forge such passages, how they turn familiar cultural instruments to unfamiliar account, how they let and make others fall into disuse, how they understand the complex interweavings of continuity and change – and put them to use.

Whether or not such a quest was a utopian dream was, and is, hardly the point. The practical consequences that matter have been at least two. One has been to provide an increasingly complex and subtle understanding of a moment of major importance in European and world history: major, because of the *actual* effects of its debates and their resulting practices. The other has been, I think, to begin to make available the grounds for questioning the nature of modern Western civilization *from within*, in *its own terms*. Those convinced that some

(at least) of the activities of post-medieval Europe have been pernicious, have responsibilities of different kinds, according as they are
themselves within or without, as they benefit or suffer, as they are (it
is said) 'victors' or 'victims'. Those within have a responsibility to understand it and to change its relationship to those it has harmed and
continues to harm. That understanding cannot but be both historical
and contemporary. Its effect must eventually be contemporary. In this
regard one must assume (and hope) that work in one area of attention affects, as it responds to, work in others. For the sphere of one's
action can obviously result only from one's particular circumstances.

   What follows here is an exploration of largely sixteenth-century
debates about the nature of language and of linguistic meaning, about
the failure of language as a tool for discovery, and its eventual replacement, in this epistemological domain, by mathematics and a new idea
of rational method. To my knowledge, this is an unfamiliar argument.
It deeply queries findings of two books that have been and remain
important catalysts for scholars in these centuries and, as importantly,
for general readers as well: Noam Chomsky's *Cartesian Linguistics*
(1966) and Walter Ong's germinal *Ramus, Method, and the Decay of
Dialogue* (1958). It tries to show not just how that sense of failure
emerged from medieval debate, but how its replacement did too, even
though, to do so, thinking had to take old tools in very new directions.
Its companion volume does the same for what it calls 'Mirages of the
Self', exploring the nature of a 'subject' whose kind and meaning were
very different from what Europeans and most North Americans tend
to have in mind when using the word. Both are followed by a broader
exploration of the new establishment and instauration that took place
over the late sixteenth and first half of the seventeenth centuries in
Europe, focusing on the figure and work of Descartes, and by two
meditations on contemporary cultural situations (contemporary to us,
that is to say), which try to be more precise about the effects of what
are there called 'cultural instruments', not only with respect to the
culture in which they developed but to their passage across cultures.

   These last two works also concentrate more on a concept of the
'*fictive imagination*' whose underlying claims and assumptions matter
as well in *Knowledge, Discovery and Imagination* (whose original title
of *From Trivium to Quadrivium* was perhaps rightly deemed too arcane,
but did catch movements as named by their own history). Here, the
phrase naming these claims and assumptions is used only occasionally
and the issues it indicates are not often foregrounded. Still, they are
implied early and grow in importance as the discussion proceeds. So
they do need at least an introductory explanation here. The two works
mentioned concern contemporary 'literary texts', exploring their

cultural function. But to put *literature* in inverted commas is also to approach the meaning of *fictive imagination*. For in *The Meaning of Literature* (1992) I argued that what the West (and more) has called – calls – literature grew in Western Europe, at first mainly in France and England, in the seventeenth century in response to quite specific pressures and in service to equally specific goals. I also argued that this role of literature had by and large ended in Western Europe by mid-nineteenth century, even if divers inertias seemed to belie such an argument. My point was that literature, and 'the arts' more broadly, no longer played the *organic* role in cultural creation that they had for the previous two centuries.

This argument produced at least four dilemmas. One evidently involved saying what part 'the same sort of' texts or other art works *now* served if it was not the same. For when people nowadays talk of 'literature' they do *seem* to mean something for which familiarity and tradition let them dispense with explanation. But phrases like 'the same sort' need unpacking: are art works 'the same' by their style? their content? the status of their makers? the nature of their receivers? their contexts? the institutions into which they fit? their modes of production? their relation to other sorts of cultural products? and so on. In what ways, maybe more baffling, is the *Don Quijote* written by Jorge Luis Borges' twentieth-century 'Pierre Menard', whose words are identical to those of Miguel de Cervantes' early seventeenth-century novel of the same name, the 'same sort of' text even though its 'meaning', Borges must write, is utterly different? What of a long *Tristram Shandy* passage when Kamau Brathwaite embeds it in a meditation on *lo real maravilloso* ('MR', 19–20)? How much more the same sort of text could they be? James Fenton puts the query in a parable of exactly remaking a Donizetti opera's début. It has its original audience and occurs in a time bubble. For one new term alters the sense of the very text. Part of the matter, *Meaning of Literature* urges, is that the complex cultural role such an artifact enacts has been transformed – so much so that it would be useful and wise to use a term other than *literature* to name it. The two books I mention try to get at what this other term may connote.

This raises other dilemmas. If *literature* named a societally and historically placed cultural practice, one had to try and say what came before that practice, and what came elsewhere. *Meaning of Literature* sought to evoke something of the first. To show it in detail is a longer project, if shorter than what is wanted to approach 'elsewhere' (which the two 'meditations' also begin to attempt). As urgently, one had to find a term able to serve the generalizing purpose 'literature', and 'the arts', had seemed to possess – at any rate, in Western thought and practice. It appears after all that every known human culture embeds practices

connoted by these terms; even though, Arnold Schoenberg long ago
held, not only were ideas of 'order, clarity, and comprehensibility' with
which Westerners defined the 'beautiful', pleasing, or desirable in art
themselves tied to time and place, but so too was the very thought of
using such criteria at all (*Theory of Harmony*, 30). Yet if all these
terms are to be defined by and in the context of a given history and
society (not just *literature* in the book named, for example, but 'the
modern system of the arts' of Paul Oskar Kristeller's eponymous essay
arguing growth of such a system in post-Renaissance Europe, mainly
the eighteenth century), then how can one grasp the similarities that
nonetheless *seem* – it may be no more – to lie across this human
capacity for 'making fictions', for creating 'possible worlds' and testing
them – as it were – in relation to a felt 'real world'?

These inverted commas do not mean fatuously to suggest that this
real world does not exist, simply that it can only ever be defined against
a time's and a place's possible worlds. The term *fictive imagination* is
meant, more or less neutrally, although not ahistorically (it is after all
of ancient Greek lineage), to describe a capacity that is always and
only visible in practices particularized in specific cultural contexts under
such names as *myth, mimesis, poetry, literature*. This book examines
aspects of the making of such a cultural context. That is why its third
part, especially, raises questions of the fictive imagination and of efforts
to understand its functioning. It does so because 'we' are accustomed
to thinking of the fictive imagination as the most 'disinterested' of activities and so, presumably, as most free of local cultural constraints. To
show *that* it is not and *how* it is not are among this work's intentions.
At the same time, because Western people *have* held this view of 'art'
as 'disinterested', so to show how its domain shares the constraints and
interests of other cultural practices in a time of change should help
further to confirm both the general direction and cohesion of the
changes in the culture and the detail of their nature.

That these several but entirely interrelated researches have been
pursued over so long a time makes it hard to acknowledge all those
who have affected them. In each book I can only try to note those
who have been one way or another instrumental in my pursuit of the
specific explorations treated there. Some, interlocutors over many
years, will find themselves thanked twice. Others have been more punc-
tual. Among the latter, I thank Terence Cave, Luce Giard, Daniel
Javitch, Ian Maclean and Patricia A. Parker for their critical readings
of and comments on earlier versions of what is now part 1. David
Lee Rubin, editor of *EMF: Studies in Early Modern France*, II
(Charlottesville, VA: Rookwood, 1996), in which it appeared in its

penultimate, if very different form, was generous with his time and attentive in his editing. I thank him for permission to use the material here. About a quarter of part 2 appeared quite differently in *Humanism in Crisis: the Decline of the French Renaissance*, ed. Philippe Desan (Ann Arbor: University of Michigan Press, 1991): I thank the Press for permission to use its matter here. I am grateful to Philippe Desan for asking me for the primitive version of that chapter, although 'primitive' is the applicable qualification. I as much regret its too early appearance in print as I relish the occasion to rework it here. I also thank Peter De Bolla for giving me a first chance to rethink it for a lecture at King's College, Cambridge in 1991, and members of that audience for fruitful discussion.

Part 3 began as a talk for Donald R. Kelley's Foundation for Intellectual History group at the Folger Shakespeare Library in Washington, DC in July 1993. It benefited then and later from discussion and correspondence especially with Don Kelley, Heikki Mikkeli, Peter N. Miller, Anne E. Moyer, Ulrich J. Schneider and Philip Weller. I thank them all. A very brief part of it appears as a chapter in the *Cambridge History of Literary History*, volume III, and I thank Glyn P. Norton for his work with me on that part. These researches have been made possible by the staffs of many libraries in Europe and North America, and have been put to the test by colleagues and students in seminars and lectures at an even larger number of universities. To thank all involved would be otiose, and anyway impossible: without both, simply, these kinds of explorations and exchanges could not be done. This also goes, of course, for their indebtedness to the work of the many other researchers in their areas. These can be and are only acknowledged by textual and bibliographical reference.

Over the years, some or all of this book has benefited in particular, however, from conversations and exchanges with Daniel Javitch (who generously read early versions of almost the whole), Peter Haidu, Timothy Hampton, Peter Miller, Deniz Sengel and Eugene Vance, besides those already mentioned, or more globally than otherwise indicated. Critical, even polemical, commentary on earlier work by Marc Angenot, Anthony Cascardi and Don Kelley has improved attention to and brought revision in some arguments and claims. My deep gratitude to all for their time and care. Tim Hampton, Patricia J. Penn Hilden, Peter Miller and Deniz Sengel were gracious and patient enough to read the whole manuscript, offering comment and criticism of fundamental importance and utility. They have my special thanks. I am indebted, also, to Stephen Orgel for welcoming this book into the series he edits, and, at Cambridge University Press, to Linda Bree and Josie Dixon for their careful and caring attention, and to Hilary Hammond for the great delicacy and heedfulness of her copy-editing.

Ideas and terms like *cultural context* and *cultural creation*, and many of their implications, were originally drawn from Lucien Goldmann, in whose conversational company I many years ago was privileged to spend an intense week. His person and work were a model of political commitment, historical sensitivity, erudition, and intellectual generosity. Would that earlier awareness of what I owe him had enabled an earlier expression of gratitude. Much more recently, I have had the further privilege of association with two great writers, Kamau Brathwaite and Ngũgĩ wa Thiong'o, for both of whom the fictive imagination can only be understood and practised in its specific cultural, sociopolitical context. What I continue to learn from them of art and identity, of cultural creation and historically informed social and critical commitment, also lies in and behind this work. Acknowledgement falls short of gratitude. It does, too, as again I thank Patricia Hilden for the discussion and conversation about the same and related issues that are the background of this book, as they are the foreground of others and justification for all (to say nothing of the improvement she has wrought in my writing).

A note on the text

A few technical matters need mention. Notes give author and short title. Unless otherwise indicated, cross-reference between or to notes is within a same chapter. Full title and publication information is provided only in the bibliography, which is little more than a check-list of volumes referenced in the text or notes. I have occasionally added a title not directly cited or otherwise mentioned. I hope in this way to have further acknowledged those authors with whose works what follows is in many ways a dialogue. The index, apart from topics and names, furnishes dates for all persons who lived before the nineteenth century (corresponding, more or less, to the bibliography's 'primary sources'). Unless otherwise noted, all translations are my own.

Introduction

Since time immemorial, or at least since the mythical, religious, and legendary tales of diverse antiquities, language and wisdom or knowledge have been accounted inseparable: whether through Mercury or Moses, Adam or Prometheus, Thoth, Hermes or Jahveh – whose Logos was both speech and ultimate wisdom – language and mind have been taken as mutual and simultaneous signs of one another. Language conferred wisdom; the power of speaking was also that of knowing. Mind was manifest in language; the latter no less than reason itself was the final index of humanity.

These are clichés, but against some such generalizations, distinctions may be made to historicize this relation of language and mind (especially where sixteenth-century European writers are at issue). Endlessly repeated, the commonplace coupling of rationality and language is not itself my question, though furnishing a backdrop. For the coupling has been diversely conceived in different places and times. Here, I am concerned with a time of conceptual change in Europe when to maintain the coupling at all seemed increasingly hard. When the issue was finally resolved, the resolution produced fundamental changes and developments in how the human condition and situation were understood (indeed in how they *could* be understood).

I wish to look at a precise moment in this history, starting in the last years of the 1520s. People then still maintained these clichés, as well as what was then, but is not now, another: the assurance that the foundation of the highest human culture was *writing* and the transmission of written texts and the arts dealing with them. This had been so since at least Hellenistic times, and remained the case throughout the supposedly dark and silent European Middle Ages, the vast size and meaning of whose manuscript tradition in *grammatica*, the grounding doctrine and practice of 'learning, interpretation and knowledge', is only now becoming appreciated. The union between written language and reason was total, and *grammatica* in particular, but the language arts in general (with which it much overlapped), were always held to be '*productive*' of knowledge. [1]

By the early sixteenth century or a little before, people were increasingly distinguishing between language as means of rational communication (grammar and rhetoric) and language as means of discovery (logic), source, precisely, of 'productive knowledge'. As to the last, they were actually coming to question whether language could meaningfully furnish any path whatever to discovery (syllogistic or other), and whether some other tool might not be available. Such another tool, responding directly to linguistic failures, would be mathematics. Analyses were still rooted in the trivium and quadrivium, but dissatisfaction with both style and substance was growing apace. It was doing so under pressure from growing commerce and trade, from new geographical discoveries and resultant cultural and ethical debates, as well as from political and military projects of imperialist and dynastic expansion, from on-going historical and textual research and finds, and from the national and social rearrangements consequent on the political and economic shiftings connected with these and other motions. Such pressures differed in different places and times, and reaction ebbed and flowed variously, before settling into a more or less equally generalized new circumstance.

In our own generation, under the weight, it may well be, of analogous pressures, debates about language and meaning have had a vital role both in efforts to reach into our own dilemmas and to explain intellectual and other activities in early modern Europe. So they did in those activities themselves. But neither in content, attention, nor urgency did they involve the kind of change and dramatic rupture modern scholars have often claimed. Throughout the Middle Ages, the linguistic arts of the trivium, besides grounding literate culture, focused much complex discussion. Scholars of the fifteenth and sixteenth centuries were wholly absorbed by those arts and their past; continuity of argument and topic was essential to change. By the 1520s, especially among those pondering vernaculars, older ontological and theological knots combined with newer sociopolitical and epistemological ones to create an impasse.

Here, a short aside on the issue of continuity/discontinuity will not be amiss. The question matters for what follows, and the brief remarks of my prologue hardly suffice to offset even the two major objections: the one that the matter is idle, telling us something of historiography (perhaps), nothing about history; the other that even were it historically

---

1. Irvine, *Making*, 1–22 (quotations on 1 and 8).

important, we still know too little of the European fifteenth and sixteenth centuries to give any 'general answer to the question' of continuity. [2] The last is surely the case, but such a general answer can be built only from scraps and accumulated instances. As to the first, a reply rather depends on what one is seeking. The kind of continuity Pierre Duhem sought early in our century in the subject matter and forms of attention of natural science from Greek antiquity to European seventeenth century may not hold – or holds in ways so attenuated as to mean little. Peter Dear avers that meaningful continuity is not to be found in principal. It would demand, he says, identical contexts, method and theoretical and practical goals. This claim means there can be no continuity in history at all – or even in a single human life. [3] In some sense, historical knowledge would be impossible, since 'continuity' simply marks coherent paths from one 'place' to another, explains cohesion of times and places, the *consistency* (in every sense) of events. Here 'history' and 'continuity' are nearly synonymous, but neither, it must be said, axiomatically implies straightforward linearity of relations: the 'paths' may be winding, forking, devious and chaotic.

More recently, treating some of the questions of this book as they occurred in a slightly later era, Dear has been blunter. He opines that to say (as I just did) that people in a given time and place were 'intellectually shaped by the "learning of the schools" is surely an unquestionable proposition'. What matters, he believes, is to know how ways of formulating, here scientific, questions 'made sense' differently. For the history of science at least, concern over continuity and discontinuity is 'unnecessary' and 'unilluminating'. [4] But questions *make sense* differently *from* something, and they do so for reasons which we can – I would say must – want to understand: not from delight in speculation, but because of continuing effects. How we examine motions signalled by the phrase 'the European Renaissance' has been, willynilly, set in discussion of continuity versus discontinuity. To elude the issue is to ignore the multifold ramifications, for example, of the vehement and historically and philosophically fraught debate over the modern era's 'legitimacy': a way of defining a question of ethics and history that we may deem odd or 'wrong' but whose implications we ignore at our peril. [5] The whys and wherefores of the tangled paths

---

2. N. Jardine, 'Epistemology', 710.
3. Dear, *Mersenne*, 238 (also 232, 234–5 and his final chapters more generally). The last point repeats Peter Barker's and Roger Ariew's more detailed reply to Dear in their introduction to *Revolution*, 17.
4. Dear, *Discipline*, 15.
5. See too, Reiss, *Meaning*, especially 3–5, and 'Autonomy'. (The issue underlies my *Against Autonomy*, in progress.)

from one dominant practice and analysis of ways of social and cultural action to another (or others) embed and guide their consequences in particular, as they may also help us grasp how humans make such 'passages' in general. [6]

'Continuity', here then, speaks to the understanding of why certain cultural paths were taken, to the tracing of their routes, winding and forking as they were, and to some grasp of where they led – and still lead. It does not assume similarities – far less identities – of 'concept', 'method', 'logic' or whatever from one time to another. Continuity does suppose that the one(s) came from the other(s). It does suppose that we can know how and why they did, and to what effect. In this regard, it can and does just as powerfully concern differences, provided it enables us to see how such differences came about, what they meant and mean, what they *did* and continue to do.

Such eclectics as Charles de Bovelles, Desiderius Erasmus, Pierre Fabri, Jacques Lefèvre d'Etaples, John Palsgrave, Geofroy Tory, Juan Luis Vives and others, humanist heirs of scholasticism and most of them close to politically expansive courts, faced an infinite regress in relations of language and non-linguistic phenomena (*res*), even while they expressed notions and kinds of 'mastery' in which an ordered vernacular would have a civic role of central importance – even as (and though) they would ultimately have to turn to mathematics and a new idea of 'method' for actual validation of such order. These same humanists were indeed among those who explored, as well, these once wholly quadrivial (but also practical) areas of concern. Hermann Schüling writes that even if 'the study of language and eloquence took first place' for humanists around 1500, nevertheless 'one must speak of a certain turn of humanism towards mathematics'. Nicholas Jardine goes further, insisting that the promotion of mathematics was 'a central part of the humanist programme'. [7] Its solutions were an essential element of what became Western Europe's 'modernity'.

---

6. The phrase 'dominant practice' refers partly to argument in the first two and last chapters of Reiss, *Discourse*, the Introduction to *Uncertainty*, and more generally to Michel Foucault's work.

7. Schüling, *Geschichte*, 35; N. Jardine, 'Forging', 147. By the late 1530s, the latter continues: 'astronomy flourished as never before in the academies which fell under [Philip] Melanchthon's aegis'. Johann Sturm's renowned Strasburg academy gave mathematics a high place (the then well-known Cunradus Dasypodius was educated there and was its mathematics professor for forty years in the century's second half). Schüling names Lefèvre and Bovelles – whom Cassirer saw as a 'Mathematiker und Physiker' embedded in Scholasticism but striving 'for renewal of the empirical world model' and giving the 'Renaissance view of nature its vital grounds' (*Erkenntnisproblem*, I.77). Rejner Hooykaas and Paul Lawrence Rose make a similar point about slightly later humanists, though both Schüling (*Geschichte*) and Hooykaas

For these humanists, unlike their scholastic predecessors, the parts of the trivium were always unable to offer any element of 'a logic of discovery'. And thus distinguishing between communication and discovery, between, in Lisa Jardine's words, the 'tactical application of ratiocination to specific debating questions' and 'the pursuit of truth', meant the unity of the trivium was breaking down around those questions of the nature and use of language which were, after all, the very ground of its triple propaedeutic of grammar, rhetoric, and logic/dialectic. [8] Since Hellenistic and Latin antiquity, the tasks of these three arts, even when distinct, had been cumulative. For most of the period (and one is speaking of something like a millennium and a half), *grammatica* itself was really the foundation of the other two, and indeed did more than just overlap its companions of the trivium. [9] By the later Middle Ages and early Renaissance (let us say, fourteenth and fifteenth centuries), if things had changed a lot, distinctions of task being often made clearer, yet the three remained a cumulative source of knowledge.

Grammar, as Petrus Ramus still noted in his 1547 attack on Cicero's rhetorical authority, *Brutinae quaestiones*, dealt with etymology, syntax, prosody and orthography. [10] Rhetoric treated 'the art of good speaking', its aim being to teach public persuasion, although by the late Middle Ages it also taught the *ars dictaminis*, how to write letters. Logic/dialectic (once separate) taught the art of good reasoning and of communicating that reasoning, the *ars bene ratiocinandi*. Rhetoric and logic both taught how to find (*invenire*) and order arguments, remember them, and communicate them. Their ends were different, but their means were hard to distinguish: which was why Ramus became famous for cutting the Gordian knot of their similarities, placing *inventio*, *dispositio*, and *memoria* under logic, *elocutio* and *actio* under rhetoric. [11] That Ramus found it necessary to make such an attack tells us much about the still lingering force of a unified trivium. His emphasis

---

(*Humanisme*, 75–90) aver that mathematics in Sturm's and Melanchthon's schools was training in rigorous thinking and useful art, not an activity implying remaking of curriculum or thought.

8. L. Jardine, 'Lorenzo Valla: Academic Skepticism', 358–9. The specific notion of 'communication' implied by her first phrase was particular, as we will see, to humanist ideas of what communication was about: I use it here to help insist that we are talking of new adjustments. The reference just preceding is to her *Francis Bacon* (6), whose argument is predicated on the humanists' separation of communication from discovery (although, there, the last does not concern mathematics).

9. I refer again to Irvine's *Making*: he makes such a remark at 7–8, but the whole work is eloquent of the matter. Compare Zedelmaier, *Bibliotheca*, especially 265–6, but also *passim*.

10. Ramus, *Attack*, 17.

11. For example, ibid., 17.

on *teaching* will tell us much about the changes it was undergoing, had undergone. But he was far from the first to do this, and among other things in the second part my book explores why his work was from the start thought most crucial. (Chapter 4, especially, also explores how that same work has produced a serious, if popular, misunderstanding about just what kind of change is in question: supposedly abrupt, supposedly from oral to galactically visual and spatial.)

Crossovers between parts of the trivium in the Middle Ages were usual. Even late medieval grammarians undertook explorations that included not just etymology, syntax or other elements of what is nowadays called 'grammar', but all aspects of reading, interpretation, correction, and critical judgment. These, of course, passed into areas of *inventio* and *memoria* (although not only) that took them through rhetoric and logic to metaphysics and theology. Some of this is glimpsed in chapter 1. These kinds of overlappings made a 'unity', thought Ramus and many of his contemporaries (although they saw it in the Latins, not in the Middle Ages, whose authors they by then ignored altogether), that risked completely obscuring the *pedagogical* specificity, even identity, of the trivium. But the trivium had already started to change and sometimes to weaken at its seams, while other areas of learning were also being transformed.

The influx of Latin translations of Aristotle from the twelfth century altered the conception of *grammatica*, emphasizing logic and meta-physics. Partly as a result, theoretical grammar, poetics, and glosses on classical texts 'split apart into three nearly independent spheres of activity'. [12] In Italy by the mid- to late fifteenth century, as Rita Guerlac observes, logic and natural philosophy 'went hand in hand' at the universities of Padua, Bologna, and Pavia, while claims that dialectic grounded all knowledge grew more common. [13] Natural philosophy, of course, did not belong in the trivium. Its place in the quadrivium meant that research tying it to logic tended to connect the latter with the mathematical arts of that part of the curriculum. Pursuing such associations, Italian thinkers continued developments begun in thirteenth- to fourteenth-century Oxford, from Robert Grosseteste and Roger Bacon to Thomas Bradwardine and the Mertonians, William Heytesbury, Richard Kilvington, Richard Swineshead and Ralph

---

12. Irvine, *Making*, 463–4 (quotation on 464). Irvine promises another volume studying *grammatica* through the fourteenth century. For Aristotle, see, for example, Dod, 'Aristoteles', and Lohr, 'Medieval'.
13. Guerlac, introduction to Vives, *Against*, 13. Compare Giard, 'Aristotélisme', and various of Schmitt's essays now reprinted in his *Aristotelian Tradition* and *Studies*.

Strode, and in fourteenth-century Paris with Jean Buridan, Albert of Saxony and Nicole Oresme. Kristeller has noted the existence of many manuscripts showing that Heytesbury's and Swineshead's writings were used in Italy as textbooks from the fourteenth century: 'numerous Italian philosophers were trained in this tradition and followed its methods and arguments' – as was not the case in England, he added.[14] All these thinkers had increasingly 'mathematized' logic.

It matters that in Italy, we will see above all in chapter 5, the pursuit of these connections in and through the public universities put the new teachings at the disposal of a public world of physicians, jurists, and others 'who took an active part in the political and cultural life of their cities'. [15] For it meant that their connection with technical practice was not only quickly apparent, but that the development of these teachings in fact benefited as well from such practice. And it was especially in Italy that from the early fourteenth century the necessity for mathematics in commercial practice had led to growing numbers of *scuole d'abbaco* where it was taught to many pupils from a wide cross-section of society. Chapters 4 through 7 of the book argue that this combination with the mathematical sciences/arts was eventually to prove all-important, as an older logic based in the language arts of the trivium collapsed. Galileo will be found among those observing the vital bond between discoveries of these commercial explorations and the application of mathematics in natural science. The collapse had many reasons. Part 1 argues that to no small degree it came from vernacular pressures and from trying to use language arguments for epistemological needs of everyday life. The idea that such claims were plausible came from medieval debate about language. The need to situate them in the vernacular and in the broader social sphere came from pressures to which I referred before.

Still, non-mathematical logic had for some time seemed to be taking itself into a cul-de-sac. Lisa Jardine shows that already by mid-fifteenth century, humanists like Lorenzo Valla and Rudolph Agricola saw scholastic dialectic training in linguistically based valid inference and formal analysis as a futile ground for discovering truths that would in fact always elude them. For them, dialectic was already ever and always for communication, above all in teaching. [16] E. J. Ashworth observes how scholastic doctrines had been so flagging that in the sixteenth

14. Kristeller, comments on Murdoch, '*Mathesis*', 257–8. Replying, Murdoch added Bradwardine's work to such 'textbooks' (259).
15. Guerlac, 'Introduction', 15.
16. L. Jardine, 'Lorenzo Valla: Academic Skepticism', 358 for the first point; *Francis Bacon* 26–7 *et passim* for the second. See too Vasoli, *Dialettica*, 47–77, 147–82.

century they could eventually be reduced to little more than an introduction to Aristotle. She specifies, though, that this 'eclipse' did not
really occur decisively until after 1530 – a date interestingly matching
many of the suggestions of my argument to follow. [17]

Guerlac adds that early sixteenth-century toilers in these fields made
medieval logic (and so implicitly its companion arts of the trivium)
sufficiently obscure as to lead budding humanists to dismiss them and
their goals out of hand. Gaspar Lax, Vives' teacher at the College of
Montaigu as the sixteenth century began, was a fair instance. A butt
of his great student's early *In pseudodialecticos*, he still pursued
medieval dialectic and 'mathematico-physical' speculation in years
when many of those figuring in later chapters were working on their
myriad editions of the classics and Italian humanists. He issued his
Exponibilia and other works in 1512. Such texts, Guerlac avers, now
mystified contemporaries as much as us. She instances his analysis of
the term *immediate*, needing to be defined 'nominally, non-exponibly,
categorematically, syncategorematically, prepositionally, or conjunc-
tionally'. [18] Lax could not make clear just what purpose might be served
by this potentially endless multiplication of levels of understanding.

However, as chapter 2 suggests, Lax seems unintentionally to have
begun to negotiate a dilemma about the nature, function, and possibilities of (the Latin) language that humanists were soon to confront
with regard to the vernacular. It was a dilemma coming more or less
directly from medieval debate and for which the early sixteenth-century
humanists could yet see no solution. Simultaneously, though, some of
these same humanists were exploring areas from whence a solution
would finally be drawn. Lefèvre d'Etaples and his pupils and co-workers,
Josse Clichtove and Bovelles, devoted enormous time and energy to
arithmetic and geometry as they simultaneously worked on language,
whether grammar or rhetoric, questions of translation, or of textual
recovery. It may be, as Jean-Claude Margolin has noted, that these
three were atypical. Even Vives did not see mathematics as central,
despite the space he gave it. On the contrary, he found grammar
'an essential and still instrumental preliminary stage of the diverse
disciplines'. [19] Rudolph Agricola and Erasmus spurned scholastic

---

17. Ashworth, *Language*, 16–20. For the 1530 date, see her 'Eclipse'.
18. Guerlac, 'Introduction', 23–4 (from *Exponibilia*). Humanists' attitudes towards such
    researches have been usefully explored in Perreiah, 'Humanist Critiques'. See too
    L. Jardine's clarifications in 'Humanism and the Teaching of Logic'.
19. Zedelmaier, *Bibliotheca*, 270. He asserts that this view 'became dominant in the age
    of Reform and Counter-Reform', especially in the universities (270–1). With regard
    to the latter, he may be right. Elsewhere, and more generally, what follows
    contradicts the claim. If one equates 'philology' with history rather than grammar,

mathematical speculations outright, together with their proponents. [20] Warren van Egmond has indeed suggested that people like Bovelles and Lefèvre, with their early emphasis on Plato, in fact did to death such southern French mathematical advances as there had been in the late fifteenth century 'under the avalanche of French humanism'. [21] I will argue that their role was at once more ambivalent and more positive.

Be that as it may (for the moment), this was not the case in Italy, where in the universities and in commercial and artistic practice mathematical work had been receiving more attention for many years, although in the former, despite its apparent breadth, mathematics teaching relied even beyond the sixteenth century on texts used throughout the Middle Ages. [22] Historians mostly agree that Luca Pacioli's 1494 *Summa de arithmetica, geometrica et proportionalita* united 'academic and vernacular traditions'. [23] It was also the first printed work to give a systematic treatment of algebra, the 'key subject in the mathematical revolution of the [late] sixteenth century'. [24] Making unacknowledged use of Piero della Francesca's arithmetical and geometrical manuscripts, it was directed at an 'artisanal' and an academic audience. The most advanced practical French mathematician of the time, Nicolas Chuquet, who taught commercial calculation in Lyon, never published his writings and they were unknown until the nineteenth century (except for a 1520 work by Estienne de La Roche, who copied their practical aspects and garbled their more complex ones). At the same time, most French humanists dismissed the earlier academic mathematicians along with all other scholastics, although again rather more ambivalently than has sometimes been asserted.

Chuquet seems to have known much of the work going on in Italy, although in his day there was that short-lived flurry of productive mathematical work in southern France, of dim origin, to which I have already

later scholars like J. J. Scaliger did believe that it could incorporate 'all' knowledge. But this had little to do with 'discovery', and even the wider claim was relinquished when Scaliger was criticized by such as Tycho Brahe and Johannes Kepler (Grafton, *Joseph Scaliger*, II. 161–2, 203–5, 469–88; and Reiss, 'Towards' (11–13)).

20. Margolin, 'Enseignement', 109–11. Schüling recalls Agricola's 1476 praise of mathematics in *In laudem philosophiae et reliquiarum artium*, even though it went no further than that (*Geschichte*, 35).
21. Egmond, 'How Algebra', 139, 140.
22. Schmitt, *Studies*, V. 485–530.
23. See, for example, Flegg, Hay, and Moss, eds., *Nicolas Chuquet*, 11.
24. Whitrow, 'Why Did Mathematics?', 267. On Pacioli and other sixteenth-century Italian 'algebrists' more generally, see Rose, *Italian Renaissance*, 143–50. Schuster agrees on the great importance of 'the 'analytico-algebraic' approach' at the end of the sixteenth century, insisting on the importance of François Viète and the future of the art in Descartes (*Descartes*, 20–2).

referred. [25] And indeed, the circulation among university teachers, humanists, students and business people guaranteed vital exchanges of information over time – which is why, although some readers may wonder at the geographical passage in what follows from north to south and back again, most assuredly by the mid- to late sixteenth century, one can talk of a common Western European high culture. Problems raised first in one place could readily get their solutions in another, and if some centres might be strongly identified with certain kinds of study, these usually did not last over long periods nor were they as isolated as they have sometimes been claimed to be, as Luce Giard and Charles B. Schmitt, among others, have reminded us. [26]

By little after mid-sixteenth century, in Italy and Germany, France, Spain, the Netherlands, and even so provincial an outpost as England, matters had changed utterly. [27] Two developments were notably revealing on this score. The first was the Italian-based but European-wide debate sparked by publication of Alessandro Piccolomini's *De certitudine mathematicarum disciplinarum* in 1547. Piccolomini argued (with many) that mathematics was of the first degree of certainty, since it dealt entirely with rational abstraction, but not of strongest demonstrative power, since it could not deal with material causes. Because others were already by this time looking to mathematics for some general science of logic (an idea disputed by the many Aristotelians for whom logic was only an instrument, not a science of *causas* at all), the next fifteen to twenty years saw vehement debate spread from Italy to the north. Some, like Francesco Barozzi at Padua and Cunradus Dasypodius at Strasburg, held mathematics to be a more powerful tool, capable of more universal guidance. (The argument actually continued into the 1620s. [28])

25. Egmond, 'How Algebra', 134–9.
26. Giard, 'Aristotélisme', 283–8. For Schmitt, see bibliography.
27. I say 'provincial' for England because Augustus De Morgan's old estimate surely still stands that it 'was only towards the *end* of the sixteenth century that what were then the higher parts of the mathematical sciences began to be disseminated with effect in Britain' (*Arithmetical Books*, xxi). Cuthbert Tunstall (*De arte supputandi*, 1522) was a lone precursor. In France, Viète (save the unknown Chuquet) was the first major original mathematician, but from Lefèvre and his colleagues at century's start, through Oronce Fine and Ramus, with divers surrounding reckoners, a firm tradition had grown. Talk of a seventeenth-century English 'dissociation of sensibility' (T. S. Eliot) and rupture between 'scientific and poetic truth' has nothing to do with this provincialism or even with issues of induction and discovery (what I have called analysis and reference), but much with poets' claims of access to universal 'truth' (Schabert, 'Trennung').
28. See, for example, Crapulli, *Mathesis*, 31–62, 101–43; N. Jardine, 'Epistemology', 693–7; Schüling, *Geschichte*, 41–56 *et passim*; Vasoli, 'Introduction', xiv; Wallace, *Galileo, the Jesuits*, chapter 14 ('Aristotelian Science and Rhetoric'), especially 16 ff.

Caught up in this debate (via its Aristotelian and Aquinian references, among other things) were many of those involved in the second development to whose importance for mathematics I referred: the remarkable growth of the Jesuit college system. Although the extent of the actual teaching of mathematics in the colleges surely varied according to the availability of qualified teachers, there is no doubt of the emphasis the Society placed on it. The Collegio Romano itself always kept strong mathematicians on its faculty, and was not alone in doing so. Furthermore, the curriculum, common to all the colleges of the system, was open to new work in ways the universities' curricula seem not to have been. [29]

By the turn of the seventeenth century, France in particular saw a burst of work in algebra, raising questions of 'Why then? Why there?' which have yet to be answered. [30] But mathematical study had become a central intellectual project far more widely, intimately bound with debate over ideas of 'method' and, surely no less importantly, with music practice and theory on the one hand and with military and economic developments on the other. The first long kept specific and elaborate links with quadrivial concerns. The second required attention to technical innovation in matters of artillery, military construction, and deployment (what was called 'embatailling' in English), as well as to innovation in commerce and trade (such matters as double-entry bookkeeping, such theories as 'Gresham's Law' and more).

Music involved issues both of theory and of practice, and in both areas, because they had to do with moving and 'tuning' human passions, found links with two other fields of endeavour that in one case had

---

29. See Crombie, 'Mathematics'; Dainville, 'Enseignement'; Dear, *Discipline* 32–62; Schüling, *Geschichte*, 47–52; Wallace, *Galileo, the Jesuits*, especially chapters 8 and 14, *Galileo and His Sources*, and *Prelude*, especially 129–252. The end of chapter 4 and all of chapter 5 of my *Descartes, Philosophy, and the Public Sphere* (working title: in progress) also treat this in detail.

30. Egmond remarks that since 'algebra is nearly as old as recorded history itself' it is important to understand why it was then and there that the 'revolutionary change in its character and form' occurred that produced 'analytic geometry, the calculus, and all the varied disciplines of modern analysis'. Although algebra was known in the West as early as Fibonacci's (Leonardo of Pisa's) 1202 *Liber abaci*, except for the algebra recorded by some *maestri d'abbaco* in Italy, it led to no great flourish until the solution of cubic and quartic equations in mid-sixteenth-century Italy by Scipione del Ferro, Niccolò Tartaglia, Girolamo Cardano and Ludovico Ferrari, and then to the great outburst of late sixteenth-century France, where there had been no such tradition. 'What', he asks, 'were the conditions and events that preceded and presumably spawned this extraordinary transformation?' ('How Algebra', 127, 129). Whitrow asks the same question, noting that although Rafael Bombelli's 1572 *Algebra* was the century's most systematic treatise in Italy, it was, again, in France that these techniques were pursued and bore fruit ('Why Did?', 268–9). I hope this book will help suggest answers.

been connected with the mathematical sciences since the first half of
the fifteenth century and in the other was thought by the mid-sixteenth
century to be capable of such association. These were painting and
poetry, the first tied to mathematics through perspective theory, the
second through metrics – although as early as 1392, Eustache
Deschamps tied the 'musique naturele' of poetry to the 'musique arti-
ficiele' whose mathematically ordered 'thirds, fifths and octaves'
permitted untuned 'hearts and spirits to be cured and reset [*medecinez
et recreez*]'. [31] But at least since the Pythagoreans, music was also tied
to ideas of social order, by no means just metaphorically or allegori-
cally. A wealth of thought and connection backed Leonardo Bruni's
remark in his *Laudatio Florentinae urbis* (*c.* 1404) that as strings were
tuned to forge 'a single harmony', Florence had 'so adapted all her
parts to each other that there results a harmony of the total structure
of the republic ... everything occup[ying] its proper place'. [32] Aspects
of this 'political' turn of debate will be evident early in this book, but
Part 3 especially ties theoretical and political (or ideological) implications of arguments in music associated with this sort of view to wider
developments – as it tries as well to show the more detailed precision
and new forms people were wanting to give these arguments.

One begins to see some of the ramifications of the change we will
be exploring. It was not a change from oral to visual, from language
to spatialization; or at least, not to spatialization in any ordinary sense
of the term. Indeed, if it had been so, it would be hard to explain why,
in the area of mathematics, algebra suddenly became so much more
urgently important than geometry. It was a change in the claims of
discovery, from natural language to the 'measurable' language of mathematics. It was a change, too, in what was taken to be the nature of
discovery: not a finding of something that already existed, but a making
of a new rational order for the comprehension of what existed. No
distinction was made between inference and a logic of discovery – nor
would it be, by and large, before the second half of the nineteenth
century (and I will try to keep that elision in what follows). [33] It was,
though, a change in what such discovery was taken to let one do:
control and master the objects and processes entering into such order.
And precisely inasmuch as these new propositions tied up with assumptions about the nature and function of human passions and actions, so

31. Deschamps, *Art de dictier*, 269–70.
32. Quoted in Edgerton, *Renaissance Rediscovery*, 36.
33. Stephen Gaukroger has observed that lack of distinction between inference, deduc-
    tive reasoning, and a logic of discovery is crucial to understanding Cartesian inquiry:
    Cartesian Logic, 7 *et passim*. In *Discourse* I argued that their combination was funda-
    mental to 'modernist' ('analytico-referential') practices.

they were an essential element in the development of new ideas of the human subject and self.

To some extent, I have in mind, with regard to this last issue, millennia-long thinking about the intimate relation between a universal macrocosmic harmony and the equanimity of the human organism, the fine tuning of the microcosm's passions and temperament, as they eventually yielded to a quite different account of selfhood. But at the same time, if it could be held by the European Middle Ages that 'wisdom' was most exactly defined as contemplation of the divine order and of humans' coherent and cohesive place within it, but also that that contemplation depended on readings of language and meanings set in the mind by God, then breakdown in the language arts enabling such readings meant the collapse of that idea of wisdom. Too, it created an imperious demand to rethink the nature of the human whose ideal that wisdom and those arts had defined and described. Discovery had been defined as 're-membering' a universal order (whether 'divine' or not), and language had been its basic tool: finding the meanings that described, *in*scribed, that order. The humanists were now showing that even for such discovery language was inept.

As argument became stronger that language and discovery were not codependent but that 'knowledge' and discovery were, on the contrary, intimately related, so 'failures' of language implied – certainly at first – that those who still felt the language arts central to human action had to turn elsewhere to understand what human 'wisdom' might be, and to comprehend what was defining of the 'human' itself. This may largely explain that 'transformation of wisdom from contemplation to action, from a body of knowledge to a collection of ethical precepts, from a virtue of the intellect to a perfection of the will' that Eugene F. Rice, Jr. describes as 'humanism's chief contribution to the development of the idea of wisdom in the century between Bovillus's *De sapiente* and [Pierre] Charron's *De la sagesse*'. [34]

This way of putting the matter rather understates that what was at issue was something like a path from 'being' to 'doing'. For the conception of human reason as most fully realized in contemplation of knowledge (divinely) given in the intellect matched description of human psychophysiology in terms of passion and temperament. Both set the human inside an integrated 'web' of relations over which *its* individual or singular control was the last matter at issue. One might 'read' such relations, understand them through the language that along with reason defined humans as a species. But that language was part

---

34. Rice, *Renaissance Idea*, 149.

of those relations. It did not discover the 'new'. It revealed the familiar
(or once-familiar). It did not manipulate. It showed. This could no
longer do when unfamiliar pressures required new responses, when the
language arts showed themselves incapable of producing them, and
when new notions of 'discovery' seemed needed. That may explain why
'specialists' in language, the humanists, turned to action, *not* so much
to 'collection of ethical precepts' as to efforts of ethical praxis, from
intellect contemplating to will acting and persuading to act.

Language moved from discovery understood as a 're-membering'
of a universal order to communication separated from knowledge production or discovery. What it might *communicate* was doubtless open
(it could surely, for example, communicate knowledge gained by other
means). But it perforce took for fields of *action* those human ones in
which it could have an *effect*, ones of human action itself. They could
be defined as those of civil society. The kind of 'wisdom' once associated with 'knowledge' (*scientia*) became the natural philosopher's
domain; civic practice the humanist's – where before the *grammaticus*
and the *philosophus* had often been thought the same person with
a single field of operation. [35] The one would use mathematics for
discovery. The other would use language to identify and communicate
'a code of personal ethics, a moral guide to an active life of successful
virtue'. [36]

Indeed, a Charron would eventually identify true wisdom with the
second, dismissing with some scorn the 'knowledge' to which humanists had access: 'the great heap and stock of other peoples' wealth,
studied gatherum of things seen, opined, and read in books', amassed
willy nilly in 'the memory'. Wisdom was a quite different 'rule of the
soul' that educated to civic virtue. Book learning (communication)
could to some degree be at its service – but it must never pretend
more. [37] Charron would have nothing to say of a natural philosophical
scientia for which discovery was independent of natural language and

---

35. Irvine, *Making*, 6: he refers specifically to a ninth-century manuscript.
36. Rice, *Renaissance Idea*, 165.
37. Charron, *De la sagesse*, 687 (III. xiv):

> Science est un grand amas et provision du bien d'autruy, c'est un soigneux recueil
> de ce que l'on a veu, ouy dire et leu aux livres ... Or le gardoir et le magazin, ou
> demeure et se garde cette grande provision, l'estuy de la science et des biens aquis,
> est la memoire. Qui a bonne memoire, il ne tient qu'à luy, qu'il n'est sçavant: car
> il en a le moyen. La sagesse est un maniment doux et reglé de l'ame: celuy la est
> sage, qui se conduit en ses desirs, pensées, opinions, paroles, faits, reglemens, avec
> mesure et proportion.

> The next pages elaborate on the vanity and servility of book *science*, but also on
> what services it *can* render *sagesse* (III. xiv: 687–98).

whose practitioners increasingly turned towards the virtues of rationally regulated analysis. He aimed his disdain at such humanist critical philologists as Joseph Justus Scaliger, who made absolutist claims for the virtues of historical knowledge, but made, he thought, no contribution to the kind of *sagesse* needed for life in social concord (see note 19 above).

Knowledge acquired through language and through the study of language had nothing to do with the human *will* required for action in the community. It had, indeed, little to do with the intellect on which the will would operate and through which it would function. It had everything to do with a memory that Charron, in the passage previously quoted, saw as the passive 'storehouse' ('le gardoir et magazin') and 'case' ('l'estuy') of mostly useless learning. This was a faculty whose powers differed utterly from those that earlier thinkers had granted a memory whose divine purpose was to enable humans to 'get back to' the knowledge and wisdom their souls once had. *Wisdom* had become a sort of transumed 'prudence' (including but surpassing Ciceronian *prudentia*), *knowledge* would (eventually) be natural discovery – 'science'. The kind of active civic virtue people like Charron had in mind by the end of the sixteenth century thus referred to forms of doing and acting that ultimately redefined being, the very nature of the *person* involved in them.

Not all of these matters can be dealt with here. The last topic in particular is the matter of this book's companion volume, attending at length to private and public implications of sixteenth-century debates about the 'self'. Nor do I, here, write much about the technical issues of military and economic developments. The former is the object of a long chapter in my forthcoming volume around Descartes, *Descartes, Philosophy, and the Public Sphere*, that explores wider and later changes (in which book I also discuss issues of mathematics and method in the light of different, if analogous, developments). Economic matters receive no more than this mention. I focus here on the passage from 'trivial' to 'quadrivial' sources for methods of rational analysis and discovery, on its reasons and consequences, and on what it tells us about how societies make use of what I call 'cultural instruments' to rethink their establishment, both in theory and in practice.

Because it seems to me to provide the strongest – even most startling – evidence of the importance both of this change itself and of this way of seeing it, I have chosen to emphasize in this book's last three chapters the way in which changes it explores led directly to the elaboration of what can be called a rational aesthetics. It offers the strongest evidence because what I call the 'fictive imagination' (producer of what the late seventeenth century and on tended to call 'arts and [good] letters') is an area of endeavour contemporary Western peoples ordinarily have some difficulty associating with the ordered processes that 'mathematics' means to them. Yet their developments were wholly dependent upon one another, and led directly to later researches in the same area. We would expect this close relation in the natural sciences, in economic theory, in demography and geography, and elsewhere; in those activities, that is to say, that post-seventeenth-century thinking has all too often kept increasingly rigidly separate from those of the 'arts' (and that earlier centuries had included – where they existed as doctrinal activities – in the quadrivium). We expect it less, if at all, in the arts we now tend to think of as having come from the trivium.

When Peter Dear remarks how 'a mathematical philosophy that [in the seventeenth century] had ambitions to the measurement of all things became [in the nineteenth century] a science that attempted to grasp everything', he seems to catch our modern way of seeing this. [38] But the case of 'aesthetics' suggests that the 'later' grasp was in fact an explicit assumption from the start, that *in practice* the expansive claims of a Barozzi, an Adriaan van Roomen or a Johann Heinrich Alsted had won: claims for what the last called a 'mathematica generalis' and the second a 'prima mathesis' able to grasp not just abstract quantities but the real 'causes' of all concrete phenomena involving measurable times, sounds, tones, places, motions and all and any other quantitative elements. [39] It may be the case, as Dear (and others) argue, that the thoroughgoing institutionalization and imperial spread of the mathematical sciences were nineteenth-century phenomena, but both their 'operational ideal' and absolutist claims were endemic from the beginning. [40] To see that this new tool in fact produced what can only be delineated as an *aesthetic* sphere furnishes evidence that it was indeed here, in this passage from 'language' to a 'mathematics' both practical and theoretical, that one major set of transformations was worked out.

---

38. Dear, *Discipline*, 9.
39. On Roomen and Alsted here, see Crapulli, *Mathesis*, 101–46. Alsted explored his 'universa mathesis' in *Methodus admirandorum mathematicorum* (1613), Roomen offered his in *Universae mathesis idea, quae mathematicae universim sumptae natura, praestantia, usus et distributio brevissime proponuntur* (1602). My last clause refers to Crapulli 112 and 146. Van Roomen was born at Leuven, educated there and by the Jesuits at Cologne, and taught at both as well as at Würzburg. Alsted was the leading light of Herborn.
40. Dear, *Discipline*, 1.

Part 1

Problematizing the language arts

1   Grammarians' dreams

In the last years of the 1520s several debated issues about language seem to come into notably sharp conflict in vernacular works of a representative group of humanists by and large sharing education and values. I take the particular cases of three notably important works by Pierre Fabri, Geofroy Tory and John Palsgrave. But I place them against the background of much wider and longer debate and the screen of some contemporaries: most especially Charles de Bovelles. Many others, broadening also the geographic spread, will of course receive attention in the rest of the book.

Of those just mentioned, Fabri was somewhat the older: he had probably helped found the Puy des Palinods at Rouen in 1486. He died just before the 1521 publication of the work examined here. Bovelles was born early in 1479 and lived until 1567. [1] The other two were both born about 1480, Tory dying in 1533, Palsgrave in 1554. All four were thoroughly familiar with medieval debate in their field. All participated in the new learning. They looked no less to the one than the other as they tried to resolve problems. Rather, though, than solve them, they began to offer the terms through which they might one day *be* resolved.

Trivium and quadrivium were their sources. Indeed they were their contexts: as to form, their works fit quite well within the tradition – however unique in other ways Tory's and Palsgrave's were. Using old instruments taken from the familiar disciplines of languages, they moved towards new paths. Perhaps they (and others) exhausted the potential of those old instruments. So that even in the areas of language with which they dealt, future conceptual developments, it may be, were to owe less to issues raised in the trivium than to debate within the

---

1. Bovelles' dates have until lately been confused. His birth was put at around the 1480s, his death in 1529, 1553, 1556 or 1565. We now know that he was born in 1479 (before 28 March) and died 24 February 1567 (n.s.): Musial, 'Dates', 31–57. Although he apparently became quite senile in his very last years, it is pleasant to think that Bovelles may have known most of the vast changes we are exploring.

quadrivium, from which others would draw more than has usually been recognized. This chapter and the next analyze elements of a passage between fundamentally different conceptual worlds, the creating of new mechanisms with instruments and elements used for and taken from the old, the play of change and continuity.

The 'holistic' tendencies of medieval thought and society, at least theoretically, have often been noted. Here, I apply the adjective to a scholastic age running roughly from the eleventh to the fifteenth century. As R. H. Robins has put it: 'Scholasticism was a system of thought reinforced by and reinforcing the Christian faith of the day, which could serve to unify within itself all branches and departments of learning and in which the claims of reason and of revelation could be harmonized. Probably not before and certainly never since has the fabric of knowledge been so undivided at its heart'. [2] In a world created by God, where all creatures came from and tended towards Him, human rationality was no more (nor less) than an activity mediating an obscure return to the Divinity, for whom alone the world was fully comprehensible.

Yet in such a paradigm of human ignorance in the here and now but of eventually full knowledge hereafter in eternity with God, language and reason were strangely comforting. In a world so made, language and reason had somehow to fit the divine ordering of all nature. The fit was usually taken to be semantic. Words could more or less securely be understood to mean what they said. The problem was to find the meaning implanted in us by God: knowledge and reason as memory; language as the tool of memory – as Augustine and others reiterated. To find truth was to overcome forgetfulness and recall what one 'previously knew above', as one major source put it. 'We are then', Macrobius continued, 'relearning those things that we naturally knew before the influx of matter intoxicated our souls as they approached their bodies'. [3]

Even in the later, highly complex and subtle theories of the Modistae, the chief issue was to understand the relation between three levels or *modes* by which world and reason were in touch, just so that the precise functions and *meanings* underlying the *partes orationis* might be classified and understood. The three levels in question, or rather the

---

2. Robins, *Short History*, 74–5. Although dated, this work is still useful. In terms similar to those used here, I have discussed the 'patterning discourse' of the 'Middle Ages' in *Discourse*, 55–107.
3. Macrobius, *Commentary*, 135–6 (I. xii). I do not claim this was the only theory at hand; just that it was typical – however rapidly I have reviewed it. Mary Carruthers has indispensably detailed the specificity of the Middle Ages as a memory culture.

categories through which these levels might be grasped, were the *modus essendi* (relating to the *res* denoted, as it is in itself and prior to contact with any mind: this is the category of 'Firstness' in Charles S. Peirce's ontological semiotics), *modus intelligendi* (*res* as apprehended by the mind: Peirce's category of 'Secondness'), and *modus signandi* (*res* as it has been apprehended and now acquires a sign, *dictio*, potentially able to signify it: Peirce's 'Thirdness'). The *dictio* generated at the last, still pre-grammatical level is a universal concept: it has not yet, that is to say, become any particular *pars orationis*, and is not yet manifest in any language-specific phoneme (so being quite different from Saussure's 'signified'). The analysis of such *voces* falls, at the last, under *modus significandi*: only there did practical grammar's task begin – what preceded was philosophical or 'scientific' grammar's.

This series of concepts offered a way to comprehend how *partes orationis* meant and related to each other, to grasp the rational semantic principles underlying actual linguistic communication. The Modistae held these to be universal and the substance of all languages. The claim 'that languages are identical in substance' meant 'that the semantic universe from which these are invented is the same for all mankind'. The parts of speech were thought comparable in all languages because 'they represent semantic notions which exist in the universe'. [4] The Modistae were not interested in investigating individual terms *per se*, recognizing that these differed from language to language ('accidentals'). Nor were they, quite evidently and for wholly similar reasons, concerned with the social or cultural aspect of language. They sought to analyze the common sets of significant ideas taken to underlie the terms, ideas forming a single universal 'grammar', the sets, as it were, of the *dictiones*: 'for the Modistae at least, grammar meant a categorial semasiology'. Because meanings, like all nature, came from God, a grammar founded on their exploration was looked on always 'as dependent on the structure of reality'. [5] (The broader question of

---

4. Breva-Claramonte, *Sanctius' Theory*, 45. More generally here I refer to Bursill-Hall, *Speculative Grammars*. For these remarks, see especially 88–113. This work, too, is subject to the correction of later work by many scholars. The most useful recent overview is Rosier's *Grammaire spéculative*, but too many scholars to acknowledge here have contributed to a vastly and rapidly growing body of knowledge about medieval grammatical and logical theory.

5. Bursill-Hall, *Speculative Grammars*, 331. Previous quotation, 77. Rosier, too, emphasizes that the Modistae were interested in the grounds of meaning, not meaning (in utterance) itself: *Grammaire spéculative*, especially 10, 23–37, 199–200 (and see note 10 below). Besides Robins' *Short History*, the most accessible, though also dated, work in English on medieval linguistic matters is his *Ancient and Mediaeval Grammatical Theory*. Apart from works given in note 4, see Pinborg, Cerquiligni, Murphy, *Rhetoric*, Stock, *Implications*, and Irvine. These last three move us from

the structure of that reality then matters: it cannot be considered here.)
Speculative grammarians explored, but always assumed, 'the abiding
link between language and the real world', and, as G. A. Padley put
it, felt that 'grammatica est de signis rerum' ('is about the signs of
things'). [6] Such things and the intellectual concepts realizing them were
equally derived from God.

This emphasis on a philosophical and logical grammar was new and
– for the Modistae – really concerned a highly technical Latin. Prior
to the eleventh century, *grammatica* had been an altogether different
'science of interpreting the poets and other writers and the systematic
principles for speaking and writing correctly; it is the source and foundation of the liberal arts', as Martin Irvine neatly sums up ninth- to
eleventh-century views in his book's epigraph. These were, in fact,
views that came down from ancient Greece and Rome and were transmitted not only through Cicero and Quintilian, but through such as
Donatus, Priscian, Macrobius, Boethius, Cassiodorus and especially
Isidore of Seville – 'whose *Etymologiae sive origines* became the most
widely used grammatical encyclopedia of the Middle Ages', transmitted
integrally but also in its separated first book, *De grammatica*, and,
as well, in 'a set of excerpts from it' incorporated into many other
writings. [7]

These and others made a commentary tradition of *grammatica* that
trained an ability to read, interpret, rectify, and evaluate texts correctly.
It was an *ars recte loquendi et scribendi*, 'the science', wrote Isidore in
his authoritative compilation, 'of speaking correctly'. In that sense it
lay at 'the origin and foundation of liberal education' – a quite different
project from that which we have just seen. [8] Here, *grammatica*'s purview
was vast. It was nothing less, as Irvine shows, than the central vehicle
of cultural knowledge and its various institutions for a millennium
and more, until about the twelfth century. Indeed, despite the fact that
so early a thinker as Anselm had already tended to turn grammar

---

what might be thought 'linguistic' matters, and the number of works on medieval
grammar, rhetoric, and logic has grown dramatically over the past few years (my
bibliography gives others, but only those used in preparing this book). Still, these
works give a good overview of texts and issues. More general but very important
is Zumthor, *Essai*. A most useful bibliography may be found in Giard, 'Du latin'
52–5.

6. Padley, *Grammatical Theory ... Vernacular Grammar*, I. 234. By *res*, medieval
   commentators (after Cicero, the *ad Herrenium* and Quintilian) meant any referent
   besides the word itself.
7. Irvine, *Making*, xiii for the epigraph; 209, 212 for the comments on Isidore; 209–43
   for his whole discussion.
8. Isidore, *Etymologiae xx*, I. V. 1: 'scientia recte loquendi est origo et fundamentum
   liberalium litterarum'.

into a branch of speculative philosophy, [9] throughout the European Middle Ages grammar stood as the first of the seven liberal arts, at the head of the *trivium*: the grounding element in the triple prope-deutic to the quadrivium. And even for the Modistae, if grammar had lost its foundational cultural sweep, it yet retained a different kind of centrality. For it was taken to provide access to the bases of thought itself. Language and language study, that is to say, were still thought '*productive* of knowledge'.

But taken as the first element in the trivium, grammar could also be reduced to little more than a servant of the other six liberal arts, gate-way to the paths of real knowledge. Despite – or because of – the Modistae's philosophical claims that to study grammar gave access to the very foundations of thinking and was no less essential a part of philoso-phy than dialectic, by their time grammar in its older understanding often (usually?) received reductive interpretations: especially in texts not particularly aimed at Latinate scholars. [10] Now that that grammar had become 'speculative', it had to be separated from its old, broader cultural claims. These were diverted into poetics and glosses on the clas-sical tradition, neither of which had a place in the school curriculum. This did not leave much matter for less-speculative study of language as such (although some did try to continue the older *grammatica*).

Thus, in 1392, a good century after the speculative grammarians had been at their height, Eustache Deschamps wrote of grammar as first of the arts: 'par lequel l'on vient et aprant tous les autres ars par les figures des letres A, B, C, que les enfans apraннent premierement, et par lesquelz aprandre et sçavoir l'on peut venir a toute science, et monter de la plus petite letre jusques a la plus haulte'. [11] Although this could be clearer, Deschamps seems to be saying that grammar teaches

---

9. Elsky, *Authorizing*, 25.
10. I thank Luce Giard for reminding me that late medieval thinkers about language dealt more with a learned technical language than with languages in general. Irvine echoes the point (*Making*, 464). Bursill-Hall notes that thirteenth-century pre-modist grammarians like Grosseteste, Ralph of Beauvais, Hugutio of Pisa, Jordan of Saxony, Nicholas of Paris, Robert Kilwardby and Roger Bacon already made Latin 'tanta-mount to a metalanguage, so that [it] became for them the specification of the general grammar, the word-classes and syntax of the perfect language' (introduction to Thomas of Erfurt, *Grammatica*, 19). Jensen adopts this view of the Modistae in his *Rhetorical Philosophy*, 51–2. That said, other grammarians did not ignore vernac-ulars (Lusignan, *Parler*). Still, by the thirteenth century many felt that real grammar (represented by Isidore) was being banished in favour of philosophical logic. A mid-thirteenth-century poem has grammar embattled at Orléans and finally defeated by the forces of logic and the quadrivial arts from the University of Paris. Grammar withdraws to Egypt (Andeli, *Battle*).
11. Deschamps, *Art de dictier*, 266: 'through which one reaches and learns all the other arts by the figures of the letters A, B, C, that children learn first, and by whose

us our letters so that we can then move on not deeper in *grammatica*, but into the other written 'sciences'. A few years later an anonymous author was even less precise and clear in delineating the aim of such linguistic study, seeing it both in narrowly practical terms, producing familiarity with and for use, and in broader theoretical ones, enabling knowledge and authority (to be sure, this author was concentrating on poetics): 'MERCURE fu dieu de langage. Tient on que il estoit dieu de sagesse, maiz il estoit de pesant somme tendant et pratique, et de ses jours tenoit l'estude de langages divers; et regna en toutes les parties de l'Orient.' [12]

Behind such a comment, almost surely, lay Martianus Capella's enormously popular allegorical textbook, *De nuptiis Philologiae et Mercurii*, which, with Boethius' writings, provided a foundation for the medieval schools' teaching in *trivium* and *quadrivium*. For both writers, as for Isidore a century and a half later, grammar had been that doorway to and ground of all learning that many equated with philosophy. [13] But simplification in Deschamps' direction seemed to be Coluccio Salutati's view, as well, when he penned a letter to a friend in 1406 on the trivium and quadrivium, and on pagan and sacred poetry. Grammar, he wrote, was 'the gateway to all the liberal arts and to all learning, human and divine'. 'How can one', he asked, 'know letters without a knowledge of grammar?' 'The art of grammar comes first in order and in [ease of] perception.' This did not mean that it was inscribed onto an empty slate, however, for 'grammar itself is in great part unintelligible without a knowledge of general facts [*rerum*], of how the essential nature of things changes, and how all the sciences work together – not to mention a knowledge of terminology.' For Salutati, chancellor of Florence, grammar, like all learning, grounded public prudence and service to the political community, but 'ease of perception' was not how any of the older grammarians would have characterized the higher reaches of their discipline. [14]

---

learning and knowing one can reach all knowledge, and climb from the smallest letter to the highest'. By Deschamps' time, nominalist thinkers had dealt major blows to the philosophical underpinnings of modist speculation.

12. Anonymous, *Regles*, 97: 'Mercury was the god of language. It is held that he was god of wisdom, but he was profoundly active and practical, and in his time led the study of different languages; and ruled throughout the East.'

13. For a modern translation, see Martianus Capella, *Marriage*. On grammar and philosophy, see Irvine, *Making*, 6.

14. Salutati, 'Letter to Giovanni Dominici', 351, 355. For the letter's dating, see 6 n. 8. On Salutati's relating of learning to active civil life, see above all Baron, *Crisis* (1955), especially 81–94, but Salutati is a central figure throughout this book's two volumes. For a brief and clear appraisal, see the revised one-volume edition with the same title (100–18) and Rice, *Renaissance Idea*, 36–43.

The simpler views of writers like Deschamps and Salutati, as well as the ambiguity of claim of my second quotation, continuing an older tradition of grammatical theory and apparently largely ignoring more recent philosophical trends, may also have reflected a development that some modern historians of language argue as the primary source of Renaissance linguistic theory. This was the rise of a grammatical tradition in Provence and northern Italy from about the eleventh century that emphasized 'lexicographic and grammatical writing . . . oriented towards rhetoric rather than dialectic'. The rhetoric in question was 'not the art of forensic eloquence but the techniques of written composition, or the *ars dictandi*, as it was called in those days'. [15]

Targeting actual practice (which also explains why Provence of the troubadours and post-Norman Britain saw the earliest efforts at vernacular grammars), this work grew to understand language as a historical process, and undermined universalist views. By the mid-fifteenth century, Lorenzo Valla was denying any logical basis for grammar, relying on a forthright pragmatism that sixteenth-century grammarians were to criticize. He urged that actual usage took precedence over any 'law' supposed to precede and legitimate it. [16] But this claim by no means sapped the semantic basis of linguistic analysis. Contrary, for example, to the rather radically constructivist conclusions Richard Waswo seeks to foist on Valla, drawing an assertion that the Italian thought of language as 'making' reality from a heavily belaboured analysis of a passage on names and things in Valla's *Dialecticae disputationes*, the humanist strove to keep a clear

---

15. Percival, 'Grammatical Tradition', 233. Quoting Percival, Padley opposes southern rhetorical simplicity to northern (French and German) dialectically-oriented 'logic chopping' (*Vernacular Grammar*, I. 2–4). Part 1 of his *Vernacular Grammar*, II. 5–153, discusses this chiefly Italian tradition. From it came the first major vernacular grammar, probably by Leon Battista Alberti *c.* 1443, fifty years before Elio Antonio de Nebrija's *Gramática castellana* (1492), long thought the first. Alberti's manuscript was not, however, published until 1908 (23–7). On this, see Grayson, 'Leon Battista Alberti' and the same scholar's edition of the work: *La prima grammatica*. Matters of precedence are always dubious. One may mention work in Provençal grammar between 1200 and 1350, especially the third book of the *Leys d'amour* (Law, 'Originality') and work in England and France, starting with what seems the first written French grammar, the *Donait françois* commissioned by John Barton *c.* 1409 (Kibbee, *For to Speke*, 85–92, and Lusignan, *Parler*, 111–15). Nebrija's was the first *printed* vernacular grammar.

16. Giard, 'Du latin', 43. See, too, Waswo, *Language and Meaning*, 88–113 – a work marred, it seems to me, by some forced misreadings, however much Waswo may acknowledge the contemporary interests that lie behind his analysis (see note 17 below). On Valla, for these matters, see above all L. Jardine, 'Lorenzo Valla and the Origins'; Vasoli, *Dialettica*, 37–77; and Jensen, *Rhetorical Philosophy*, 52–5.

distinction between the two – and to rely upon it for his understanding of meaning. [17]

Valla's younger contemporary, Niccolò Perotti, based his work on a similar pragmatism. His 1468 *Rudimenta grammatica* (published in 1473), defined grammar as but the 'art of speaking correctly and writing correctly as observed by the reading of writers and poets'. W. Keith Percival calls this work the 'first comprehensive Latin grammar ever produced by a Renaissance humanist'. Influential deep into the next century, like his posthumously published *Cornucopiae*, such a work provided a pragmatic resource for effective writing and speaking. [18] These writings ultimately emphasized the production of *elegantia* in writing, and directly fed both the long debates about Ciceronianism and those about creating vernaculars to rival Greek and Latin that peaked in the second quarter of the sixteenth century in works by such as Pietro Bembo, Juan de Valdés and Joachim du Bellay. In a very

---

17. Waswo, *Language*, 105–11. Valla was separating the names 'wood', 'stone', 'iron', 'virtue', 'genus', 'species', 'substance' from their corresponding referents – or 'things', as he wrote, following normal usage (see note 6 above). He told his reader that one is a word the other is not: 'illud non vox, hoc vox est' – of which Waswo makes heavy weather, unsure whether Valla intended a 'fact', 'joke', or 'genuine contradiction' (108). What if he meant what he said (minus our punctuation)? Then 'ergo vocabulum inquies est supra res, quia res vocabulum est etiam, sed significatum rei supra significatum vocabuli est' (given by Waswo as 'therefore, you will say, the term is above the thing because "thing" is also a term; but what is signified by "thing" is more than what is signified by "term"') infers something like the doctrine of supposition (hidden here by different translations of *supra*). Contrary to what Waswo urges (after Gerl, *Rhetorik*, 217–24), Valla does not collapse word and thing. Both, he wrote, must be written as *res*. *That* is why he was anxious to make his reader see not only that they are not the same, but that the word is under (*sub*) the thing, which is *above* (*supra*) it, signified by it. The passage is incomprehensible if one ignores its manifold effort to keep the distinction. Waswo uses his reading to claim that Valla and others held a theory that language structures our reality and that concepts do not exist beyond words. This would differ wholly from scholastic ideas. It is nonsense. Waswo was taken to task for such reading by Monfasani, 'Is Valla?' He replied that if Valla had not been heterodox he would not have been attacked by his contemporaries: 'Motives'. The trouble with such a claim (to which I do not do entire justice) is that you cannot exhaust the forms of heterodoxy or the motives of attack. For useful comment, see Maclean, *Interpretation*, 3–4, 212–13.

18. Percival, 'Place', 233: 'ars recte loquendi recteque scribendi, scriptorum et poetarum lectionibus observata'. Paul Grendler has also studied this work and its impact (*Schooling*, 162–72). According to Karl Rosen, the *Rudimenta* had some thirty editions from 1471 to 1541 in France alone ('On the Publication', 265). The *Cornucopiae* was a kind of combined dictionary and commentary on the first book of Martial's *Epigrammata*. Jean-Claude Margolin notes that it had at least twenty-four editions between 1489 and 1536 in Italy (chiefly Venice), France and Rhenish Germany, and was mined by Pico, Erasmus, Budé and Vives among others ('La fonction pragmatique', 124, 126). Percival's 'Changes' is a useful summary of many of these developments.

real way, they picked up the relation between grammar and civil society where Salutati had left it.

The full impact of this work was not really to be felt, however, for a half century or so beyond Valla and Perotti, once Erasmus, Vives, Guillaume Budé and others began to pick up on it and explore its implications. Indeed, Lisa Jardine observes that although Valla's work and Agricola's equally influential *De inventione dialectica* 'were completed, and accessible by the last decades of the fifteenth century, their popularity and influence date only from the late 1520s and 1530s': a fact whose importance we will soon see. It is worth noting, too, that emphasis on actual usage was typical of debates about jurisprudential interpretation and meaning, for almost always, as Ian Maclean has shown, they referred to the needs of particular cases.[19]

If I mention, rather rapidly and cavalierly, these medieval concerns and concepts, it is because the beginning of the sixteenth century confronted a number of difficulties in conceptualizing language and thought. Their past lay in the Middle Ages. These traditions were not alternatives or opponents: all were available at once. It is not only that the 'distinction . . . often made today between humanism and scholasticism in the Renaissance is an analytical tool of our time', whereas 'the sixteenth century did not necessarily see the two as incompatible', as Kristian Jensen writes. It is also that other, seemingly new ways of thought, such as 'Euclidianism' and Platonism, had already woven strands deep into and through the Middle Ages. Future solutions to difficulties drew on a variety that prevented any mere chronological divide, even as they resulted as well from later sixteenth-century debate, in the Latin grammars of Thomas Linacre, Julius Caesar Scaliger, Ramus and Francisco Sanchez, and culminated in seventeenth-century epistemological writings of such as Francis Bacon, Descartes, Port-Royal and John Locke.[20]

---

19. L. Jardine, 'Lorenzo Valla and the Origins', 147; Maclean, *Interpretation*: the last studies commentary aimed at real practice (although a brief examination of Francisco Suárez (179–81) explores an important case of wholly theoretical concordance). Like Jardine, Jensen shows that even in grammars by writers directly associated with Valla, things hardly changed. He implies, in fact, that real change was even later than she suggests (*Rhetorical Philosophy*, 61–80, 86–7). Ashworth's 1530 date, mentioned in my introduction, may usefully be recalled here ('Eclipse', 787, 790, 795–6).

20. The Jensen citation is from *Rhetorical Philosophy*, 186. Naming these grammarians and philosophers, especially the first, I accept the findings of Padley's *Latin Tradition*. Of equal importance, on vernacular issues, is Chevalier's *Histoire*. Padley's volumes on *Vernacular Grammar* are essential. For parallel rhetorical debate, Howell's *Logic* is still basic. For the period directly contemporary with that of the works analyzed here, see Chomarat's ponderous but informative *Grammaire*. More generally, Apel's *Idea* is useful. This translates *Die Idee der Sprache in der Tradition des Humanismus*

Such solutions will break with the semantic analogy between language, thinking and being. Between the three a separation will occur and a new concept of methodical ordering will be invented. This concept will enable a manipulative knowledge to be founded not on the assumption of a semasiology whose ultimate guarantor is God, but on a claim that the 'proper' ordering of language makes it a transparent mediation of an identically ordered process of reason, itself echoing the mechanism of the material world. *Meanings* may then be arbitrarily (which is *not* the same as wilfully or deliberately) set according to what is useful for the new 'practical philosophy' aimed at making material, and therefore spiritual, life better for all humanity. But their *ordering* is set by the nature of the world (which is why a concept of *laissez-faire* will be inevitable: the individual within such an order is literally unable to contravene a process that is universal, and what it does *must* conform with that process). Language, then, could no longer be the tool of discovery which people had earlier often hoped and strained for it to be – in that regard it was reduced by such as Galileo and Bacon to a mere trope: an 'analogy' of material order. Language could now be 'no more' than a perfect definitional and descriptive instrument. [21]

They will not write, like older grammarians and compilers such as Donatus, Priscian, Martianus Capella, Cassiodorus and Isidore, that writing gave access to and produced all knowledge; like Deschamps or Salutati that learning language was a first step to acquiring such knowledge through the other arts; like others, that grammar provided a means to know the sources and derivations of terms and a way to write with elegance; or like the Modistae, that grammar and logic were both paths towards an ultimate 'knowledge of existence'. Rather will they construe the relation between language and ordered community in a rather particular way, giving it an inflexion that the isolated Salutati early and the sixteenth-century Ciceronians later hardly had in mind. They will say that right speaking confers and is the mark of a *mastering* of knowledge gained by other means (other than linguistic, that is to say), but according to a sole process of order. This is so whether the 'other means' involves the senses, as it will for some, or innate and universal

---

von Dante bis Vico (1963), which various mishaps have stopped me seeing. Maclean, too, insists on the evidence for change and continuity: *Interpretation*, especially 203–14 (but it is the entire volume's theme).

21. Reiss, *Discourse* (especially 203–12 for Bacon's claim *re* language), introduction to *Uncertainty*, *et passim* in the first three chapters of *Meaning*. Galileo's remark about mathematics as the language of matter is renowned. Thomas Hobbes and Descartes made like comments, as did Johannes Kepler, although he certainly had in mind something other than the analogy intended by the others.

ideas, as it will for others. Elio Antonio Nebrija's 1492 remark that language was the 'companion of empire' did not attend simply to political, economic, or religious empire, but also, he went on in his dedication to Isabella, to control of both knowledge and history: it alone could describe and record them for now and for posterity – *'para nuestra recordación y memoria'*. [22]

In medieval schools, grammar and knowledge of syllogistic logic were essential – while such logic did not alone preoccupy medieval thinkers, it was certainly primary. [23] True knowledge was assumed as given once and for all. To achieve it one worked inwards with means *already there*. By the end of the sixteenth century, syllogistic logic and semantically oriented grammar were being replaced by a logic of inquiry or discovery, whose methodical basis was drawn largely from the mathematical arts of the quadrivium, and by a grammar aiming to *express* (not permit) discovery in a syntax whose proper order was supposed identical to that of the underlying logic. Grammar might remain first in pedagogy (since without access to linguistic communication no learning of knowledge could occur), but it was no longer first in epistemology, far less in ontology. No more was the word in the beginning – a change that took 'discovery' from the purview of *all* the disciplines of the trivium. Not for nothing was Descartes to invert the medieval order and assert that the proper method of reasoning would inevitably produce the exact language to accompany it. [24]

For most medieval teaching, then (and this is the case, if less explicitly so, in non-modistic writers as well), a knowledge of grammar was taken to provide *some* kind of semantically direct access to concepts and to the world of 'being'. It did so by virtue of the universality of the conceptual ground. It did so regardless of the precise ways in which different commentators and thinkers described such access: to elaborate exegeses was to obtain the only knowledge available to humans, and to walk the only path possible towards the Divinity. Such an assumption vitally

---

22. Nebrija, *Gramática*, 97, 101.
23. See, for example, Ashworth's many essays, but more concretely the different kinds of argument discussed in the most popular textbook of the mid-thirteenth to mid-sixteenth centuries, Peter of Spain's *Summule logicales* (1246), especially Tractates 4 to 12, although these do not always concern what one might call 'arguments' (*Tractatus*, 43–232. See, too, Dinneen's English translation of this edited text.) L. Jardine reminds us that the *Summulae* were widely used into the 1520s; in some places as late as the seventeenth century (*Francis Bacon*, 19). Ong earlier explored the *Summulae* and its impact on sixteenth-century humanists in *Ramus, Method*, 55–91.
24. In his letter to Marin Mersenne of 20 November 1629 (Descartes, *Oeuvres*, I. 230–2). Similarly, L. Jardine notes a passage from 'certainty to probability as the focus of intellectual attention' ('Lorenzo Valla and the Origins', 164).

underlay medieval hermeneutics, indicating a concept of understanding
still present in Pierre Fabri's *Rhetoric*, written a full century after the
anonymous text quoted earlier (which dated from between 1411 and
1432), and contemporaneously with the work of such writers as Niccolò
Machiavelli, Erasmus and Thomas More.

Fabri asserted, fully in accord with the grand hermeneutic tradition
dating back at least to the Stoics:

> Et sainct Hierosme dit que es parolles n'est pas l'euangile, mais au sens, et
> soubz l'escorche est la mouelle. Encore a la saincte escripture tout le texte
> est exposé en quatres manieres: la premiere literalement, comme Hierusalem
> au sens literal signifie cité de Hierusalem qui est en terre de Iudée; la
> seconde moralement, il signifie ainsi loyalle et chrestienne; la tierce maniere
> alegoriquement, et adonc Hierusalem signifie l'eglise militante; la quarte
> maniere anagogiquement, et ainsi Hierusalem signifie l'eglise triumphante. [25]

That Dante, Boccaccio and many others (especially biblical exegetes)
had made use of this commonplace example is not the point. [26] What
matters is that this critical assertion recalled a principal condition of
the linguistic sign for most thinkers even of the late Middle Ages
(although I am aware that this is a perilous generalization): that very
condition which had been the object of such intense theoretical speculation. The concept of semantic analogy of which I have been writing
did not imply any kind of similarity (far less 'identity') between something like a Saussurian signifier and signified, between, as Deschamps
called them respectively, *semblance* and *signification*, *terme* and *sens*
as they were named around 1501 by l'Infortuné, author of the *Jardin*

---

25. Fabri, *Grant et vray art*, 12–13:

    And St Jerome says that the Gospel is not in words but in sense, and the pith is
    under the bark. Further, in Holy Scripture the full text is explained in four ways:
    the first literally, as Jerusalem in the literal sense signifies the city of Jerusalem in
    the land of Judea; the second morally, where it signifies loyal and Christian; the
    third allegorically, and then Jerusalem signifies the Church militant; the fourth
    anagogically, where Jerusalem signifies the Church triumphant.

    Future references will be in my text by 'PF' and page.
26. Henri de Lubac argued that the fourfold exegesis originated in the work of the
    Church Fathers: *Exégèse médiévale*, I. 171–207. This is inexact. Through Varro's *De
    lingua latina* the idea goes back at least to the Stoics (Reiss, *Discourse*, 80–1). The
    De lingua itself was known to almost none throughout the Middle Ages, but Varro's
    '*Disciplinarum libri* IX, which began with a *De grammatica* (now lost), was the most
    influential encyclopedia in the Roman world'. Its disciplines modulated into the
    medieval trivium and quadrivium. 'His classification of the *artes* and his model of
    grammatica' had become 'authoritative', his views incorporated into the tradition
    (Irvine, *Making*, 51). Given my point about the complex ways in which medieval
    patterns and humanist researches inspirit one another, it is worth recalling that Varro
    was a major source of material and inspiration as much for Lorenzo Valla early as
    for Erasmus later, not to mention his constant use by Augustine in *The City of God*.

de Plaisance. [27] Rather, grammatical 'science' explored the 'signified', specifying and gathering meaning: what Fabri here also called *sens*. Grammar, allied with dialectic, did not presuppose, either, any observation of external phenomena. No effort to find such external referents was implied – they were given in and by the *significatio*, the *dictio*. Focus was on the linguistic grounds of valid inference and formal analysis from assumptions that 'discovery' of truths was essentially their *recovery*. Even if language since Babel no longer possessed the immediate relation of identity with the world that it had before, some such relation remained, however hidden, and maybe could even be recovered etymologically – although it mattered little whether one actually did so, for God still stood as final Guarantor. In 1521, Fabri still confirmed – or hankered for – such a view.

Indeed, what I most wish to stress of these early sixteenth-century writers is how they produced notable change while staying often confusingly (but not confus*ed*ly – *this* confusion is ours, not theirs) embedded in past authority, how they used, as I suggested, old instruments for newly emerging ends – and we shall briefly glimpse at the end of this chapter how even these quite fundamental 'medieval' forms of conceptualization stayed alive still very much later. We shall have several reasons to hesitate before Ong's now widely accepted idea of the overwhelming impact of the visual metaphors and even conceptualization of Ramus' work. He argued that they indicated a growing separation between thought and its object (and between thought and language as its expression) and gave evidence of an essential transformation in mentality – in what Foucault was to call 'episteme'. Mathematical thought and a wider debate over method seem to me almost surely more important, that mathematical thought whose renovation and revival Rose could refer to as a humanist 'obsession'. All the same, some such distancing was already becoming apparent at the very beginning of this century. [28]

---

27. Deschamps, *Art de dictier*, 277; [l'Infortuné], *Jardin* I. iiij v.
28. The last reference is to Rose, *Italian Renaissance*, 1, the earlier to Ong, *Ramus, Method*. In *Discourse*, I adopted Ong's view, but now feel this analysis needs serious review. This book attempts it. Among other things, we will see both the ambiguity of the use of visual metaphors and its antiquity. Giard comments that Lefèvre d'Etaples made much of 'Ramus'-style tables and 'trees' as early as 1520. She credits his Lullist interests ('Mise', 71). Bovelles used such devices in his 1509 Lullist *Ars oppositorum*. So had Llull (not to mention Porphyry) – Ong was, of course, fully aware of all these, but tended to downplay them or see them just as hesitant precursors (*Ramus, Method*, 76–91). If they are epistemologically important, the issue is to know when, if ever, they came to dominate ways of thought and analysis, not as visual aids but as basic cognitive processes. The evidence that they did so is unconvincing. (The mass of emblem books in the 150 years between the 1520s and 1670s

L'Infortuné was thus able to write that Second Rhetoric was 'un regard scientifique' that 'donne sa clere vision / Aux erreurs nubileux.' [29] To be sure, these 'obscure errors' were still no doubt *within* the sign itself (after all, l'Infortuné was discussing the analytical purpose of poetics). Yet it remains that such a 'clear view', combined with an idea of *science* as an ordered, general, and *useful* knowledge, implied a view from above, a potential mastery of *sens* and of *terme*, of *signification* and *semblance* that had rarely been quite so explicit. Before, one might have hoped for a clear enough *understanding* of meanings, a 'correct' interpretation of signs, but their control was in the hands (and sight) of God, via human memory. The fourfold course of medieval criticism repeated by Fabri was a model of how to work by stages through letter, moral habit, allegorical authority and memory to anagogical illumination and one's final humble bow before God's Grace.

Such a sequence was possible because every aspect of the universe corresponded in some way with every other. Divine Creation had instituted a singular harmony, whereby every detail found some analogy among a myriad other details. Since God's gift of Christ, humanity had been brought back into that scheme. And throughout the Middle Ages another powerful tradition reinforced Christianity's claim. This was a Graeco-Latin antiquity whose 'Pythagorean' number harmonies imbued the quadrivium as it had come through Ptolemy, Martianus, Boethius and Cassiodorus, and which had left a mystical philosophical legacy that found its way into the trivium through Porphyry and into theology at least via Augustine. Edgar de Bruyne, discussing (and paraphrasing) Boethian aesthetics, has noted that

it is through divine Reason that all things were settled in harmony according to the order of numbers: before revealing themselves to the senses, they existed in the eternal and intelligible model of the creative intelligence and it is this pre-existing mathematical law that gave birth to the innumerable combinations of the elements, the harmonious sequence of the seasons, the course of the stars and the heavens. [30]

This combination of Christian and 'Platonico-Pythagorean' traditions often makes it difficult to judge the source of seeming novelty in texts

---

is far more impressive: but they suggest quite other sorts of relation between verbal and visual.) Further, as Irvine observes, the visual was of huge importance in the manuscript tradition, whose texts we should consider a 'total system of verbal and visual meaning' (*Making*, 17; see also 371–93). We will later see further complications.

29. *Jardin* I. ij v: 'a scientific look [that] gives its clear view/To obscure errors'.
30. Bruyne, *Etudes*, I. 9.

by early humanists. Ernst Cassirer has argued at length that this mathematical tradition was transformed by Nicholas of Cusa, leading in one
direction towards a mystical metaphysics, in the other to a new science.
But John E. Murdoch has shown how in writings of Bradwardine,
Heytesbury, Swineshead and others the mathematics of natural philosophical questions of continuity, finite and infinite, motion and
kinematics, changes of various kinds of quantity and quality were
readily applied to issues such as how to *measure* the relative perfection of species and to divers theological questions. Once again, that is
to say, it remains exceedingly hard to pick single figures or exiguous
moments that mark transformation.[31] Indeed, I mean to insist on
this complexity, and on the fact that we are dealing with what one
can think of as multiple continuities. For one of the major new strands
of influence came from the 'neoplatonism' consequent on the influx of
scholars and works during the decay and after the fall of
Constantinople.

A first impulse sometimes appeared to exaggerate strands already
present in medieval thought, even while giving rise, in a Cusa, a
Valla, a Pico, a Ficino, a Lefèvre d'Etaples, to quite unaccustomed
works. Such a one, too, was the remarkable *Champ Fleury*, published by
Geofroy Tory in 1529. His aim, he wrote, was to glorify the French language, establish it on firm rules, and teach how to speak it with elegance:
goals that appear to situate the work in both grammar and rhetoric,
although Ramus would not hesitate to call it 'a kind of [Gaulish or
French grammar] treatise'. Indeed, the work's goals align it with the
older medieval tradition (and such treatises as it is on the symbolism of
the alphabet were common), even as it stretches towards the new.[32]

In Paris, in the first decade and a half of the century, Tory had
moved in the circle of the first French humanists. It included Lefèvre

---

31. The quotation is from ibid., I. 14. The other references are to Cassirer, *Individual*,
    14, 41, 48–59, and Murdoch, '*Mathesis*', especially 239–46. This kind of mathemat-
    ical exploration was quite different from the logical 'quantification' of which Ong
    writes, although they were connected via suppositional theory (*Ramus, Method*,
    53–73). Cusa's name will recur. He was a central figure in the studies of Lefèvre
    d'Etaples and his circle and an authoritative name for many later mathematicians
    (Cassirer, *Erkenntnisproblem*, I. 52–77). Antonio Pérez-Ramos suggests that Cusa,
    like many others later, got his notion of 'the truth of mathematical propositions'
    from Proclus' commentary on Euclid's first book (*Francis Bacon's Idea of Science*,
    56). Chapters 4 and 5 of this book show how this matters.
32. Tory, *Champ fleury*, title-page verso. Future references are by 'GT' and page. Ramus'
    comment is in the 1572 dedication to Catherine de' Medici of his *Grammaire
    françoise*, reproduced in Waddington, *Ramus*, 417–20: 'Geoffroy Tory, maistre du
    pot cassé, lors imprimeur du Roy, en [de la grammaire gaulloyse ou françoyse] mit
    en lumière quelque traicté' (419). For 'treatises and poems on the symbolism' of
    letters, see Irvine, *Making*, 103.

himself, with his pupils, the mathematicians, philosophers, and theologians Josse Clichtove and Charles de Bovelles. Lefèvre's concerns were
manifold, his energy prodigious. His exegeses on and editing of biblical
books, especially but not only New Testament (Psalms in 1509, Pauline
Epistles in 1512, Gospels in 1522), were as reforming as those of
Erasmus. At the same time, further aided by such formidable scholar–
printers as Jodocus Badius Ascensius and Beatus Rhenanus, he brought
to print both patristic writings and those of several medieval mystics
(Elizabeth of Schönau, Hildegard of Bingen, Richard of St Victor, Jan
van Ruysbroeck, Ramon Llull, and others). Lefèvre had met Pico in
Paris in 1485, and in the winter of 1491/2 he travelled to Italy to talk
with him and the Venetian Aristotelian Ermolao Barbaro. There, he
also conversed with the third member of this 'triumvirate', as he called
them: 'Marsilio Ficino, the first and true propagator of Platonic philosophy among the Italians.' [33]

Early in the next century, Lefèvre, Clichtove and Bovelles were deep
in the study of Llull and Cusa. From 1499, seven books by the former
issued from their workshop, which also printed parts of the *Corpus
Hermeticum*, and works by Athenagoras, pseudo-Denis, Heraclides
and Cusa. Bovelles wrote the first printed biography of Llull in
1511, and his 1551 theological dialogues showed how great was Llull's
and Cusa's influence on that area of Bovelles' thought still years
later. [34] At the same time, the group was concerned to bring to light
an Aristotle freed of medieval accretions, refined directly from the
Greek: 'For knowledge of natural philosophy, for knowledge of ethics,
politics and economics, drink from the fountain of a purified Aristotle,'
Lefèvre urged in his 1506 commentary on the *Politics*. His friend
Barbaro had translated the entire *Organon* by the time he was
thirty, and joined humanists like Lefèvre in scorn for what he saw as
the futile calculus and logic of such medieval thinkers as Swineshead:
'the sophistical rubbish and Suisethian inanities commonly called
empty quibblings'. [35]

The group's own interest in mathematics was considerable. They
edited and wrote on Euclid, Boethius' *Arithmetica* and *De musica*,
the pseudo-Boethian *Geometria*, and Jordanus Nemorarius' arithmetic
and music. Clichtove and Bovelles wrote Platonizing philosophical
and mathematical works. Maurice de Gandillac scorns Bovelles'

---

33. Lefèvre d'Etaples, *Prefatory Epistles*, xii n. 6; also Gandillac, 'Lefèvre', 156–8. Vasoli
    has written on the logical work of Lefèvre and 'sua scuola' (*Dialettica*, 183–213).
34. Llinarès, 'Lullisme', 127; Gandillac, 'Lefèvre', 163.
35. Lefèvre, *Prefatory Epistles*, xv–xvi, 204, 227: 'sophisticae quisquilae et suisetica inania
    quae vulgo cavillationes vocantur'.

studies in this area as 'far beneath Cusa's thought', and that of a 'mere amateur'. [36] But these works, maybe above all Bovelles' own *Geometry*, reprinted a number of times in Latin and French, also had their practical intentions, and it does seem the case that Bovelles later quite reduced Platonic aspects of his mathematics. In this regard, an intellectual link is suggested with growing Italian interest in the practical benefits of mathematical techniques, and with researches that would one day provide an exit from linguistic *hallucinationes*, 'errings' or 'babblings' – to use Bovelles' eventual term for the dilemmas we will soon explore.

Before doing so, however, one must stress that Lefèvre and his circle did not confine such practical intentions to mathematics. On the one hand, their efforts to return to more pristine religious sources and to offer readers the personal experiences of medieval mystics were associated with reformist movements whose political and social impact were already becoming apparent, and were soon due to become dramatically more so. Lefèvre's patron was the reforming bishop Guillaume Briçonnet. In 1521 Briçonnet brought him to Meaux to help effect 'a comprehensive programme of diocesan reform', as Eugene Rice calls it, and in 1523 the bishop made him his vicar-general. That same year, the Paris faculty of theology detected errors in his Gospel commentary. Summoned two years later to appear before Parlement on suspicion of heresy, Lefèvre fled to Strasbourg. The next year, however, François I brought him back as royal librarian and then as tutor to his children. Under royal protection, Lefèvre finished his translation of the Bible (Antwerp, 1530). He spent his last years at the court of the king's sister, Marguerite de Navarre. [37] She and her associates (François Rabelais among them) were not Lutheran, as some chose to imagine, but they assuredly urged reforms one could think of as 'Erasmian'.

On the other hand, Lefèvre and his friends had not hidden their political views. The idea of an early Christian *communitas*, deduced both from their medieval mystics and their New Testament and patristic readings, could readily be joined to arguments drawn from Aristotle to the effect that a legitimate politics had as its goal a right ordering of the *republica*, acquiring, establishing, and conserving it. It was like a household, πόλις/*civitas* being a large-scale version of οἰκία/*domus* (subject of an 'Economics' as the former was of a 'Politics'). The *communitas* that was the *res publica* echoed the ideal

---

36. Gandillac, 'Lefèvre', 164.
37. Rice, introduction to Lefèvre, *Prefatory Epistles*, xiii–xiv.

'unity' that marked Creation itself. So Clichtove prefaced Aristotle's
Politics in 1516, mainly summarizing Lefèvre's 1506 commentary on
the same work. [38] In his own preface, Lefèvre repeated Aristotle – that
the commonwealth's purpose was to be useful, honest, pleasing. But
his commentary argued that the only legitimate commonwealth was
one of people working together for the common good and for those
three ends. The best life involved a public service whose steps were
those of deliberation, judgment, magistracy. All citizens were called to
occupy some kind of public charge, and all could, in this sense, achieve
that balance between the active and the contemplative life which was
the good, and whose attainment was the reason for the commonwealth's
existence. [39]

The *domus/civitas* association meant that although the place of chief
magistrate, be it prince or other, was 'natural', it equally bore 'natural'
duties and obligations. At the same time, community itself meant an
equal exchange of mutual tasks, whose final purpose was the good
(Christian) life: one that involved active involvement along with the
opportunity to contemplate the wider universal order whose mainte-
nance one thus enabled. That Lefèvre dedicated his 1506 *Politics* to
the reforming Briçonnet is of a piece with Clichtove's dedication of it
in 1516 to the President of the Paris Parlement, Charles Guillart. [40]
One is reminded of Salutati's earlier ideals, not to mention those of
Bruni, his successor as Florentine chancellor, of Leon Battista Alberti,
and others from the same city and (less) from Venice. [41] Their once
idiosyncratic and unique ideal of active civic humanism now had
growing appeal. It would grow even more thanks to the fact that in
the early years of the sixteenth century, Lefèvre's circle also included
Erasmus, publishing major works in Paris (by Valla among others),
Budé, already the foremost Hellenist of his age, and, besides the learned
printers mentioned, Henri Estienne (for whom Tory at one time
worked). Their varied origins, wide travels, and surging reputations
ensured the ideal's dissemination. The matter will return, for the ideal
was intimately tied to their linguistic researches.

Like all these, Tory worked as a teacher and editor: three editions
of ancient geographical texts, a Quintilian, and an Alberti (*De re*

38. Ibid., 367–8.
39. Stegmann, 'Politique', 305–9.
40. Lefèvre, *Prefatory Epistles*, 150–5, 366–9.
41. Rice, *Renaissance Idea*, 49. The connection may well be tighter. The *domus/civitas*
    bond shares much with the mercantile/humanist ideal that many have seen in early
    Renaissance Florence, linking political order, family life, and a careful idea of civic
    libertà (e.g., Bec, *Marchands*, 280–4, 301–30). Hans Baron remains the chief source
    for the scholarly debate here.

aedificatoria) being perhaps the most noteworthy. In 1515 Tory went off, a second time, to Italy. The Paris humanists were by now being attacked by many enemies among more conservative academics. The issue of translating the Bible posed a special threat to the established Church and its interpretive monopoly. We saw how Lefèvre's work was later taken as just such a threat. Dangers of this kind may explain Tory's departure, but many other things could do so equally – including a wish to return to the source of so much of their thinking. Lefèvre himself travelled thrice to Italy and Bovelles had explored Llull and other things with friends in Spain, besides travelling in Germany and Italy. How long Tory stayed in Italy is not known, but he was anyway back in Paris by February 1523, when he signed a lease on premises to be used as the printing shop that he now established. He was to work there as a printer (being named *imprimeur du roi* in 1531) until his death in 1533. [42]

This learned academic background and these relationships, his own clear early interest in language (a Latin grammar as well as his Quintilian), in geometry (both geography and architecture were in that part of the quadrivium), and in history (he had edited two such texts) may well explain both Tory's desire to make use of that training and to unify it in a text such as the *Champ fleury*, with its mixture of artwork, mathematics and linguistic discussion. For its part, the nature of his earlier contacts and his own work may help explain why later commentators have found Tory's book so hard to place in a tradition, whether medieval or Renaissance. As I have already insisted, one may best consider it as neither, and both.

Language and knowledge did considerably more than accompany one another. No distance lay between them – as it would, say, for a Sanchez. Seemingly like many older thinkers, Tory found knowledge literally contained in language. It was in the very letter:

Le nombre Imper, comme dict Macrobe au premier liure De Satur[n]alibus, est prins pour le masle, & le nombre Per pour la femelle, qui est a dire, que par coniunction de masle & femelle lhomme est engendre. Aussi par con-iunction de lettres les syllabes sont faictes, & par coniunction de syllabes les dictions. Et Loraison par assemblement de lettres, syllabes & dictions bien accordees se trouue bonne, elegante, et bien coulant. (GT fo. x r) [43]

---

42. Most of these details are from Reichenberger's and Berchem's Preface to the 1973 Slatkine reprint of Tory's *Champ fleury*, but also Bernard, *Geofroy Tory* (2nd French edn., 1865: a work Gustave Cohen considers unreliable: Introduction, Tory, *Geoffroy Tory*).

43. The uneven number, as Macrobius says in the first book of the *Saturnalia*, is taken for male, and the even number for female, which is to say that by joining male and female man is conceived. Thus by joining letters are syllables made, and by

Tory made this assertion in order to explain that the ancients placed the letter *A* first because it is composed of a triangle (an odd number) set on a square (that is, 'de nombre per'), male on female giving life to all subsequent language and knowledge. 'Science' was thus born from the letter, and lay within it:

Lesditz triangle & Quarré sont aussi compris en ung rond, qui est la figure contenant plus que nulle autre figure, qui nous denote que la parfaite & ample cognoissance des Muses et bonnes Sciences est & gist en bonnes lettres, par lesquelles on peut lire & estudier, escripre & assembler en livres & memoire, comme ont fait iadis les bons Philosophes & autheurs anciens, & comme pouvons faire en nous exerceant iour & nuyt a lire & escripre les susdites bonnes lettres & Sciences. (GT fo. x r) [44]

In its turn, the 'rond' was of course an *O*, a letter Tory described as most perfect, 'representing' Apollo and 'lodging' the nine Muses, seven Liberal Arts, four Cardinal Virtues and three Graces. This letter, in its 'concathenation et ronde perfection' ('organization and circular perfection'), symbolized how the Muses, Arts, Virtues and Graces were 'inspirées & noriées par Apollo' ('inspired and nourished by Apollo'), the sun – or better yet, 'par nostre vray Dieu & createur qui est le vray Soleil' ('by our true Lord and creator who is the true Sun': GT, xxxiii v–xxxix r). Tory drew his *O*, and the other letters, inside a squared grid: line and curve, he wrote, were the essential elements composing all letters. *I* and *O* had come first: as symbolized by the myth of Io, raped by Zeus and changed into a cow by enraged Juno, who revealed herself to her father Inachus by tracing *I* and *O* with her hoof in the sand (she actually formed omega, not omicron, as Tory observed in the long passage of his first book, where he told and interpreted the myth). [45]

---

syllables words. And discourse, by the association of well-tuned letters, syllables, and words, is good, elegant and smooth.

The association of odd and even numbers with male and female dated from the early Pythagoreans. As Tory said, a major source for this as for much else was Macrobius: 'An odd number is called male and an even female; mathematicians, moreover, honour odd numbers with the name Father and even numbers with the name Mother.' Or again: 'Since the uneven numbers are considered masculine and the even feminine, God willed that the soul should be born from the even and uneven, that is from the male and the female' (Macrobius, *Commentary*, 99 (I. vi), 192 (II. ii)).

44. 'The said triangle and square are also enclosed in a circle, the figure containing more than any other, which denotes that perfect and full knowledge of the Muses and good learning is and lies in good letters, through which one can read and study, write and assemble into books and memory, as once did good philosophers and authors of Antiquity, and as we can do by practising day and night to read and write the aforesaid good letters and learning.'

45. For a discussion of Tory, and especially a detailed analysis of *O*, see Bowen, *Words*, 27–44. On *O*, 30–5, 38–40.

The combination of Christian, pagan and mathematical elements was fundamental to Tory's argument. All knowledge was thus held in the alphabet, whose good letters ('bonnes lettres') summed up the geometrical and arithmetical relations between humanity and the world (a human figure formed the background to each letter – within the grid). But Tory made geometry the ground, and began by teaching his reader, 'que c'est que Rond, que Quarré, que Triangle, et consequement qu'il sache les figures plus generales de Geometrie. Car nosdittes lettres Attiques en sont toutes faictes & figurees comme ie le monstreray aidant nostre seigneur' (GT, fo. xi r). [46]

Furthermore, this 'geometry' of the letter was not at all abstract. On the contrary: the geometrical order was taken to exist concretely in the world, an immanent mark of God's mind (which is no doubt why, at this point, Tory called on God to help him). The analogical medieval world, in which this geometry was, we saw, embedded, had its concrete existence separate from and subsuming of the human mind – which was simply its exegete. That may explain, in Tory's work, why the depiction of humanity and the world (what we might think of as 'content') became a function of the geometry of the alphabet. This itself may correspond to an order drawn from Martianus Capella (an acknowledged major source), in whose system grammar was first in the *trivium* just as geometry was first in the *quadrivium*. This was not the order others gave them, and tradition was to split, we saw, as to their relation to one another – whether the first was a mere servant, or an essential philosophical foundation. Tradition was also split, we will see in a moment, on the actual order internal to the quadrivium, but by Tory's time, a Bovelles, whatever that case, was clear enough about an overall relation of subordination and subsumption, which he summarized finely in a French text on geometry first published in 1511:

La science et art de Geometrie, est en proportion pareille & respondante & subalterne & la noble science Darithmetique, & comme dependant dicelle. Larithmetique est dediee aux nombres, lesquelz sont gisans & situez en lame. La Geometrie considere les mesures, les quantitez & dimensions corporelles, lesquelles sont posees & situees au corps, & en toute chose solide & materiele. [47]

---

46. 'what is a circle, a square, a triangle, and next all the most common geometrical figures. For our aforementioned Attic letters are wholly made up and figured from them, as I will demonstrate, God helping.'

47. Bovelles, *Livre singulier*, fo. 3 v:

The science and art of Geometry is proportionately like, respondent and subalternate to the noble science of Arithmetic, as if dependent on it. Arithmetic is dedicated to numbers, which lie and are situated in the soul. Geometry treats measures, corporal quantities and dimensions, which are set and situated in the body, and in everything solid and material.

Tory drew the geometrical elucubrations with which he began his second book, thenceforward basing his analysis and creation of letters on them, from this 1511 work of Bovelles (praised as having immortalized his name by writing a geometry in French: GT, fo. xi v). This may be why, introducing *Champ Fleury* (xii–xiii), Gustave Cohen argued that Tory's geometrical ideas prefigured 'the seventeenth century, age of geometric architecture and of reason', but the claim was manifestly erroneous. Indeed, Cohen contradicted himself, having already remarked that 'Tory cannot consider anything, letter, form, drawing, without wanting to discover its moral meaning and symbolic value, and in this he is less a man of the Renaissance than a continuer of the scholastic Middle Ages' (GT, ix). One could, indeed, readily understand Tory's third book (GT, fo. xxxi r–lxvi r) as a literal description of letters (their writing and pronunciation) whose moral and allegorical interpretations he had undertaken in the preceding second book. There, for example, he affirmed that the horizontal bar of the letter *A*, 'couure precisement le membre génital de lhomme, pour denoter que Pudicite & Chastete auant toutes choses, sont requises en ceulx qui demandent acces & entree aux bonnes lettres' (GT, fo. xviii v). [48]

We have seen how he described the letter *O*, with Apollo, the Muses, Liberal Arts, Graces and Virtues. The other letters received similar treatment. But one may add that the entire alphabet, with its twenty-three letters, corresponded to the nine Muses, the seven Liberal Arts, the four Cardinal Virtues, and the three Graces. [49] These twenty-three letters (with what they symbolize, therefore, and their moral significance) were situated in the human body, each letter and its interpretations fixed in its 'proper' place. [50] These arguments surely signal the first three levels of interpretation, literal, moral and allegorical. Albeit more implicitly, Tory also recalled the fourth level: concluding the book just mentioned, for example, with the sentence, 'en cet endroit louant nostre seigneur Dieu, Ie feray fin a nostre Segond

---

This 1542 work apparently reprints *L'art et science de géométrie avec les figures sur chacune règle par lesquelles on peut facilement comprendre ladite science* (Paris: Henri Estienne, 1511): see Dumont-Demaizière, introduction to Bovelles, *Sur les langues*, 34–5. Tory praised this, along with Bovelles' Latin mathematical publications, begun in 1500 and 1503.

48. '... covers exactly man's genital organ, to denote that Modesty and Chastity, before all else, are required of those who seek access and entry to good letters'.

49. The twenty-three letters are our modern twenty-six less *W* and the doublets *I/J* and *U/V*, distinguished as vowel and consonant, but not as letters – as any reader of early printed texts knows.

50. See the two plates 'l'homme letre' (*GT*, fo. xxii v) and 'l'homme scientifique' (*GT* fo. xxiii v).

liure' ('here praising God, I will put an end to our Second book': GT, fo. xxx r); showing how the letter *O* figures the divinity of humanity (GT, fo. xxi v); ending his third book with another acknowledgement of divine inspiration; or, indeed, by claiming that the very existence of the alphabet referred us constantly to God. [51]

We should, however, be careful of ascribing Tory's symbolism, 'ethical' analysis and numerology only to belated medievalism – or more precisely, of accepting a now traditional notion of a rupture between medieval learning and humanist research (a notion owed in part to humanist claim). No such *rupture* occurred, and this volume continually seeks to emphasize how profound change grew from within firm continuities. Progress through the medieval Liberal Arts cursus had certainly been progress towards an understanding of God's universe and realization of God's will: Tory surely echoed this movement. No less was it the case that many made the *quadrivium* central to this: as we may feel Tory did through his geometry. As Michael Masi writes, introducing Boethius' *De institutione arithmetica*: 'For the schoolmen of Chartres, mathematics was the link between God and the world, the intellectual key which unlocked the secrets of the universe'. [52] Tory agreed that, 'Confe[c]tum est numeris, quicquid natura creavit', whatever nature has created is composed through numbers, or, as Tory paraphrased: 'every natural thing is, and is contained in, number' (GT, fo. xvi v). Such number, we know, was for Tory, too, the path from and to God. Arithmetic, Boethius had written, was 'mother to the rest' of the *quadrivium*, because God had created 'this first discipline as the exemplar of his own thought and established all things in accord with it'. [53] But tradition was not only Christian.

Boethian tradition also viewed arithmetic as an introduction to music, dealing no longer with quantity alone, but with quantity in motion – and more, with the harmonious order of the universe. In Capella's (Boethius' rival in medieval influence) earlier ordering of

---

51. In *Words*, Bowen berates those who 'classify Tory as a medieval, rather than a Renaissance, author', arguing rightly against the authors of a widely used manual that Tory did not turn the fourfold exegesis on each letter (29). But that does not alter the fact that *Champ fleury* was otherwise imbued with this exegesis. Bowen urges Tory's consent to values we now think of as 'Renaissance', notably the recovery of ancient texts whose ultimate purpose was to enable a Christian civic life founded on *vérité* and *vertu* (41). Tory and his colleagues saw no such clear opposition. However some may have emphasized the novelty of their explorations, they took whatever means came usefully to hand.

52. Boethius, *Boethian Number Theory*, 32–3. Chartres and Orléans, at the same time, taught a pragmatic grammar whose aim was to teach right speaking and writing (Elsky, *Authorizing*, 25).

53. Boethius, *Boethian Number Theory: De institutione*, 74.

the quadrivium, indeed, music was the final, culminating science. In both cases, numerical proportions were fundamental, deriving from Pythagorean/Platonic tradition, intimately relating arithmetic, geometry, proportions of the human body, motions of the human mind, harmony of the spheres and movements of the planets, with music as the sensory and rational foundation and evidence of order. 'Musique', said Deschamps, 'est la derreniere science ainsis comme la medecine des .vii. ars'. It comes, we saw him write, 'to cure and reset' hearts and spirits exercised on the other six arts, tuning them 'by the charm of its science and the sweetness of its sound, singing its delightful and pleasing songs in its third, fifth, and octave notes'. [54]

With the humanists' rediscovery of Plato, their fascination with Plotinus and other sources of mystical numerology, much of this medieval tradition was simply reabsorbed (humanist editorial activity, we saw, was instrumental): Ficino, Pico and their successors, Lefèvre, Bovelles, Clichtove and later neoplatonists drank afresh from the same or neighbouring sources. [55] That this kind of mathematizing would later be marginalized (*much* later: Johannes Kepler, Johann Faulhaber and others still followed allied paths) was hardly clear to those writing in the early sixteenth century. No great divide was occurring. Neoplatonism and hermeticism may sometimes have been perceived as new, but they easily absorbed many quadrivial concepts and intentions: including a non-Christian idea of universal harmony.

Unique in its form, guided by old traditions but urged by new needs and projects, Tory's text dramatically combined what we now tend to consider as separately medieval and humanist ways of thinking. Through the composition of letters, their moral value, and their symbolic depth, humans acceded to the meanings embedded in language. Tory continually reminded his readers that the final meaning and reference of language and thought were to be found neither in the mind nor in the world, but in the interpretation of signs (letters and their combinations) that came from God. Their geometry was neither

---

54. Deschamps, *Art de dictier*, 269: 'Music is the final science and so like the medicine of the seven arts.'

55. Pico claimed his use of 'the ancient system of philosophizing through numbers' to be 'new' and essential to assertions of truth (*Dignity* (1487), 25–6). For a recent translation of Boethius' work on music, see Boethius, *Fundamentals*. Boethius' quadrivium went: arithmetic – music – geometry – astronomy; Capella's ran: geometry – arithmetic – astronomy – music. The first took the order: numbers, numbers in motion, spatialized numbers, spatialized numbers in motion. The second involved what was understood to be an ascending order of completion (as we saw Deschamps imply).

just rationalizing design nor mere description: although it was *also* that. But first and foremost it signalled some tight relation with the world that made geometry both substance and order, an integral part of and a real link within the 'Great Chain' binding the material, moral and social spheres to the divine intellect: 'Ie ne puis icy passer oultre sans montrer que nosdictes lettres ont este inuentees par inspiration diuine ... [une] Chaine dor pendant du Ciel iusques a noz pieds ... de la longueur & largeur bien proportionee & conuenable a la symmetrye de nostre lettre proportionnaire I.' The Chain embodied 'toute infusion spirituelle & corporelle que pouuons auoir icy en bas', which 'vient & procede du souuerain createur de tout le monde' (GT, fo. xxv v). [56]

Such discourse did not come to an end with Tory. In his 1548 *Art poétique françoys*, Thomas Sebillet, we will see in chapter 4, moved in the same patterns. They remained clearer still, if anything, even in a text as late as Claude Duret's *Thresor de l'histoire des langues*, printed in 1613. For of course conceptual worlds do not just disappear, and the 'commemorative' concept of knowledge (and resultant action), for example, was still vital in so crucial a later figure as Jacopo Zabarella, whose name and work will recur here in rather different contexts. In his posthumously published commentary on Aristotle's *De anima* (1605), he asserted 'that our knowledge of universals is not acquired by inference from observations. Rather sense experiences give rise to images that render the "possible intellect" (*intellectus possibilis*) or rational soul receptive to representations of the universals present in the mind of God. The vehicle of this inspiration is the "active intellect" (*intellectus agens*).' [57] Not wholly different views may be found even later in the work of the Cambridge Platonists and those influenced by them. Then, too, the seventeenth century still saw Peter of Spain's *Summulae* being used (as we saw above, note 23), whose *Tractates* emphasized 'the impression ... that *truth* resides in

---

56. 'I cannot go further here without showing that our aforesaid numbers were invented by divine inspiration ... [a] golden Chain hanging from the heavens to our feet ... of length and width well-proportioned and suitable to our proportionate letter I.' It embodied 'every spiritual and corporal infusion we can have here below [which] comes and proceeds from the sovereign creator of the whole universe'.

57. N. Jardine, 'Epistemology', 691. His 'Galileo's Road' (301–3) takes this thought pattern to explain Zabarella's 'demonstrative regress' (see chapter 5 below) – after Skulsky, 'Paduan Epistemology', 354–61. Some analysis of such thinking is in Reiss, *Discourse*, 60–94 and, on the idea of *self* related to it, in my forthcoming *Mirages of the Self*. Cassirer argued that 'active intellect' was a passage to a modern idea of consciousness, especially in Zabarella's *De anima* commentary (*Erkenntnisproblem*, I. 108–13, 120–1). Perhaps here was another instrument pulled two ways. The matter needs more study.

language'. [58] They urged that one worked into language, as it were, to recover the memories whose previous embedding we are thus enabled to recall.

These continued the kinds of argument put forward by Tory. But he had begun his work by telling another story, a pagan one, at length. Lucian's tale of a 'French Hercules' depicted the hero as an old wizened man leading along a great crowd of people by a different golden chain from the one of the passage cited a moment ago. This chain began at Hercules' tongue and was attached to the ears of all those following him. It denoted the power of eloquent language. At the same time, it connoted the linguistic power and mastery of the *human* Hercules. [59]

---

58. L. Jardine, *Francis Bacon*, 24.
59. GT fo. ii ff. The complexities of 'French Hercules' have been traced in Jung, *Hercule*. Given Tory's admiration for Bovelles, one may note that a major source for Lucian's story (which the text in *Champ fleury* translated) was the *Antiquitatum variarum volumine xvii* (Rome, 1498) by Annius of Viterbo, which Tory edited in 1510. In his *Aetatum mundi supputatio* (Paris, 1520), Bovelles also used Annius as a source. Budé issued a translation of Lucian's text in 1508. In 1509, Jean Lemaire de Belges, whose importance we will see, published his *Illustration de Gaule et Singularités de Troie*, its first part reproducing Annius and the Hercules myth: Jung, *Hercule*, 43, 52–4, 52 n. 41, 76. It may not have been indifferent that Christine de Pisan's *Epistre d'Othea la deesse a Hector* had been printed in Paris by Philippe Le Noir in 1522. She did not write of Hercules as linguist, but much of him as Christian knight: caps. 3, 27 and 66 (for example) – see Christine de Pisan, *Epistle*, 10–12, 38–9, 80–1.

I am reminded of an unusual text in a slightly later work by Tory's hero, Bovelles. He titled the penultimate chapter of his *De vitiis vulgarium linguarum liber* (in *De differentia*, 1533) 'Ab arbitrio primi parentis Adae primam voluntate dei emanasse mundi linguam' ('By God's will, the world's first language issued from the decision of our first ancestor Adam'). He added that Adam's naming the animals showed us first how, by God's gift ('munere dei'), Adam had the *arbitrium* voluntarily to establish a first tongue ('primae totius mundi linguae voluntariae institutionis arbitrium'), and second, how God endowed humans with 'libero arbitrio'. [1] Marie-Rose Logan remarks of this passage that in 'no other work paraphrasing Genesis does there seem to be a word so explicit as "arbitrium" used to designate Adam's gesture'.[2] Well, yes and no. For Bovelles could in fact have found his terms, if not Adam's actual gesture, in a celebrated work by one of his teacher's Italian triumvirate.

Pico may not have been writing specifically of language, but he was undoubtedly paraphrasing Genesis at the start of his oration *De hominis dignitate*. Nor can we doubt that Bovelles knew Pico's imaginative record of God's word to the Pentateuch's first human:

We have given to thee, Adam, no fixed seat, no form of thy very own, no gift peculiarly thine, that thou mayest feel as thine own, have as thine own, possess as thine own the seat, the form, the gifts which thou thyself shalt desire. A limited nature in other creatures is confined within the laws written down by Us. In conformity with thy free judgment [*pro tuo arbitrio*], in whose hands I have placed thee, thou art confined by no bounds; and thou wilt fix limits of nature for thyself. I have placed thee at the center of the world, that from there thou mayest more conveniently look around and see whatsoever is in the world. Neither heavenly nor earthly have We made thee. Thou, like a judge appointed for being honorable [*quasi arbitrarius honorariusque*] art the

---

1. Bovelles, *Liber de differentia*, 46.
2. Logan, 'Bovillus', 662. Waswo has also noted the unusual nature of Bovelles' analysis (*Language*, 286–8): he claims it to be typical of current 'challenges to orthodoxy' (287).

molder and maker of thyself; thou mayest sculpt thyself into whatsoever shape
thou dost prefer. [3]

Such passages as these rouse deep ambiguities, and however ancient
the Hercules tale may be, it also serves to emphasize how much
Tory manipulated and mastered his geometry – drawn from Bovelles.
We may be reminded of l'Infortuné's similar claim of mastery
mentioned before (page 32), and of those forms which were yet to
come (pages 27–9 above). Regarding the use and control of language
a definite gap had been opened between God and humans (although
we should avoid the rapid assumption that humans had therefore
been set up as *their own* masters: such notions still lay in the far
future).

Indeed, Adam's voluntary use of his *arbitrium* to forge names
emphasized that opening. Such wilfulness caused the Fall that first
separated humans from God. It was directly to cause the scattering of
tongues at Babel. Bovelles' *De differentia vulgarium linguarum*
(in which the above-named work was one of three brief treatises)
examined the on-going process of linguistic decay and dissolution.
That very process, he wrote in his preface to his friend Martial
Masurier, was what made its study so necessarily piecemeal and him
so loath to undertake it: there was, he echoed Plato's *Phaedrus*, 'nullus
rationis temo, nulla ibi fixa & certa mentis aurigatio' ('no rational
rudder, no fixed and sure way to guide the chariot of the mind'). [4]
Vernacular words (*voces*) and names (*nomines*), from which speech
and discourse were woven ('ex quibus texturae fiunt sermonum &
orationum'), had no other origin than the spontaneous and varied
arbitrium of humans ('quàm spontaneum & varium hominum arbitrium'). Every day, he added, the flaws of humans' tongues cut,
changed, adulterated the crowd's disorganized language ('quotidie
humanorum labiorum vitia secant, variant, adulterant incompta vulgi
idiomata'). Every day, the errors 'of popular language' (*popularis*

---

3. Pico, *Dignity*, 4–5; *De dignitate* 8–10:

   Nec certam sedem, nec propriam faciem, nec munus ullum peculiare tibi dedimus,
   o Adam, ut quam sedem, quam faciem, quae munera tute optaveris, ea, pro voto,
   pro tua sententia habeas et possideas. Definita ceteris naturae intra praescriptas a
   nobis leges coercetur. Tu, nullis angustiis coercitus, pro tuo arbitrio, in cuiùs manu
   te posui, tibi illam praefinies. Medium te mundi posui, ut circumspiceres inde
   commodius quicquid est in mundo. Nec te caelestem neque terrenum, neque
   mortalem neque immortalem fecimus, ut tui ipsius quasi arbitrius honorariusque
   plastes et fictor, in quam malueris tute formam effingas.

4. The echo of *Phaedrus* 245b (as clear as the previous remark's echo of Pico) is of
   Plato's comparison of the soul to a chariot and reason to the charioteer (Bovelles'
   aurigatio) who must guide it past passion and desire.

linguae) grew, deformed 'by the tongues of the ignorant' (*in labiis imperitorum hominum*). [5]

That was why, wrote Bovelles, any study of vulgar tongues was obliged not to follow rules, only actual usage (reading Valla may have left an impact on his linguistic as well as his philosophical studies – although we have seen that Valla was far from alone in such observation: so the growth of vernacular grammatical work itself attested). As he repeated at the end of his second essay, neither rudder of authority nor oars of reason ('nec authoritatis temo, nec rationis remigia') were at hand when the crowd's whim/will/decision made new words daily ('arbitrium vulgi novas quotidie voces effingit'). [6] This vulgar *arbitrium*, which had unsettled languages and cut them off from an original ancient *homophonia*, worked 'by inattention to rules, distance of place, and errors of speech'. [7] Vernaculars, that is to say, were the precise result of peoples being left to their own devices, divided from one another as well as from God. Indeed, Bovelles' choice of *'effingit'* no doubt responded to Pico's use of the same verb to characterize the *arbitrium* given to Adam (see note 3 above: *'effingas'*). Now characterizing all humans, to it was ascribed inevitable deformation of language. Bovelles, we readily see, held vulgar tongues in no favour. But his condemnation of their faults, arbitrariness, barbarity, babble and confusion drew on the claim, constantly and repeatedly asserted, that humans were responsible for, controlled, their language. [8]

This, *per se*, was not new. Legal doctrine habitually argued the impact of usage on interpretation and meaning. So, wrote Bovelles' Toulousan contemporary, Pierre Rebuffi: 'consuetudo enim et usus loquendi potest

---

5. Bovelles, *De vitiis*, 3.
6. Bovelles, *Quae voces*, 90.
7. Bovelles, *De vitiis*, 5.
8. Bovelles' third work was entitled *De hallucinatione Gallicanorum nominum*. *Hallucinatio* meant both wandering in mind and babbling in speech. This titular linking of *ratio* and *oratio* echoed theoretical developments (see notes 11 and 23 below). Cassirer and Bernard Groethuysen both analyzed Bovelles' broader thinking on human responsibility. Groethuysen held him 'the great thinker of the French Renaissance', in whose metaphysics 'the new man seems to become fully conscious of himself' – a view taken up by Rice, who argues that Bovelles best showed 'the encyclopedic capacities and Promethean nature of the [new] wise man', making of his *De sapiente* the 'Renaissance culture hero' (*Renaissance Idea*, 106, 122). Groethuysen ignored Bovelles' specific claim that *only* the wisest (a minute élite) were actually capable of working the mind to its 'full humanity' by ever-fuller ('mythic') knowledge of the order of the world and the universe. This further explains Bovelles' isolation, for among the 'masses' such wilfulness led to chaos. Groethuysen sees Bovelles' thinking as forward-looking, Cassirer insists on its transitional nature: Cassirer, *Erkenntnisproblem*, I. 77–85, *Individual and Cosmos*, 89–93; Groethuysen, *Anthropologie philosophique*, 190–200 (quotation on 194).

vocabuli significationem immutare et novam dare' ('custom and word
usage', Maclean translates, 'can change the meanings of words and
confer new ones on them'. It matters, though, that 'vocabuli', 'significationem', and 'novam' are singular, for Rebuffi was not suggesting endless
ambiguity). There was nothing uncommon, that is to say, in the view
that concepts and words both had a history, and that any understanding
of linguistic meaning had to account for some sort of evolution. Indeed,
juridical argument formally incorporated rules to specify agreement on
the meaning of both concepts and words, and to make a place for adjustments to custom and equity. Bovelles was less deploring the implied
authority and freedom than finding himself obliged to analyze in
pragmatic detail (like Palsgrave) what he saw as its consequence. [9] What
was new here, then, after Valla and Perotti, was not so much the concepts being used as their deployment in a new context for new ends:
usage and language history were made fundamental to the very understanding of what *meaning* was or could be.

In Pierre Fabri's 1521 *Pleine Rhetorique*, distance and mastery
became marks of a quite new development in the conceptualization of
language and discourse: eloquence came to operate *as* a position of
power. Such was what Tory's Hercules now seemed to embody as he
had in earlier Lucianic – and Italian – tradition, and as now did
Bovelles' Adam four years later. This was certainly in part, as Padley's
discussion of the Latin grammatical tradition suggests, merely an *effect*
of a change in contextual emphasis. By the early sixteenth century, he
writes, 'in accordance with the newly found emphasis on rhetoric and
on oratorical rather than dialectical training, grammar is commonly
defined as the art of writing and speaking correctly'. And he concludes
by asserting that by the end of the first decade of the century, 'by the
time of Aldus Manutius, the new approach is well established.
Grammar is determined not by the application of medieval categories
of logic, but "by usage, reason and authority".' [10] I have, of course,

---

9. Maclean, *Interpretation*, 104–9, 142–58 (rules defining concepts), 133–4 (concepts
   having a history), 171–8 (on custom and equity). These arguments about language
   quite evidently echoed those against Protestant reform. After the first decade of the
   century, Bovelles himself lived in isolation – which is why his life has been so badly
   known (see chapter 1 note 1 above). His choice may have come from a wish to
   avoid nasty dispute. Royal protection may have solved Lefèvre's troubles, but the
   menace of persecution was ever present. We know the suspicions often raised about
   Erasmus (whose translation of the biblical *sermo* (see note 12 below) was harshly
   attacked on theological grounds). That such issues were joined in every intellectual
   domain is no surprise. We shall see their vehemence in Ramus' case.
10. Padley, *Latin Tradition*, 30–1. Whatever other disputes may continue this is not one
    of them. Elsky, L. Jardine, Waswo, and others all agree that usage had taken over
    from rule.

been suggesting that at least in vernacular thought matters were less than clear cut.

Padley argues at length that humanist grammatical theory quits the medieval doctrine of signs and of *consignificatio* (semantic and syntactical meaning), to anticipate seventeenth-century theories dependent on a concept of separation between language, mind and world. Then will come an idea of language as transparent mediating instrument for thought processes whose logic echoes the syntax of a rightly used language, at the same time as it is able adequately to represent the mechanical order of the world.[11] Padley speaks here of the Latin tradition, but similar developments were to be found in vernacular writings. This is because once emphasis had been placed on the communicative aspect of language (grammar as an *ars recte loquendi*: Tory's Hercules or Bovelles' conversation-directing Adam), rather than on its epistemological side (grammar as a form of dialectic, means towards interpretive knowledge), then a concept of language as a way to persuade or to order what it speaks of grew to predominate.[12] Thus language tended towards a form of control and of authority.

To this development, the social context of such writers as I am discussing here was surely not indifferent. We have already seen something of Tory's case. I may add that by 1531 he was printing works 'par le commandement du Roy nostre sire'. François I had established

---

11. This anticipation was a main concern. Padley began his three-volume work partly against Chomsky's *Cartesian Linguistics* and its avatars:

     A good deal, in fact, of what has hitherto been regarded as the specifically seventeenth- or even eighteenth-century contributions to grammatical theory is found to be already present in these earlier authors, more particularly in Melanchthon. In his work the logical proposition is already being taken as the norm for the grammatical *oratio*, the seventeenth-century *thing/action* dichotomy is already in place in the definitions of noun and verb, and the treatment of the latter solely in the semantic, extra-linguistic terms of the signification of *agere* and *pati* anticipates Vossius' identical definition of the 'essence' of the verb by over a century. Even late sixteenth-century 'innovations' such as Sanctius' treatment of ellipse, with its implied recognition of a 'deep' and a 'surface' structure to language, a *verbum mentis* underlying the *verbum oris* of actual discourse, are given full-length treatment in Linacre's *De structura* as early as 1524. (*Latin Tradition*, 56)

     Fabri and Palsgrave just assumed some such relation between *ratio* and *oratio* (see note 23 below and corresponding text).

12. Logan avers that Bovelles' use of *sermo* in his chapter on Adam had 'all the force of "conversation exchange", a sense which it had been given by Erasmus in his famous "In principio erat Sermo"' ('Bovillus', 661: cf. Jarrott, 'Erasmus', and Waswo, *Language*, 146–50, 286–8). L. Jardine insists that once Valla's and Agricola's work began to have wide impact in the 1520s, rhetoric texts modelled on it, starting with Melanchthon's and Johannes Caesarius' widely used manuals, assumed 'detailed knowledge of [a] dialectic' itself meant for instruction *not* discovery (*Francis Bacon*, 13, 25, 26–36).

the Imprimerie Royale in late 1530. Tory became Imprimeur Royal by
October 1531, but before then he had probably started work on a fine
manuscript genealogy of Catherine de' Medici, betrothed to François'
son, Henri d'Orléans, in June 1531. Its aim was to refute those who
derided the duchess as bourgeoise, daughter of merchants, by demon-
strating her royal French ancestry (she was the daughter of Madeleine
de La Tour, countess of Boulogne). [13] Like other major humanist
figures, Tory became close to king and court.

Even more had this been so for John Palsgrave, who wrote his
immense grammar (1530), he said, to fulfil the wish expressed by
'Geoffroy Troy [*sic*] de Bourges (a late writer of the French nation)
in his boke entituled *Champ-Fleury* [for] some studious clerke [to write
down] the rules and preceptes grammaticall' of French. [14] Palsgrave
certainly suited Tory's description. But besides his erudition, he may
have been a son of ranking East Anglian gentry, not distantly
related by his mother to the Dukes of Suffolk (one of whom later
married Princess Mary, Henry VIII's sister). [15] Whatever that case,
he was certainly 'scolemaster' to Princess Mary by 1513, and may
have been so earlier. As her 'secretary', he was at Abbeville for her
marriage to Louis XII (François I's father, who was to die in 1515).
Might he then have met the poet Jean Lemaire de Belges, whose patron
had been Mary's deceased predecessor (see note 19 below)? He was
a friend of Giles Duwes, royal librarian from 1509 who had been a
teaching colleague of John Skelton in then Prince Henry's household.
He was a friend of More and Erasmus, on occasion acting as go-
between on their behalf. Partly through the former's graces, he was
recipient of several church benefices. One way or another, he was associated with the court for years: he tutored Henry VIII's illegitimate
son, Henry Fitzroy, and the sons of the Duke of Norfolk and Thomas
Cromwell. He narrowly escaped punishment later for writing against
Cardinal Wolsey. Printing of *L'eclaircissement* was contracted with
Richard Pynson, the king's printer: Tory's English counterpart.

---

13. Bernard, *Geofroy Tory*, 34–5, 130–3; Cohen in Tory, *Geoffroy Tory*, 14–19.
14. Palsgrave, *Eclaircissement*, viii (The Authours Epistell). Since he seems to have had
    Tory dead before his time, we may suppose them unacquainted; although 'late' could
    mean 'recent', not 'deceased'. Future references to *L'eclaircissement* are by 'JP' and
    page.
15. These details and others come from P. L. Carver's introduction to *The Comedy of
    Acolastus*, ix–liv. A brief but useful biography can be found in Kibbee, *For to Speke*,
    199–201. Mary wed Suffolk secretly after the death of her first husband, Louis XII.
    She had agreed to the political marriage to the old king on the understanding that
    on his death she could marry for love. Henry was not pleased when he found that
    she had indeed pre-empted another political marriage.

Not just a grammar, the book was, says Douglas Kibbee, 'a monument in linguistic method and linguistic detail'. Further, it provided, writes Gordon Kipling, 'by means of frequent allusions and generous quotations, a critical guide to such authors as Palsgrave esteemed "to be most excellent in the French tongue" (fo. 21 v). It is, in short, the nearest thing we shall find to an official statement of the poets with whom a Tudor courtier was expected to become conversant'. As Kipling notes, these belonged mainly to the group of 'Franco-Flemish rhetoricians' and their preferred poets, Lemaire the most popular, followed by Octavien de Saint-Gelais. After them ranked three others, Alain Chartier, Jean Froissart, and Jean Meschinnot, all 'either fostered by the court of Burgundy or honored there'. The Bruges court was the object of Henry VII's fondest emulation. [16] Skelton himself, perhaps of Palsgrave's personal acquaintance, is argued by Paul Zumthor to have adopted the poetic principles of those *Rhétoriqueurs* among whose 'heirs' the same critic includes l'Infortuné and Fabri. [17]

Although not much is known of Fabri, apart from his spending most of his life in and around Rouen, of whose Puy des Palinods he became 'Prince' or president, his connections were similar. Zumthor remarks that his *Grant et vrai art*, so popular as to be reprinted six times before 1544, in its second part codified the rules of the Rouen competitions: 'but its general conception of versification is precisely the same as that implied, in many of its aspects, in the work of the rhétoriqueurs'. [18] Court poets (like Skelton in England), they dealt with essentially courtly themes: power, justice, glory, peace, princeliness, virtue. In their way and with their particular instruments, they carried out the ideal of serving the political community echoed and re-echoed in the thinking of early sixteenth-century humanists.

Fabri's, Tory's and Palsgrave's object did not differ far from that of the poets whom they found exemplary. The French and English languages (Palsgrave used both) were illustrated through the work of those poets who themselves echoed courtly virtues. Jean Molinet was official historian of the Burgundinian court until his death in 1507. He was replaced by Lemaire, best known for his 1513 *Concorde des deux*

---

16. Kibbee, *For to Speke*, 201; Kipling, 'Henry VII', 130. Reference is to Palsgrave's first edition. Henry VII's father-in-law, Edward IV, had married his sister Margaret of York to Charles the Bold in 1468. Her step-daughter Mary of Burgundy (Charles' daughter by his first wife) wed the emperor Maximilian: Mary was paternal grandmother to the emperor Charles V. His aunt, Mary's and Maximilian's daughter, Margaret of Austria, was Lemaire's penultimate patron: she made him her historiographer (and see note 19 below).
17. Zumthor, *Masque*, 21, 19.
18. Zumthor, ed., *Anthologie*, 277.

langues (French and Italian).[19] In its intertwining of two languages
and cultures, this work may well be taken as the direct precursor
of Palsgrave's *Eclaircissement*, different as the two otherwise were in
ostensible purpose and content. We earlier saw how Lemaire's
Illustration de Gaule overlapped issues taken up by both Bovelles and
Tory.

Of the four authors whose work is chiefly discussed in this section,
then, Fabri, Tory and Palsgrave at least were certainly not figures
looming from some cobwebbed corner to become pedantic objects for
a dusty archivist. And even if Bovelles proposed a life of solitary
contemplation as the ideal of wisdom, later in life indeed retreating
into more or less isolated seclusion, for his first forty years he fully
shared the travels, relations, and labours of Parisian humanist circles.
Indeed, Bovelles' closest friend in the Spanish circles he visited early
in the century was Cardinal Jiménez de Cisneros, archbishop of Toledo
and regent of Castile, an 'ardent Lullist' who had, no doubt to his
friend's joy, created a chair in Llull studies at the University of Alcalá
de Henares – which he founded.[20]

If these scholars are less known than such contemporaries and friends
as Erasmus, More, Lefèvre or Budé, it is largely because they confined
their work to editions, debated language and mathematics, and aimed
them at a scholarly community – however much they echoed courtly
concerns. But the group to which they belonged was a source of

---

19. There is a MS of the work dated 1511. It was reprinted some fifteen times before
    the 1549 collected edition of Lemaire's works. His intention was vast. By 'langue'
    he meant the whole of culture: an idea not after all so very different from still
    familiar and widespread assumptions about the trivium's scope. After falling out
    with Margaret of Austria (see note 16 above), Lemaire was able to find a new patron
    in Anne of Britanny, queen of France (Louis XII's first wife), whose historiogra-
    pher he became in 1512. She died in January 1514. We know nothing of Lemaire
    after that, but suppose he died not much later.
20. Bonner, 'Llull's Influence', I. 79–80. On Bovelles' lone sage and wisdom as search
    for 'higher knowledge', see Rice, *Renaissance Idea* 106–23, but also Cassirer and
    Groethuysen as mentioned in note 8. The relations of Lefèvre's group to Spanish
    humanist circles seem to have been extensive, but Bovelles' especially so. In 1501,
    he dedicated his *Introductio in Geometriam* (printed with his and his colleagues'
    edition of Boethius' arithmetical writings) to Jacobo Ramírez de Guzmán, bishop
    of Catania. They had met when Ramírez was studying philosophy and theology in
    Paris in 1499 (Rice in Lefèvre, *Prefatory Epistles*, 90–1). In April 1506 Bovelles was
    with Cisneros in Spain when Lefèvre wrote to him at the cardinal's home. Marcel
    Bataillon thinks Bovelles began his travels in late 1505. Cisneros seems then to have
    given him several works by Llull, which were later published in Paris. Writing in
    1509 to express his and his colleagues' joy at Cisneros' victory over the Muslims at
    Oran, Bovelles recalled his stay with delight. In Cisneros' circle Bovelles had acquired
    the reputation of a prophet, foretelling Christianity's renewal. The cardinal's battle
    at Oran was a first step, on which he had a full report sent to Bovelles in 1510
    (Bataillon, *Erasmo*, 53–8).

humanist modernity. Its support lay in these late medieval/early Renaissance courts, where the new learning found its first foothold and the present and future authority of people like Erasmus, More and Budé was enabled. [21] Such writers' views on language and meaning knowingly and deliberately reflected and illustrated grammatical, rhetorical, and poetic explorations establishing new learning. One day these would lead to new forms of rationality. Equally knowingly, they set one foot in court, the other in school; one eye on the old and familiar, the other on the even older but unfamiliar.

Their proximity to government authority explains, too, the choice of the vernacular. Not only were they addressing those who held and acted on it, but they wanted to affect the daily life these orchestrated. Analogous reasons lay behind vernacular *abbacus* treatises aimed at a business community. Not by chance, maybe, was Bovelles from the north-east, and his morphological analyses emphasized Picard and 'Franco-Flemish' dialects; even though he wrote almost always in Latin. His dismay was perhaps the counterpart of Lemaire's Belgic optimism. Where Bovelles was to withdraw from the world, Lemaire not only participated fully in court life but wrote on culture as *proceeding* from the vernacular (hence, perhaps, *his* recounting of the Hercules myth). Such ambivalence is readily explicable.

Placed at such a crossroads and seeing it from such a context, these earliest writers in the vernacular tradition unsurprisingly brought ideas of control and authority to bear on the mystery of language. Their problems were not thereby reduced. The question of the relation of language to reason and reality did not simply go away, and sooner or later it had to be resolved. At first, I will argue, the difficulty led to an infinite regression (although not wholly unrelated to modist conceptual levels), as the theoretical relational levels of word, thought, and thing tended to multiply without limit. These two aspects, language in terms of control and authority and the multiplication of levels in the sign, will absorb the remainder of this chapter.

With Tory and Bovelles, I mentioned Fabri in connection with the first of these. But the start of his *Rhetorique* seems anodyne:

Tulles, en son premier livre De Officiis, dit que le lyen qui tient les hommes conioinctz en benigne communité, c'est raison auec oraison ou eloquence, laquelle eloquence conduite de raison enseigne, apprent, communique, dispute,

---

21. One aspect of this authority's creation lies in the activities of Erasmus and his circle in the late 1510s and twenties, as Lisa Jardine describes them (in *Erasmus*). Whether or not quite so much of their work as she implies was a matter of public relations is hardly the point. What matters is how much they were aware of having to create an audience and establish their authority in relation to it.

iuge entre les hommes et les conioint en naturelle compaignie. C'est pourquoy qu'entre les dons de grace divine, raison, prudence et eloquence sont donnees a l'homme, sans lesquelles les royaulmes et chose publique ne peuent [sic] estre maintenuz et l'homme n'a maniere de viure. (PF, 5) [22]

According to this introduction (which recalls Tory's later French Hercules tale), reason, prudence, and eloquence lay at the same level of mental operation. Nonetheless, to the extent that humans lived in society, that they were *created* to live in society, it was the last, eloquent communication, that was to be emphasized above all (Adam's *sermo* in Bovelles – but also, of course, the constant threat of vernacular decay when *sermo* did not follow authority and rules).

This order was not a heuristic or methodological preference, as it might have been in the Middle Ages. It was determined by the very articulation of the three activities: reason guided eloquence, which in turn persuaded the prudence necessary to the beneficent, peaceful, and happy community – 'benigne communité'. It is the case that one of the major features distinguishing humanist concern with language from scholastic interests was precisely this social focus: thereby matching the historical and practical analyses of language, as it also mightily complicated the issues. Reason and the kind of human action suitable to the social order (the meaning of *prudentia* in the *De officiis*) were mediated, but also enabled, by the proper use of language. For it is clear that Fabri saw mental operations in terms of their communicated and communicable results, of the fact that these last alone made possible 'les royaulmes et chose publique', dominions and ordered society. Thinking, judging and speaking (well) existed only to the degree that they were *seen* to do so – in the language expressing them and making them functional. I think much the same set of ideas induced the following formula in Palsgrave: 'of these letters, lyke as in all tonges, be made syllables, of syllables wordes, of wordes sentences or reasons' (JP, xxiv). [23] Sentence construction according to a correct grammar

22. Cicero, in the first book of his *De officiis*, says that the bond which keeps men joined in a happy community is reason with speech or eloquence. This eloquence, directed by reason, teaches, communicates, disputes, judges between men, and joins them in a natural society. That is why among the gifts of divine grace, reason, prudence, and eloquence are given to man, without which kingdoms and commonwealth cannot be maintained and man has no way of living.

23. It is the case that the term *ratio* also had the sense of sentence, phrase, enunciation throughout the Middle Ages. Peter of Spain approaches this, when, having at the outset defined *oratio* as 'vox significativa ad placitum cuius partes significant separate' ('an utterance significative by convention whose parts signify separate things'), he begins his fifth tractate (*De locis*) by writing of the many meanings of *ratio*, one of which 'idem est quod oratio ostendens aliquid, sicut rationes disputantium' ('is the same as the *oratio* which demonstrates something, such as the *rationes* of

(elaborated in the 1,200 pages of the *Eclaircissement* – as already suggested, far more than just a grammar) produced right reason. Indeed, Palsgrave thenceforth wrote indifferently 'partes of speche' and 'partes of reason', in an assimilation the *OED* avers quite rare – instancing only Caxton besides Palsgrave.[24]

The emphasis Fabri put on seeing good usage, on the fact that eloquence produced and established the reason that enabled society, rapidly became the mark of a kind of *mastery*. Initially, the question was one of a social mastery, a mastery, so to speak, of the discursive network: 'car eloquence est la royne des hommes, laquelle conioincte auec sapience et science, peult enflammer ... restraindre ... paciffier ... reduire' (PF, 6). He added emphasis:

Et combien que l'homme ayt beaucoup de convenience auec bestes brustes, si y a Dieu donné grande difference par le langage, par lequel l'homme peult exprimer le concept de sa pensee, et *qui mieulx le sçait exprimer, il a excellence sur les aultres hommes* ... Et *qu'est il chose plus magnifique* que les peuples, les iuges, senateurs et princes, par la grauité et prudence d'une oraison, *reduire et conuertir a raison ...?* (PF, 7: my italics)[25]

He ended by observing that the ignorant 'debueroient considerer que rhetorique est science, comme i'ay dit deuant, de noblesse royalle, de magnifique auctorité et de tresgrande antiquité entre les hommes practiquee' (PF, 9).[26] We need not wonder that he linked the art of writing, the science of rhetoric, and military order: 'Moyses, qui fut homme de discipline militaire, remply de merveilleuse doctrine et deliura les Hebrieux des Egiptiens, lequel pource qu'il fut inuenteur des letres et de l'art d'escripture, il fut des Egiptiens appellé Mercurius Trismegistus, se monstre vng grant orateur et poete'

---

disputers'): *Tractatus*, 3, 55. But Palsgrave was writing after such as Fabri and Linacre (whose 1524 *De structura* he must have known). The conclusion of his sentence is an addition to the commonplace series, letter – syllable – *dictio*, as other cases show: Molinet (or De Croy), *Art de rhétorique* [1493] and [Anonymous,] *Art et science* [1524–5], in Langlois, *Recueil* 216, 265 (see note 11 above).

24. But see Elsky, *Authorizing*, who argues that Aristotle wholly 'intertwined knowledge and language in logic' (11, and to 21 for the argument as it is taken into and through the Middle Ages).

25. 'For eloquence is the queen of men, which joined with wisdom and knowledge can enflame ... restrain ... calm ... defeat.

And however great a similarity man may have with brute beasts, yet God has made a great difference through language, through which man can express the concept of his thought, and he *who can best express it, is excellent above other men* ... And *what more magnificent thing* can there be than to *reduce and convert to reason* judges, senators and princes, by the gravity and prudence of a speech.'

26. '... ought to consider that rhetoric is a science, as I said before, of royal nobility, magnificent authority, and practised among men since the greatest Antiquity'.

(PF, 10). [27] Bovelles might have taken solace in thinking such discipline possible. He found it denied by actual usage.

Certainly in Fabri's case, then, a 'new' rhetoric and grammar began to develop as a power of possession and an avowedly *political* mastery: 'rhetorique donc est science politique' ('So rhetoric is a political science': PF, 15), a science of the *polis*, of civil society and community. For this to be possible, it was essential to conceptualize the way in which language could be said to express 'le concept de la pensee', and in which it could be claimed as adequate to the world – social or material – it supposedly controlled. One had to know how language might be said to accede or refer to what was taken as outside it. One needed a theory of 'signifying' or of 'betokening', as Fabri and Palsgrave called it respectively. As the former wrote, while speaking of the activities of 'orateurs et acteurs auctorisez', 'il conuient auoir science pour approprier leurs termes a la chose selon son propre significat' ('it is good to have a science to make their terms suited to the thing according to its proper *significat*': PF, 23).

To express the issue in these terms, however, suggests why these early vernacular writers proved unable to answer their own question. Instead of developing a concept of reference or of denotation such that a sign could be supposed (ideally) in a one-to-one relation with its referent or denotatum, levels of mediation were multiplied in an increasingly complex but impotent effort to explain how some element of language could in any sense be said to signify some other linguistic or non-linguistic element. Indeed, the question might even become that of knowing what such an 'other' element could be. We saw Lax exemplify a version of the same sort of multiplication. Whatever different solutions there may be in the abstract to such a potentially infinite regression, the one people actually used, in this late European Renaissance, was that of cutting the knot, declaring more or less by axiom a clear theory of representation.

According to Padley, Latin grammarians had such a theory quite early. Referring for example to J. C. Scaliger's *De causis linguae latinae* of 1540, he shows that while grammar was firstly concerned with use and spoken word, its scientific aim was 'the seeking out of *rationes*' and the 'true object' of the grammarian's 'study [was] the *communis ratio* of language'. For Scaliger, *verbum mentis* and *verbum oris* were ideally 'congruent'. Of Scaliger, indeed, Padley goes yet further, adding

---

27. 'Moses, who was a man of military discipline, filled with wondrous learning, and delivered the Jews from the Egyptians, and who, because he was inventor of letters and the art of writing, was called Mercurius Trismegistus by the Egyptians, is shown to be a great orator and poet.'

that with this assumption of congruence between what we saw Palsgrave conflate as *ratio/oratio* (possibly the modists' *dictio* and *vox*), was 'a further one that language, and hence mental concepts, [were] a faithful reflection of natural phenomena. Truth [was] arrived at when there [was] an exact coincidence of speech with things.' That was why Scaliger used the word *veritas* both in our sense of 'truth' and in that of logical and grammatical *meaning*. In this, Scaliger anticipated arguments of works like the Port-Royal *Logic* and *Grammar* by over a century, viewing 'language as the superficial and variable actualization of an underlying and unchanging mental structure that is the same for all men everywhere'. [28]

Some approach to this kind of assumption was made by Fabri and Palsgrave. When the latter compared languages by their relative 'perfection' for instance, he meant, Kibbee observes, 'that one language has a more explicit and less ambiguous representation of the underlying semantic structure'. He was moving to 'a greater appreciation of the logical/semantic forms underlying the morpho-syntactic structures and systems' of language. The perfection of languages (what Louis Meigret was to call their 'elegance') lay in the extent to which they did or did not require circumlocution to reveal that underlying layer. [29] Such notions presupposed at least *some* thought of a potentially definable – and reliable – relation between the orders of words and concepts. Yet writers like Fabri and Palsgrave still seemed to feel insecure with these notions. They continually inserted new signifying levels, in what comes across as something like a desperate effort to anchor meaning.

In the sentence I quoted earlier from Fabri, where he tried to define his scientific project ('il conuient auoir science pour approprier leurs termes a la chose selon son propre significat'), a separation was signalled between a thing ('chose'), having its proper and natural

---

28. Padley, *Latin Tradition*, 62–5. Jensen, *Rhetorical Philosophy*, 111–84, has a more nuanced view of the *De causis*. While accepting this kind of general statement, he gives short shrift to Padley's 'contradictory' claims that Scaliger was at once Thomist, modist, and ancestor of seventeenth-century philosophical grammar (189 note 13). At the end of this chapter (page 69), I shall suggest that the turn to mathematics and the reasons for it complicate claims like Padley's about 'anticipation' and those like Jensen's about 'contradiction'. On the one hand the anticipation was less direct, on the other its indirection and the eclecticism of all these thinkers make ideas of simple contradiction hardly more than anachronistic projections of the 'clear and distinct reason' of Enlightenment claim.

29. Kibbee, 'John Palsgrave's "Lesclaircissement"', 37, 39, 53. The issue became central in grammars: a theory of ellipsis developed, based on the premise that its possibility depended on such an underlying structure. See, for example, Sanchez de las Brozas, *Minerva*, 25 ff, and Breva-Claramonte, *Sanctius*, 57 ff.

meaning, and a word, arbitrary, that was to signify the thing's meaning, its *significat*. For syntactically the word *significat* belongs with the term *chose*, not with the phrase *leurs termes*. *Significat* indicated some middle term between a thing and a discursive sign (word, *oratio*, *vox*): a concept perhaps not wholly removed from Saussure's *signified* – except that as the theory became more complex it could no longer retain such a status. For in Fabri's text the term needs distinguishing from *signification*, and even from what he calls *signifiance*. This last, he wrote, should be considered not in relation to the thing, but to the sign: 'Signe est vne demonstrance qui donne presumption que la chose fut ou sera selon la signifiance d'iceluy signe et sont tels signes selon les cinq sens du corps, comme: "Il y a ycy grant pueur, il y debueroit auoir quelque charongne." Et: "Quant l'en [*sic*] monstre les plais, il s'ensuit qu'il a esté nauré"' (PF, 100). [30] (Fabri was clearly not without a sense of humour.)

In this last case, of course, the sign was not a verbal one: it was in fact defined in a way almost akin to Peirce's indexical sign. But *signifiance* could also refer to a word, and it then seemed to mean something like a 'proper sense' of the sign. This was likewise the case in Palsgrave who, speaking for example of negation, wrote: 'they put also after theyr verbes *pas*, *poynt* or *myé*, which of themselfe signifye nothyng, but onely be as signes of negation' (JP, 110). The distinction here between signification and sign (whether substantival or other) is quite clear, although in this particular case Palsgrave was speaking about the 'absence' of such signification. *Signification* or *signifiance* was a matter of relation, while *sign* was an element considered in itself. The signifying relation may be that of word (sign) and mental concept, or it may be between material object and its apprehension in the mind. Examples of both usages are legion.

Despite such confusion, the vocabulary appears at the start to lead toward a rather simple and clear conceptual scheme or model for the fundamental operation into which grammar and rhetoric were to be inserted. Fabri wrote, for instance: 'Encore est a entendre que aulcuns des termes dependans du latin ont aultre signification que le latin ne sonne, comme de *oratio* vient *oraison*. Et *oratio* en latin signifie toute *proposition* ou *sermon* ou *dicté*, ou *lettres missiues*, mais *oraison* en françoys n'entent que *priere*, et *sermo* en latin signifie *parolle*,

---

30. 'A sign is a demonstration that gives a presumption that the thing was or will be in accordance with the significance of that sign, and such signs are according to the five senses of the body, as: "There is here a great stench, there must be some carrion." And: "When one shows wounds, it follows that one has been injured."'

et *sermon* en françoys n'entent que *preschement* ...' (PF, 16). [31] All these diverse examples authorize the composition of a schema such as the following:

terme (*mot, signe*) → *signification* (*signifier, entendre*) ↔ *significat* ← *chose*

Palsgrave used arguments readily lending themselves to this schema. Let us take, for example, a passage where the grammarian was explicating gender usage: 'for, if the substantyve betoken any name belongyng onely to man ...' (JP, xxiv–xxv). The word *betoken* has the sense of 'signify', but what it signifies is a name, itself attached to a thing. So he similarly indicated later, when writing 'of every substantyve endynge in *e*, betokenynge the name of any frute ...' (JP, 185). One is reminded irresistibly of the White Knight explaining to Alice the naming of his song:

"The name of the song is called '*Haddocks' Eyes*'."
"Oh, that's the name of the song, is it?" Alice said, trying to feel interested.
"No, you don't understand," the Knight said, looking a little vexed. "That's what the name is *called*. The name really *is* '*The Aged Aged Man*'."
"Then I ought to have said 'That's what the *song* is called'?" Alice corrected herself.
"No, you oughtn't: that's quite another thing! The *song* is called '*Ways and Means*': but that's only what it's *called*, you know!"
"Well, what *is* the song, then?" said Alice, who was by this time completely bewildered.
"I was coming to that," the Knight said. "The song really *is* '*A-sitting On a Gate*': and the tune's my own invention." [32]

In fact, Fabri did get himself into just such a regression, one potentially in Palsgrave as well, and whose analogues can readily be found elsewhere. For the moment, the first example I quoted from the English grammarian gives a schema exactly similar to Fabri's:

'substantyve' → 'betoken' ↔ 'name' ← 'man'

Later on, the word Palsgave would use to indicate the activity of 'betokening' was the very term used by Fabri. Indeed, he said so himself when referring back to the passage I have examined and to other times when he referred to it: 'where I shewed how the gendre of substantyves may be known by reason of their signification ...' (JP, 188).

---

31. 'One must understand, besides, that many terms coming from Latin have a different meaning from their Latin one, as *oraison* comes from *oratio*. And *oratio* in Latin means any *proposition* or *speech* or *matter spoken*, or *written epistles*, but in French *oraison* only means *prayer*, and *sermo* in Latin means *speech*, while *sermon* in French means only *preaching*.'
32. Carroll, *Through the Looking Glass*, rpt. in *Works*, 196–7.

For the most part, the distinction in Palsgave was not between the verbs 'to signify' and 'to betoken', but between the verb and corresponding substantive. He tended to use the noun *signification* in a more general sense than the verbs *signify* or *betoken*. The noun implied *meaning* in a rather broad but imprecise way, the verbs referred to the way in which particular parts of speech put their meaning (only potential until actually expressed) into action. So, speaking of how French reflexive verbs differed from active verbs, Palsgrave noted that they were different as to their 'signifycatyon, for where as the verbes actives betokyng [*sic*] some acte to passe from the doer without forth, by which acte some other thyng doth suffre. The acte of the mean [reflexive] verbes passeth nat from the doar [*sic*], but retourneth to the doars selfe agayne' (JP, xxiv).

The two verbs *signify* and *betoken* were interchangeable, and part of the difficulty was that they referred indifferently to the relation between two words, between word and action, between word and concept, or between name (*significat*) and thing – and so forth: diverse relations whose confusion was constant in both Palsgrave and Fabri. The fact, for example, that Palsgrave could refer to French adjectives terminating in *u* as *signifying* 'plenty or store of the substantyve that they be formed of, as *barbu*, plenteously or moche bearded' (JP, 301), and thereby emphasize a relation between words that elsewhere he indicated as one of subsumption (writing of the 'many sondry wordes [that] be contayned under eche' pronoun: JP, 74), did not prevent him using the same term to refer to all those other sorts of relations mentioned. This confirms Ashworth's observation: 'In post-medieval texts one of the biggest barriers to the development of an adequate theory of meaning in general or of distinctions between sense and reference in particular, was the use of the word "*significare*" to convey all notions connected with meaning.' She asserts that this led to a confusion of different levels of meaning. [33] In these vernacular writers, as we have seen, it also produced an endless regression. At the same time, it implied that the need to make such distinctions was felt with some urgency.

Indeed, the fact remains that both Palsgrave and Fabri seemed to achieve a fairly simple basic model. It assumed a word to be in a relation of signification or signifiance with a name or *significat* itself attached to a thing – 'man', 'frute', or whatever. Here the term *significat* may be interpreted as a concept in some undefined way produced by a material object. It seems somewhat akin to the modist *dictio*,

---

33. Ashworth, *Language*, 47.

although with the added complication of being 'properly' attached to
the thing. Palsgrave confirms such an interpretation by the way he
defined the verb 'to signify' later in his work, in his 'dictionary of verbs':
'I signifye, I betoken. *Je signifie*, prim. conj. and *je designe*, prim. conj.
I sawe a marvaylouse thyng in the ayre yesterday what so ever it doth
signyfye: *je vis hyer une chose mervailleuse en layr, quoy qu'il [sic]
signifie*, or *quoy qu'il designe*. And *je denote*, prim. conj.' (JP, 718).
There appears to be a kind of cross here between Fabri's notion of an
indexical sign like that we saw earlier and some vague idea of a meaning
attached directly to a material thing, whether or not one might interpret its signification. One could select many examples of such an idea
of 'proper' meaning in both Palsgrave and Fabri, although more in the
former.

In such a conceptualization, Palsgrave seems closer to Tory's arguments than he does to the future. And this idea of 'properness' surely
invited the separation of such an element of signification into a diversity of functional levels, simply because of the need to find and fix the
property in question. Such was precisely what occurred. Fabri found
himself confronting a need to complicate the semiotic relations into a
regression quite akin to Alice's and the White Knight's. As I have
several times suggested, they were the more complicated by two conditions especially. The first was the continuing failure of many as yet to
distinguish between communicative and cognitive functions of language,
even though a distinction was made between grammar and rhetoric on
the one hand and dialectic on the other. Of course, the clearer the
distinction became, the more stripped language was of *any* cognitive
function whatsoever: at least to the extent that this might involve
anything like 'discovery'. The second complicating condition involved
this use of an ever more complex and yet insufficiently defined vocabulary.

First, the term *significat* was not associated only with a material
'thing' – or in no simple way. Fabri wrote: 'Exornation se faict, quant
le propre et naturel langaige est mué élegantement de son significat
en aultre' (PF, 25). [34] Any given linguistic element was thus supposed
to possess a *significat* that was 'proper and natural': a *significat*, we
may imagine, that accorded on the one hand with usage and authority,
that was 'appropriate' on the other to the thing. In the example just
quoted, *significat* was clearly tied to word. But when Fabri wrote of
the 'appropriateness' of signs, then *significat* became attached to thing:

---

34. "Exornation" occurs when proper and natural language is elegantly turned from its
significat into another.'

so we need a 'science' (rhetoric) 'pour approprier leurs termes a la chose selon son propre significat' ('to make terms fit the thing properly according to its proper *significat*': PF, 23).

The use of the verb *approprier* and of the adjective *propre* was obviously not accidental. If such was the case, there had to be some kind of ambiguous correspondence between a term's *signification* and the name that was the *significat* of the thing: its 'proper' *significat*. This latter term would thus point to a 'discourse of the thing', or at least of the *significat*s of the thing. And that would explain why one *significat* could be changed into another. At the same time, that it *could* be so changed tells us that the *significat* was in no permanent or fixed relation, but was available for rhetorical adjustment. Such flexibility and laxity in the attachment of *significat* to thing utterly contradicted any concept of 'properness'. The exploration of *significat*, that is to say, led to the destruction of the tight link whose need was so strongly felt (as much in Fabri as in Tory and Palsgrave, or as in Bovelles' fear of *hallucinationum*), and implied that other levels of mediation could be inserted more or less limitlessly – indeed, they would have to be.

Thus, too, while *significat* clearly often meant the referent of a term, it could equally well mean not just the *signified* of a verbal sign, but also what Peirce might call a social *interpretant* both of a term and of an action or object that was the term's referent:

> Or il est a noter qu'il est plusieurs termes qui de soy sont honnestes a proferer et leur significatz sont abhominables, comme l'en [*sic*] peult honnestement dire homicide, boutefeu, meurdrier, sacrilege, herese [*sic*], etc. Et les aultres termes sont de soy deshonnestes a proferer et leurs significatz sont honnestes, *ymo* necessaires, comme des membres de nature sont cul, v ..., c ..., f ..., chier, petter, etc. (PF, 70–1) [35]

Here the term *significat* was not even the name of an action or an object. It signalled a moral or social judgment made of the action or object. *Significat* pointed, then, to many different mediatory levels. It could be the concept signified by a given term (*signifiance*), it could be a meaning in some manner 'properly' attached to a material thing, as some *property* of that thing, it could be the concept one acquired as one apprehended such a thing, it could be a social judgment applied to the object or action itself, to the concept, or to the term. The word

---

35. Now, it is to be noted that there are several terms that are in themselves decent to pronounce whose *significats* are abominable, as one can decently say homicide, seditionist, murderer, sacrilege, heresy, and so on. And other terms are in themselves indecent whose *significats* are decent, indeed necessary, such as the natural parts are butt, p ..., c ..., f ..., shit, fart, and so on.

significat thus became a kind of general conceptual 'operator', enabling the transformation of any one semiotic level into any other. [36]

It is as though, for Fabri at least, the concept of *significat* were a means to *prevent*, by its own semantic overdetermination, the infinite regression with which he was otherwise threatened. The term's huge ambiguity – not to say confusion – both said and denied that levels of semiotic mediation could be infinitely multiplied. It was, then, something rather different from the 'barrier' Ashworth found *significare* to be. One can in fact establish a quite sophisticated model of what lay behind these arguments:

In cognition, the external thing acts as a sign producing a *significat* for mental apprehension, and an object, action, or whatever becomes fixed in the mind as meaningful (or as potentially so, since in some circumstances one may not be able to interpret such a sign).

In communication, the concept, a mental *significat*, is translated into a verbal sign that *signifies*, by some *term*, *name*, or *voice*, the *significat* in question. It does so in such a way that the recipient can apprehend the *signifiance* of the verbal sign in just the same way as she or he apprehends a significant phenomenon. But each level of these activities can be referred to as a *significat*. Using the same schema as before – or a similar one – one discovers the following pattern:

```
              significat            significat         significat
sign of the thing ──────────→ mental apprehension ──────────→ concept ──────────→ verbal sign
```

The model, of course, worked in both directions, according as one was going from cognition to its expression and communication, or from the understanding of such an expression towards cognition. The term *significat* entered at all levels as a means to avoid their endless multiplication. [37] It finally failed to achieve this just because of its own complex ambiguity. But it also failed, perhaps, because of its simultaneously 'individualist' and 'social' frame of reference, its simultaneous dependence on a particular mental operation and a general communal

---

36. I refer to the 'totemic operator' used by Claude Lévi-Strauss, which I have used as a term indicating an element specific to what I call 'patterning discourse' (*Discourse*, 86 *et passim*). Roughly and rapidly put, it is an instrument by whose means what later Western European thought would consider quite different levels of activity or categories of phenomena are found not just to converge, but to function without such difference coming into play.

37. *Significat* also operated, we saw, between a thing and whatever was its sign as actually apprehended. I have not included that in the schema because human minds had no access to the process of that relationship (however it might exist). The rest shows sufficiently how medieval *significatum* had been stretched. Bovelles would have thought this an error confirming his sour view of what happened to words when they passed into the vernacular.

judgment: that very judgment, it may be, that Bovelles himself
(but much less his colleagues) had condemned as absent from all but
a social élite. Indeed, it was hope of a stable communicative medium
among equal members of such an élite, enabling a stable civic polity,
that now spurred these researches, as much as the fading hope of a
language of discovery.

Fabri's rhetoric and Palsgrave's grammar, like Tory's analysis of the
alphabet and its meaning – and like the medieval grammatical logic –
were efforts to understand human communication and cognition in
terms of how verbal signs used by humans came to be *meaningful*.
They attacked the issue first and foremost through an emphasis on the
semantic aspect of those signs. In doing so, by the early years of the
sixteenth century, I have been suggesting, these writers found themselves confronting a bad regression whose consequence was to make
utterly impossible any explanation of how language could be in some
kind of 'adequate' relation with 'reality', or rather, with any reality
other than a purely conceptual one. Even in this latter case, the grasp
remained yet tenuous. Furthermore, the linkage of language and
reason, of *oratio* and *ratio*, meant that the inability to forge such an
adequate relation also applied to thought itself.

This may explain, for example, the rather contorted way in which
Bovelles turned to a visual metaphor at the end of his 1509 *De sapiente* to 'explain' how the sage (the *sapiens* of his title) learned to
accommodate exterior vision to interior contemplation. The human eye
was sighted outward, but blind inward; the wise person learned how
to free the 'eye' of its cecity and form it free to float in the air, like
the sun, illuminating and seeing with both sides of its orb – 'que extra
et que intus sunt': things both outer and inner. [38] The image was
Platonic and Christian and appealed to older familiarities. For the
linguistic and lay philosophical research I have been exploring it emphasized the tenuity of reason's grasp on the actual – and so of language's.
For vernacular writers the grasp was the more tenuous because of a
seeming lack of linguistic rule. But Bovelles' rather belated pessimistic
dismay about the vernacular, perhaps the other face of his earlier
'Platonic' appeal, was already being answered by such as Alberti and

---

38. Bovelles, *De sapiente*, in *Livre du sage*, 298–310 (302). Once again, he surely got his
    metaphor from Pico, who wrote that the eye had some internal light of its own yet
    needed external light to function, and compared it to the intellect, whose internal
    light needed 'the forms and ideas of things, like invisible light, for the intelligible
    truth to be clearly discerned' (Pico, *Heptaplus* (1489) vol. I, in *Dignity* (etc.), 128.
    Cf. 122 (IV. 4)). Cassirer looks at other sides of Bovelles' debt to Pico, notably that
    of humans' self-creation (*Individual*, 89–93). Rice discusses 'Janus' aspects of
    Bovelles' idea of wisdom (*Renaissance Idea*, 115).

Nebrija, not to mention Palsgrave. [39] The call for vernacular grammars was precisely for an understanding of linguistic rules surely, it was thought, no less thoroughgoing – and valid – than those of Latin.

So it was that in works like those of Fabri and Palsgrave, in spite of this incapacity, possibilities of a solution were already being indicated. If one could simply remove such ambiguous concepts as those of *signifiance* and *significat*, concepts that attempted to 'explain' the relation between a sign at one level and a sign at a different level, the difficulty would at least be palliated. If one could then simply lay down a priori some sort of inescapable similarity between different levels, the difficulty would be to a considerable degree resolved. Actually, of course, it was not so much resolved, as avoided. The terms were changed, and the older difficulty was sidetracked once and for all. Padley argues that the Latin grammarians were starting to achieve this a mere decade after those of whom I have been speaking (indeed, at the same time, in Linacre's case). Chomsky asserts that it was the accomplishment of Port-Royal. And certainly the 'Cartesian' *mathesis universalis* seemingly behind Port-Royal's work appears to offer the readiest way to assert identity between material, conceptual, and linguistic levels. But Padley's work has shown convincingly how some of the necessary elements were in place long before. In turn, they were developed out of yet older ones.

Referring to Ramus' *Grammatica* of 1559, some twenty years after Scaliger's *De causis*, Padley argues that 'nature, method and practice ... are cardinal tenets of Ramus' system. On the level of logic these correspond to the faculty of reason ..., the establishment of rules, and the formation of habits in accordance with these rules.' So he can affirm that Ramus' grammar excluded meaning as a basis for classification. Indeed, it assumed an underlying *ratio* analogous in implication to a notion of *mathesis universalis*. [40] In effect, what happened was that the mediatory notion of *significat* (and its companions) was simply excluded. It was 'replaced' by an a priori assumption of the identity of orders. One is tempted to say that to assert such an underlying *ratio* was the first and last claim of discursive mastery – of that mastery we earlier saw as incipient in Fabri. It was first, because it provided the

---

39. In part 2 I will suggest that in his mathematical writings Bovelles eventually wrote of an adequacy between signs and things that had no need of Platonic grounding. His ambivalence about language and human *arbitrium* was thus perhaps resolved by seeing in mathematics a system that was independent of such *arbitrium* even while subject to its rational control. He found in mathematics, that is, a strictness of rule that where languages were concerned might be found in Latin, never in the vernaculars. For Alberti and Nebrija, see chapter 1 note 15.

40. Padley, *Latin Tradition*, 83, 90.

essential way to cut through the infinite regression of meaning. It was
last, because it had afterwards to seem part of the natural and objective world order, not an imposition of a discursive 'system'.

In the early sixteenth century, the emphasis on meaning placed grammarians and rhetoricians before the difficulty of having to explain the
passage between signs presumed to be on different functional levels.
It led directly to the unlimited multiplication of such levels. [41] The old
semantic universalism of the modists had largely gone, as had any sense
that some Divine *sermo* guaranteed linguistic meaning. Pragmatists like
Valla, in his *Elegantiae linguae latinae*, or even Bovelles later, destroyed
any idea that meaning inhered 'naturally' in language. The question,
'qu'est-ce que signifier?' required urgent solution. [42] The later claim
that identical structural laws ruled all and any different levels meant
that the adequacy of the relations between them could then be presupposed. It meant that the levels of world, concepts and language could
be counted susceptible to the *same* logical analysis.

That development occurred later, after people had broadened their
search to other areas of thinking as well and in response to the problems confronted by such writers as Fabri, Bovelles, Tory and Palsgrave.
To us, these writers may appear overwhelmed by contradictions, caught
between an array of ancient, medieval, and prospectively modern ideas.
They faced a bewildering mess of old and new notions on language
and reason, on civic virtue and public authority, on humans' place in
the world, and on relations between all these matters. This may explain
why, as Ashworth puts it, the 'most interesting work [in logic] of the
[post-medieval] period ... was done at the end of the fifteenth century
and the beginning of the sixteenth century', mainly, she adds, 'in Paris'.
It may also explain why Valla's and Agricola's work became influential, L. Jardine observes, only in the late 1520s and early 1530s. [43]
To solve problematic issues, writers used tools and information from
the material at hand. Starting to sort out conflicting tales, they often
fell into *hallucinationes* and tortuous ambivalence, torn between

---

41. This phenomenon of multiplication, I have argued in *Discourse*, is a mark perhaps
    typical of historical moments that see the start of a shift from the dominance of one
    discursive model ('class') to that of another, although it is not necessarily levels of
    meaning that multiply. In his superb study of Renaissance writers (Erasmus, Rabelais,
    Ronsard, Montaigne), Terence Cave explores the phenomenon of 'plural narratives',
    whose theoretical model was the concept of *copia* as used and transformed mainly
    by Erasmus (*Cornucopian Text*). This plurality is a poetic and narrative counterpart
    of the formal explorations we have been examining. It is surely also counterpart to
    Bovelles' fears about the growing decay of the vernaculars – a multiplying of error.
    Chapter 3 begins with these matters.
42. Giard, 'Du latin', 43.
43. Ashworth, *Language*, 21; L. Jardine, 'Lorenzo Valla and the Origins', 147.

pessimistic reaction and an optimism that became sometimes flamboyant: I think of Lemaire's vernacular daring as much as of Tory's all-inclusive alphabetical art or of Palsgrave's enormous grammar. And Lemaire's courtly context recalls the other side of these vernacular researches.

When Nebrija published his Castilian grammar in 1492, he wrote in his dedication to Queen Isabella that on an earlier occasion at court (yet again) she had asked him what it was for. As he told the nowadays often misquoted anecdote, the Bishop of Avila leapt in on his behalf. He spoke (prophetically) of Spain's coming rule over peoples of divers languages, of a conqueror's need to impose laws that must be understood, of the need of all those, Europeans and others, who would have to treat with Spain to know its language. Contrary to contemporary myth, Avila did *not* say 'language is the perfect instrument of empire'. Rather, beginning his dedication, Nebrija himself summed up the Bishop's remarks as he later recorded them: 'que siempre la lengua fue compañera del imperio'. [44]

The term Nebrija used is actually more interesting than later avatars and agrees better with the arguments we have seen. Language and empire were equal *companions*. The difference perhaps shows that need to hide the 'mastery' of which I wrote earlier: required among other things to cut through the infinite regress of meaning, so that the *ratio* it had asserted as underlying linguistic order 'would afterwards seem part of the natural and objective world order, not an imposition of a discursive system'. To call it an 'instrument' is, exactly, to view it merely as the 'transparent' instrumental operator of later European claim about the nature of language and its mediation between mind and world. Early humanists were more direct. In 1572, Ramus still told Queen Catherine de' Medici how Henri II's command that he work on a French grammar (among other things) was wholly equal to a king's 'expansion of his monarchy by great conquests and dominations'. Even in 1635–7, Richelieu would make the (political) righting of language and letters the purpose of his new Académie. [45] On other

---

44. Nebrija, *Gramática*, 101–2, 97. I gave this before in English. Hanke gives the 'instrumental' version (though recording, inexactly cited, the term *compañera* in an endnote (*Aristotle*, 8, 127 note 31), as does Elliott (*Imperial*, 128). He is quoting Hanke, who is quoting J. B. Trend's *The Civilization of Spain* (1944), who is quoting . . .? So are myths promulgated.

45. Ramus, dedication to 1572 *Grammaire françoise*, in Waddington, *Ramus*, 418: 'tel commandement n'est point moins digne d'ung bien grand monarque, que d'amplifier sa monarchie de grandes conquestes et dominations. Car la grammaire est non-seulement la première entre les artz libéraux, mais elle est la mère nourrice de tous.' A careful reading of this passage actually suggests that Ramus was subtly equating grammar with the queen herself, persuading her to be just such a 'mère

places and peoples, power of and over language had clear, direct
results. These writers' iteration of language's ordering force, their
moves to defeat its incapacities, Fabri's bond of military and linguistic
authority had practical implications. [46] The 1492 date is emblematic.
And it is worth noting that the court of Burgundy was birthplace
and home of Isabella's grandson, the emperor Charles V. [47] The benefits of control through language might be many. Not all concerned
issues of rationality.

This new social embedding of language was not, of course, perceived
merely as an issue of imperial control, be it pernicious or beneficent
– far from it, however useful a *bon mot* the thought may have provided
for a courtier. The humanists' claim 'that the mind's perception of
reality is, under the proper circumstances, guaranteed by the partici-
pation of the voice in a social or political community sanctioned by
convention' was fundamental to a new idea of civic responsibility and
action. [48] Language was indeed a 'companion' rather than an instrument (yet), but even less was it the tool for and of discovery that it
had been in medieval doctrine. [49] These humanists' awareness of the
complexity of the issues at stake is why, sorting out these confusions,
these authors became an essential link in the history of thinking on

---

nourrice' to her son Charles IX as the Queen Regent Louise de Savoie had been
to her son François I, leading him to encourage the spread of those arts in his
kingdom (418–19). There is savage irony in Ramus' writing this in the year he was
to fall victim to the Saint Bartholomew massacre. On Richelieu, see Reiss, *Meaning*,
chapter 3, especially 70 ff.

46. The connection between rhetoric and empire has been explored in Cheyfitz, *Poetics*.
And see the last pages of Reiss, 'Mapping'.

47. The son of the archduke Philip and Joanna of Castile, he was born at Ghent in 1500
and raised in Brussels (see, too, note 16 above).

48. Elsky, *Authorizing*, 222. This view is by now general. Jerrold E. Seigel has argued
that from Cicero (above all) writers of the early Renaissance developed the view
that rhetoric – social discourse – was not just a source of wisdom, but its very ground
(*Rhetoric*).

49. In this regard, Irvine makes an interesting argument about Alcuin, one of the major
representatives (in the eighth century) of the classical grammatical tradition. He
observes how Alcuin's (and others') *grammatica* represented, for Charlemagne,

the reciprocal empowerment of statecraft or law and the art of discourse: the king
authorizes and authenticates education in the *artes*, empowering those so trained to
use their pen or voice, and those skilled in the principles (*rationes*) of the knowledge of discourse (*dicendi sapientia*) uphold the laws of the kingdom. Alcuin thus
constructed a proto-feudal model of the arts of discourse, in which the king holds
the power of discourse and written knowledge and disperses it to his *litterati*.
(*Making*, 309)

This was a very different model from that we see these humanists working towards,
although it has momentary similarities with a later one, until they were replaced by
an implication that rational language, universally defining of 'the human', thereby
'authorized' itself.

all these topics and the solutions that were to produce Western modernity.

It is also why it became necessary, for knowledge but not for civic and communal action, to leave the arena of natural language and look elsewhere. For, confronted with the failure to establish in or by working on language anything like the *communis ratio* of J. C. Scaliger's hope and phrase (above pages 56–7), humanists sought elsewhere the firm ground of knowledge and discovery this concept intended. They turned to the mathematical disciplines. It may well be that by the end of what follows we shall have a sense that through the work of people like Descartes propositions forged in the arena of these disciplines were then *brought back into* that of language, grounding such later arguments as those of the Port-Royal *Logique* and *Grammaire générale et raisonnée*. This would indeed suggest that the path between Linacre or Scaliger and Port-Royal was considerably more complicated than Padley, Jean-Claude Chevalier, Chomsky and other linguists would have us imagine. It would also help explain the long-held Western belief that natural language contains somehow and somewhere within it an equally natural 'mathematical' rational logic.

Part 2

Passages

3   Rhetoric and politics

Bovelles ended his *De differentia* by remarking that when all was said and done to compare Latin with its vernaculars was an unrewarding exercise and to argue about it senseless. After all, Latin itself was presumably a vernacular to a previous language, in a regression that could cease only with that spoken by Adam and Eve: a language that might be re-learned only in the last days of the world. To seek origins in these decayed times was futile. One could only attend to how languages functioned *now* for their users. Contemporary Latin and contemporary vernaculars could tell us something about meaning and communication, and about their own organizing principles. To look for absolute rules beyond them was idle speculation. These ideas epitomized the sense that there was no surcease to that accumulation of levels of interpretation and meaning we have seen in vernacular grammatical explorations.

Valla and Perotti would not at all have dissented from this view of the limits and purpose of grammatical study and teaching. For a good half-century or more, indeed, a similar view was common to almost all areas of linguistic attention. Erasmian *copia*, one is inclined say, turned it to advantage, idealizing potentially unlimited multiplication and diversity of meanings. In this era, northern humanists especially, many have written, never wanted 'to devise a single absolutely valid interpretation of a text but to collect all remotely plausible ones'. They sought likewise to create texts whose understanding depended on such expansiveness. Margaret A. Sullivan shows how the effect became used by painters as well, so that by mid-century a Pieter Bruegel would use images enabling, necessitating 'multiple associations and a wide range of referrents'. [1]

---

1. Sullivan, *Bruegel's Peasants*, 55. The first citation, provided by Sullivan, is from Anthony Grafton, 'Renaissance Readers and Ancient Texts: Comments on Some Commentaries', *Renaissance Quarterly* 38.4 (Winter 1985): 636. The most notable exploration of these textual effects remains Cave's *Cornucopian Text*. Sullivan's whole book aims to show how two of Bruegel's paintings (*Peasant Wedding Banquet* and *Peasant Dance*, both *c.* 1566) exemplify this understanding of meaning and interpretation.

Remarks made by Erasmus in his *De utraque verborum ac rerum copia* further confirm this state of affairs. So does the very popularity of the work, which, after first appearing in 1512, had 'at least eighty-five editions' in Erasmus' lifetime alone. [2] Here Erasmus insisted that the purpose of rhetorical variety (the expansiveness meant by the term *copia*) was to retain attention, the better to persuade one's listeners. Apt dealing with variety of style rather than precision of meaning was what mattered. It could, indeed, create the meanings needed as one went along: 'Nor will it be difficult, with so many formulas prepared in readiness for action, to aptly divert even a rashly begun speech in any desired direction.' Practical stylistic stock for verbal action, *copia* went beyond rhetoric, having equal weight 'in interpreting authors, in translating books from a foreign language, in writing verse'. Without *copia*, he wrote, 'we shall often find ourselves either confused, or crude, or even [woe upon woe!] silent'. [3] One sees, too, how the uses Erasmus described as right applications for *copia* crossed into those that an earlier *grammatica* had understood as its own. The question of whether they could any more be thought productive of knowledge or sources of discovery, in any sense, is what this and the next chapter will explore.

However *copia* might seem to depend on synonymous expansion, in fact, Erasmus observed, it could never be so limited: for 'scarcely anywhere will you find two words so close in meaning that they do not differ in some respect'. [4] How much more would this be the case – as it in fact always was – when one was dealing not with single words but with phrases or sentences. Certainly, wrote Erasmus in the later *Ciceronianus* (1528), one should 'care first for thoughts, then for words', and 'adapt the words to the subjects, not subjects to words'. [5] But, as the second part of the *Copia* had long since shown, practically speaking neither side of this equation was exhaustible. In actual effect and practice, therefore, *copia* was really but a limit case of language use that *always* meant diversity and diversion of meaning; an attempt, as it were, to harness it. And, of course, such multiplicity did not only engage the speaker, translator or writer. It inevitably meant, in turn, that a work's audience – listener, spectator or reader: in sum, 'interpreter' – could and would look for multiple meanings (being urged and expected to do so). There could also be no end *to* them and no singular grounding *for* them.

2. King and Rix, introduction to Erasmus, *Copia*, 2.
3. Ibid., 17 (I. viii).
4. Ibid., 19 (I. xi).
5. Erasmus, *Ciceronianus*, 81.

The idea that beauty and meaningfulness required continual reading and rereading, interpretation upon interpretation, was a commonplace at least from Erasmus on. Humanists, echoing in this many of their Greek and Latin forebears, insisted that works of the artistic imagination were more beautiful and rewarding as and to the extent that ever more meanings accrued to them. That is why Erasmus' *Adagia* were endlessly augmented, and why so many sixteenth-century writings were 'unfinished': from Rabelais' novel sequence to Edmund Spenser's *Faerie Queene*, from Marguerite de Navarre's *Heptameron* to Montaigne's *Essais* or Philip Sidney's *Arcadia*. [6] It is why humanist editions of the ancients so often seem an on-going accumulation of information: Sullivan offers the case of Bruegel's friend Theodorus Pulmannus' *Horace*, whose first edition's 13 pages of annotation grew over the editor's lifetime to 207 pages. [7] Such a view of meaning and beauty would be radically opposed and finally replaced by developments 'coming from' the quadrivial 'answer' to the dilemmas we have traced.

This view of meaning as a matter of *practice* and of language as a matter of action and effect was turned to advantage again in the arena where rhetoric was to be taken to function: it was to be an art claiming no more than to teach the skill needed to order meanings to persuasive ends. That did not mean it became – as some argued – an art or science grounded in falsehood, and for the teaching of falsehood. It did mean that decisions about true and false, good and evil were not the proper concern of rhetoric *qua* art or science. Rather were such decisions topics of different skills and their arts or sciences. The view did, of course, assume that they could and were to be made elsewhere, on non-rhetorical grounds. [8] The first were the objects of logic and of natural philosophy; the second, those of moral and political philosophy. Huge difficulties in both were manifold in the face of the lack of surety we have followed. But these massive and

---

6. See Reiss, *Meaning*, 32–4, 38–41 *et passim*, but many critics have discussed this aspect of sixteenth-century writing, from Virginia Woolf to Cave, from Thomas M. Greene to Patricia A. Parker, and many more besides. As far as I know, few or none attempt to discuss at any length the non-'literary' reasons for it.

7. Sullivan, *Bruegel's Peasants*, 69.

8. In his 1552 commentary on the *De lege agraria*, Ramus argued that Cicero, for all he had muddled logic and rhetoric in his theory, in his speeches had finely used the results of logic. His theory, not practice, was flawed (Murphy, introduction to Ramus, *Attack*, xxii–xxiv). The view, commonplace after Agricola and the others, that dialectic was prior in this way to rhetoric (L. Jardine, *Francis Bacon*, 13), assumed that the latter in actual practice relied on its 'precursor' discipline for certain of its elements. The problem was that if dialectic itself was explicitly for teaching, then it, in turn, needed grounding in some other prior discipline of discovery.

unsurprising dilemmas were not matter for rhetorical art, and are not
my topic here (as some of them will be in part 3 of this book, and
others in its forthcoming companion volume). What concerns me in
this section is rhetoric itself, the second subject of the trivium, and its
agonizing. [9]

In the *Institutio oratoria*, Quintilian had defined rhetoric as 'bene
dicendi scientiam', opining that so simple a definition caught its broad
purpose of enabling philosophical happiness and political wellbeing,
'since no man can speak well who is not good himself [cum bene dicere
non possit nisi bonus]'. To these ends, it had five parts: 'invention,
arrangement, expression, memory, and delivery or action [inventio,
dispositio, elocutio, memoria, pronuntiatio sive actio]'. [10] In 1549,
Ramus dismissed definition and division alike, calling the first 'vanam
et inanem' and the second mere confusion. After Cicero, he noted,
Quintilian defined 'good' through the four great public virtues, justice,
fortitude, temperance and prudence. To claim rhetoric treated these
widened the art not just to a general treatise on education, but to a
commentary on the whole of social and political life – an absurd
presumption. Skill in an art involved only the rules of that art, nothing
beyond. Furthermore, rhetoric had only two parts: style and delivery,
elocutio and *pronuntiatio*. Quintilian missed those limits because his
unbounded definition utterly confused grammar, dialectic and rhetoric,
mixing up their rules and eliding their objects higgledy-piggledy. [11]
A skill, rhetoric had nothing to do with political or metaphysical good,
philosophical truth, moral rectitude or epistemological accuracy. It
concerned manipulation of meaning to whatever persuasive end the
orator intended.

Ramus had already urged the same point in his 1546 inaugural lecture
as principal of the college of Presles, his *Speech on Joining the Studies
of Eloquence and Philosophy*: Cicero was so remarkable an orator
because practical rhetorical skills enabled him to put his philosophy to

---

9. One can make no pretence to be exhaustive or to follow more than one major path
   of rhetorical explorations and consequences. John Monfasani points out that 'in the
   Renaissance' (roughly between the late fourteenth century and the mid-sixteenth in
   his accounting) there were 'more than a thousand authors in rhetoric' and 'more
   than three times that number of treatises' ('Humanism', 172). Much of this
   material was repetitive, but much of it was not. Still, one can claim ever wider
   accord on the arena, powers, purposes, limits and dangers of rhetoric, whatever
   attitude might then be taken towards these. The minutest subtleties of rhetorical
   debate may be impossible to trace, not its overall direction and implications.
10. Quintilian, *Institutio*, I. 314–15 (I. xv. 34), 383 (III. ii. 1). *Actio* here meant
    all the 'gestures' (motion, body-language, expression and so on) accompanying
    speech.
11. Ramus, *Arguments*, 84, 168, 84–159.

use. Rhetoric itself was a matter of that *practice*. [12] His 1547 attack on
Cicero's theoretical ideas, the *Brutinae quaestiones*, repeated the assertion, explaining that the primary flaw was to have jumbled the arts and
their distinct *facultates* (skills) and *instrumenta*, indeed, to have offered
a 'whole systematic treatment [that] is muddled and confused in unfath-
omable darkness [totam istam τεχωολογίαν infinitis tenebris turbari &
confundi]'. [13] In Ramus' view, the disorder went back to the *fons et
origo* of Latin debate on rhetoric and philosophy, as of all later
European thought, Aristotle: taken vehemently to task in Ramus'
1543 *Aristotelicae animadversiones*, as earlier in his 1536 master's thesis:
Quaecumque ab Aristotele dicta essent, commentitia esse (Whatever
things have been said by Aristotle are absurd fabrications). [14] As for
Erasmus so for Ramus: one had absolutely to distinguish the practice
of rhetorical suasion from discovery. To manipulate an audience
required other and specific skills. These involved deploying the tropes
and figures covered by the term *elocutio* and moving the audience
with them and *actio*, demeanour and gesture: 'Haec Rhetoricae
virtus & propria & sola est [This is Rhetoric's proper and unique
excellence].' [15] On the other hand, a stop had to be put to endless
copiousness.

Some years earlier, in his 1528 *Ciceronianus*, Erasmus had already
used Cicero as a way to attack unwarranted claims for rhetoric. Even
setting Erasmus aside (whose interesting premises about meaning and
its varieties in the *Copia* certainly addressed one aspect of rhetoric –
and in a work widely used as a school textbook), and later claim
notwithstanding, Ramus was by no means the first to place rhetoric in
such bounds. [16] Rather, these were being elaborated more or less simultaneously with the debates in grammar discussed in my first chapter.
If I start here by naming Ramus, it is because he was indeed a focal
point in the larger changes this book explores, and will be the central
figure of this section. But out of the wider context – as he used often

---

12. *Petri Rami Oratio de studiis philosophiae et eloquentiae coniugendis Lutetiae habita
    anno 1546*, rpt. in Ramus and Talon, *Collectaneae*, 244–54.
13. Ramus, *Attack*, 12–14.
14. Ong discusses the meaning(s) of *commentitia* at length: *Ramus, Method*, 45–7. He
    also thoroughly questions the authenticity of the supposed master's thesis, since
    nothing was said about it during Ramus' own lifetime – an odd circumstance, given
    the many acerbic exchanges in which he participated (ibid., 37–41).
15. Ramus, *Attack*, 17. *Inventio, dispositio* and *memoria* belonged, equally uniquely, to
    dialectic (*idem*). And if one failed to get the point, Ramus urged against Cicero's
    claim that the orator had first to be a philosophically wise person, that philosophy
    of necessity came *after* rhetorical training and quite separately from it (22).
16. Izora Scott mentions the widespread school use of Erasmus' *Copia*: *Controversies*,
    Part 1, 118.

to be taken (not least because of the success of his and Omer Talon's 'publicity machine', but also because of the furore over the series of attacks on ancient authorities and the trial that followed the first, and because of his 'martyrdom' in the 1572 Saint Bartholomew's Day massacre) – just what role he played in those changes is, has been, hard to see and harder to comprehend. [17]

Nowadays scholars generally give Agricola a major role in the reworking of rhetoric's place and purpose. His *De inventione dialectica* was written in the late fifteenth century but first published by Erasmus' circle in 1515, with four further editions by 1539. Lisa Jardine reminds us that its first book 'closely resembles other teaching manuals of the period which present the logical "places", or *loci*'. More thorough though its treatment was, it still seemed to do little other than give the traditional *topoi* of *inventio*, which *dispositio* then taught to arrange for purposes of argument. Thus far one had a more or less traditional dialectic art. But Agricola had made it entirely less familiar in the book's introduction. There he wrote, in Jardine's paraphrase, 'that the purpose of argumentation (*ratiocinatio*) in public debate is to put a convincing case as plausibly as possible, so as to persuade an audience to take a particular course of action. Certain truth (the traditional goal of logic) is not, according to Agricola, of great interest to the orator.' The work's last two books developed the idea, giving 'a wide range of persuasive strategies ... concerned to sway, rather than to prove'. This move from syllogistic formalism and 'rigidly deductive' argument did not delight the doctors of Leuven. Especially as Erasmus and his circle saw Agricola's text as 'a technical grounding for *bonae litterae* to substitute for traditional theology's Aristotelian corpus of logical works'. [18]

As Terence Cave maintains, the turn from the 'disciplined argument' of Aristotle and later scholasticism towards 'affective modes' of discourse, in fact undermined the old 'constraints of dialectic' and made 'a fundamental ambiguity in his project of generating discourse'. [19]

---

17. L. Jardine makes an analogous point: 'Humanistic Logic', 185.
18. L. Jardine, *Erasmus*, 110, 121. The 'tradition' was, of course, post twelfth-century. Earlier, exploration of ancient writings had been a main function of the language arts (especially *grammatica*). This is not to say that these humanists 'largely reinstalled the earlier medieval model of literary *grammatica*' (Irvine, *Making*, 464). More accurate, maybe, is Guerlac's claim that when 'Parisian logic confronted the sister of her old adversary', Grammar, it was now 'Dame Rhetoric who carried the day' (introduction to Vives, *Against*, 31). But, we begin to see, the rhetoric at issue was also something rather new. On Agricola's 'place-logic', see Ong, *Ramus, Method*, 92–130; more generally, Vasoli, *Dialettica*, 147–82, 249–77.
19. Cave, *Cornucopian Text*, 16–17. These remarks are also quoted in L. Jardine, *Erasmus*, 131.

It also meant that not accuracy of rule but efficacity of effect bore meaning. In this, rhetoric echoed Fabri's or Palsgrave's analysis of grammatical meaning, Erasmus' discussion of interpretation and the deployment of speech, and Valla's, Perotti's or Bovelles' general view of the working of language. Such concern with efficacy in the actual world of daily relations we have seen in the court context of the *rhétoriqueurs*, in the role given to language by Nebrija and Avila, and we begin to see it in a growing emphasis on persuasion and pedagogy over discovery in realms of dialectic and rhetoric. The efficacity of a vernacular practical mathematics in the real world was, in its turn, to be a major element of its power to fill other needs.

It may be that this emphasis on practice over rule reflects not just an internal loss of older certainties but a sense of external breaches as well. The loss of theological and political securities left a need for new understandings of divine, human and worldly relations that in turn required new instruments of analysis. The abruptly perceived 'expansion' of the world added pressure: humans apparently existed such as Scripture, the Divine Word itself, had no place for; histories and times existed such as were wholly foreign to the closures of medieval eschatology; the very geography of the world was not as had been thought. To note that the European sixteenth century, especially its second half (but then after Reformation, peasant and religious revolts, Spanish, Italian and French wars, and more), was a time of deep and debilitating upheaval in politics, religion, education, economic and social order, and just about every other area of human practice, is scarcely original. As we see, scholarly realms of philosophy and philology, of grammar, rhetoric, logic and mathematics did not escape this disarray. In many ways they would be crucial to a solution: not because philosophers, philologists or mathematicians intervened practically in concrete events (even though as government officials, lawyers, printers, ecclesiastics and soldiers, many did), but because their disciplines eventually gave the analytical tools to describe and explain those events. They made new concepts and practice of meaning, and so of action.

Although this section picks up on the last and refers to the work of a century or more, Ramus and some contemporaries provide the core of discussion. This is because from the late sixteenth century until now scholars have thought the Method developed by him and his colleagues and successors was basic to the making of those tools and establishment of such new thought and practice. They may be right. But the recognition has also always been ambivalent. The same Method has been condemned as logically weak, confused and incompetent.

J. J. Scaliger considered that, like Lipsius', his work 'pleases laypeople
[*le vulgaire*]', but 'one has to be esteemed by the learned and not
just by one's pupils'. He thought Ramus a good enough orator, but
'a river of words, a droplet of wit [flumen verborum, guttula mentis]'.
Nowadays, he added, 'people admire only Ramists. Ramus was a
learned man, but he is far overrated.' He added that 'his mathematics
alone are good, but he is not their author'! [20]

Writing in 1609, and so not long after Scaliger's verbal sallies, with
less sarcasm though hardly more precision, Alsted glorified Ramus'
sharp wit, passion for method, eloquence (rivalling Cicero's) and mathematical acuity. He estimated his achievement between Aristotle's
and Llull's. Yet in the same breath he scorned the '*mutilationem*' and
'*confusionem*' of Ramus' logic. Gabriel Harvey, on the other hand,
earlier praised what he saw as Ramus' new and original 'fundamental
principle' of logic: that 'of tracing causes and not merely effects'. To
be sure, Harvey was especially interested in Ramus' rhetorical side,
seeing him as his age's pre-eminent pedagogue of Cicero's true spirit,
but he did not see that as at all contrary to Ramus' achievement in
Method. [21] Many contemporaries scorned him with savage vehemence.
Others, like Theophilus Banosius in 1576, exclaimed that 'there is no
nation in the Christian world that has not admired the wisdom of
Ramus'. Ramism's swift and extensive spread across northern
Europe is a matter of historical record. Wilbur S. Howell remarked
of his English reception that very quickly and for decades after his
death there was 'almost a complete monopoly for Ramus' logic and
rhetoric'. [22]

In our own day, judgments have been no less wildly divided, although
the negative tends to dominate. Perry Miller's idea that Ramus was
'far and away the greatest figure among the faculties of Europe' was
intemperate, whatever one's view. [23] But Ashworth observes 'how
lacking in breadth and perception [his writings] were' as compared to
'those of his near contemporary, Zabarella'. His principles, she adds,

20. [J. J. Scaliger,] *Scaligerana*, 243: 'ce qu'il (Lipsius) fait, plaist au vulgaire, comme
    Ramus; il faut estre estimé des doctes & non seulement des Escholiers'; 333: 'il
    escrivoit bien mal. Aujourd'huy on ne fait estat que des Ramistes. Ramus estoit
    homme docte, mais on en fait trop grand estat ... ipsius Mathematica sola bona,
    sed ipse non est autor.' One may suppose it no accident that Scaliger's characteri-
    zation of Ramus as 'flumen verborum' more or less parodically paraphrased Erasmus'
    notion of copiousness.
21. Alstedius, *Clavis*, 17–18; Harvey, *Ciceronianus*, 73–5.
22. Banosius is quoted in Murphy, introduction to Ramus' *Attack*, xiv. The Howell refer-
    ence is to *Logic*, 187. The work of L. Jardine and others would now impose a far
    more moderate assertion.
23. Perry Miller, *New England Mind*, 116.

were not invalid, just very limited: 'They offer nothing to the scientist, and they would serve only to bolster the dogmatism of a mind already convinced that it perceived the truth in an orderly manner.' They fell, she seems to say, more on the linguistic side than on what would later be thought of as the scientific. The suspicion is widely shared. [24] Perhaps, we will see, Ramist principles were a kind of last gasp seeking to re-establish what half a century's work (at least) had already profoundly sapped. So violent a contradiction in the historical record gives pause. Worse, it inhibits explanation of Ramism's pedagogical success in displacing older school curricula and prevents any real understanding of its enduring effect on Western philosophy.

These two chapters argue that the contradiction arises from mistaking the means for its end, and that doing so has led to a genuinely serious misapprehension about the replacement of a verbal, linguistic, epistemology by a visual, 'objective', one: a misapprehension certainly as to date, but I think, too, as to fact. To grasp the misapprehension would at the very least affect understanding of some later philosophical speculation, and, for example, of the development of optics. My argument will, however, be the stronger one that the misapprehension has in fact both hidden the actual development that took place (the passage from trivial to quadrivial debate in matters of discovery) and, surely no less consequentially, impeded awareness of how sociocultural development of thought and practice is not characterized by abrupt transformative passages, but by new usings and re-usings of older cultural instruments to the different ends demanded by unfamiliar pressures. Such usings are no doubt augmented by quite new discoveries, but it is the whole reconfiguration of relations that marks change, not odd novelties.

Here I will make a threefold case about this mistake and its ramifications. First, I want to re-emphasize the importance of the social and conceptual context within which Ramus and his colleagues were working. Secondly, it is material to dispute – or at least adjust – the now dominant interpretation of their work as marking change from the verbal to visual – or spatial. [25] Thirdly, and at most length, I will

---

24. Ashworth, *Language*, 15–16. Ong holds the same opinion. He notes that the ban on Ramus' teaching philosophy was owing to 'his demonstrated incompetence': opponents held his work to contain things 'faulses et estranges' and misrepresent 'the very meaning of what it pretends to comment on' (Ong, *Ramus, Method*, 24). Bochenski, Nelson and Prantl concur, as does Murphy (Introduction to Ramus, *Arguments*, 57 n. 90).

25. Including my own in *Discourse*, 25. In a recent work, Nicholas Hudson asserts his lack of belief in a change to a visual orientation of reason, but bases it (quite indirectly) on seventeenth- and eighteenth-century debates about the nature of writing. Unfortunately, his argument is vitiated by the assumption that before 1600 writing was conceived as 'sacred', 'hermetic', 'secret', 'divine' and forged in the crucible of

look anew at the work itself, to show its play between language and
mathematics, and how Method for Ramus was first an instrument of
pedagogy, not of discovery. The last part of this final point is not new.
It was made by Ramus' first opponent, we shall see. The distinction
itself was now in the mainstream of thinking about both logic and the
mathematical arts. But its significance, here, has been rather submerged
by the altogether more dramatic claim about the verbal/visual,
oral/spatial transformation of Europe's 'mental world', about 'the elim-
ination of sound and voice from man's understanding of the intellectual
world' and their replacement by the no doubt Pascalian 'silences of a
spatialized universe'. [26]

For Method evolved from the now-familiar effort to clarify an issue
that seemed wholly philosophical, or philological: once again, that of
meaning, or more exactly, those of denotation and reference. By
the second half of the sixteenth century, faced with almost a century
of work striving to clarify linguistically not the *fact*, so to speak,
of meaning, but its function – ground, derivation, and use –, the
'Averroists' of Padua and Bologna and the Aristotelians of Salamanca
and Coimbra had put the quest for security of a method of discovery
at the forefront of natural philosophical enquiry, making such a secure
method fundamental to the whole enterprise of knowledge. Yet even
there, method in itself was not the final goal. It was, rather, an effect
of the endeavour to set a relation between idea, word and thing on
firm philosophical and linguistic ground. Further, the quest for this
'method' began (in the Spanish and Italian centres, I mean) and
continued as an attempt not to replace but to rework Aristotle. The
issue was not new. Medieval speculative grammarians had made it
central to their study. But by the mid-sixteenth century strong internal
and external pressures gave things a new sense of urgency.

'Man was endowed with language in order to proclaim truth', wrote
Erasmus still in 1523, as if little had changed since the height of the
Christian Middle Ages. [27] He was, however, observing difficulties in a
statement of this kind by now manifest to him and almost all other
thinkers. In the colloquy quoted, a certain style of trade and commerce,
for instance, was taken to militate against the claim. Ecclesiastical
writing on those issues, to be sure, had always deplored a prevalence

---

hieroglyph and mystic symbol, so that early sixteenth-century argument that it was
a 'cornerstone' for developing 'useful and virtuous citizens' was both new and in
advance of a 'demystification' that took place only in the seventeenth century
(*Writing*, 10–54).

26. Ong, *Ramus, Method*, 314, 318.
27. Erasmus, 'Pseudochus and Philetymus'. *Colloquies*, 134.

of cheating and usurious practices. But Erasmus seemed now to be avowing their inevitable universality: after all, to accumulate interest was surely not much else than an economic version of linguistic *copia*, a surplus that was not the object nor the trade whose exchange and process it facilitated, yet somehow combined both; just as verbal *copia* was not a first concept nor just its communication, but an effect additional to and reworking both. For no less important to his readers was the already common opinion of rhetoric as teaching 'the art of lying'. In the same colloquy, Pseudocheus noted: 'clever lying is a large part of eloquence'. Because rhetorical skills were most often argued to be the basis of social order, the implications were huge. That they should have long since become matter for debate over the role of rhetoric in education, letters, and civic life was inevitable, just as was the fact of the debate's growing sharper throughout the century and its lasting well into the seventeenth century. [28]

Of even greater moment, at first, was the sense that the divine guarantees beneath the terms 'truth', 'speech' and 'man' used almost glibly by Erasmus' Philetymus, were rapidly losing their familiar ground: if they had not already done so. It would soon be impossible to claim, as a late scholastic vernacular author like Thomas Wilson still could, that the task of logic was 'to finde out the trueth', the 'perfeicte' knowledge naturally available to humans 'before the fal of Adam' by 'the secret woorking of God'. [29] Questioning ecclesiastical authority had cast doubt on the relation between the human and the divine, and thus, in the present context, on any assurance of relation between mind and world, and its presentation in language (or elsewhere). That is what we saw Tory urgently striving to hold on to. Reason and knowledge, their place, order, reliability and indeed their very nature were in grave question. Further, the mere fact of querying theological authority made humans, willy-nilly, responsible for defining such matters, and so effectively responsible *for* them. That further explains Bovelles' and Pico's *arbitrium*, and seems to lie behind Erasmian *copia*: not a search *into* the mind for meaning divinely set in memory, but outward for meaning created by the speaker in communicative action.

This sense of a breach in divine order perhaps did not lead just to the well-known linguistic explorations of the Bible and theological authority by such as Lefèvre d'Etaples, Erasmus and more aggressive reformers. It also produced those searches for new groundings and

---

28. See, especially, Fumaroli, *Age*; Javitch, *Poetry*; Reiss, *Meaning*, chapters 1–3; and Reiss, '1640'.
29. Wilson, *Rule* (1551), 8–9. We nonetheless saw before (pages 43–4) how analogous views proved tenacious.

understandings of the divine in neoplatonism, Lullism and Cusa's work that we glimpsed earlier. The same worry explains Bovelles' quest to ground theology in mathematical rule – an early transfer from trivium to quadrivium whose immediate source was again Nicholas of Cusa, but of which he at least, if not his colleagues, thought he found hints in Llull. As early as 1501, Bovelles issued a Lullist compendium, *In artem oppositorum introductio* (with a preface by Lefèvre), and for the next decade worked, with Lefèvre and Clichtove and by himself, at a series of texts on mathematical and philosophical questions – again, we have seen that this 'transfer' was historically much more complicated (above, pages 32–3).

He drew from Llull an interest in 'metaphysics and rational theology' and an idea of 'a theological system that employed purely philosophical arguments to prove beyond doubt the truths of revelation'. He also thought that all rational disciplines, not excluding theology, were 'structured in a certain irreducible common fashion'. [30] Given his concern with mathematics, he hardly needed Cusa's example to suggest how these arts might furnish or be such structures. He was early convinced that mathematics could 'demonstrate philosophical and theological truths'. [31] From 1500 to 1510 especially, he explored these ideas, but gradually over the next two decades mathematical techniques and theological and philosophical speculations seem to have separated in his mind. [32] His theology grew more mystical, his mathematics practical (hence his closer relationship with the best-known mathematician of his time, the regius professor Oronce Fine, cosmographer, astronomer/ astrologer, teacher, too, of practical arithmetic and geometry). But the long search further evidences the struggle to heal a broken divine order by grounding it in new rational certainties.

Bovelles' hopes for a universal mathematical tool were no doubt premature: nor was it at all a matter of 'discovery' in any later sense. This mathematics would have been much closer to an older idea of linguistic knowledge grounded in memory. What makes the attempt interesting here is the idea that mathematics could provide a certainty

---

30. Victor, 'Revival', 504, 522, 524.
31. Victor, *Charles de Bovelles*, 38.
32. To the extent that the practical/mystical, pragmatic/spiritual might be represented by 'Aristotle' and 'Plato' (and later on often were), Bovelles' efforts to keep the two together show well in a letter he wrote in May 1515, arguing their difference to be merely a pedagogical one of emphasis and order (printed and translated by Chomarat, 'Platon', 52–3). We saw that Cassirer also insisted on the doubleness of Bovelles' juggling, caught between his scholastic grounding and an 'empirically' oriented and mathematically inclined natural philosophy (*Erkenntnisproblem*, I. 77 *et seq.*).

of order that language had lost. That sense of loss is why the development and ever wider use of vernacular languages would no doubt of themselves have provoked closer attention to language and its functioning. As it was, they simply emphasized the urgency of the need for a stable concept and practice of meaning. They were just one of several pressures.

Among these were old and seemingly unending political uncertainties that now gave rise to new debates: about the relation between monarch and subjects, about the nature of sovereign authority and the subject's rights with regard to such sovereignty, about the relation of sovereign to sovereign, and, increasingly, of society to society – or state to state, and more. The rediscovery of Greek and renewal of Roman arguments on these subjects added to an already volatile mix. Increasingly, the ways in which humanists presented their texts on other subjects, their manner of citation and commentary, set such issues before readers even when they were not otherwise the primary matter at issue. We have already seen how this was so in Palsgrave's case. The tactic would become increasingly common. It is just one further instance of how difficult it is to separate disciplinary concerns. [33]

One must add to this mix of pressures the humanist and then Reform desire for direct access to biblical and patristic texts and commentaries (already mentioned) that produced new researches – with new intentions – in the three languages, Latin, Greek, and Hebrew, whose study eventually affected all the disciplines. [34] So it was and is small wonder

33. Adams has analyzed Ramus' *Dialectica* and a work of one of his strongest followers to show how the examples given express specific political and moral agendas ('Gabriel Harvey's *Ciceronianus*'). Many have explored how such ploys, 'ideological tactics' as we now call them, are deployed in school texts in our own day. At some level, we may suppose them unavoidable. More interesting is Adams' analysis of the political agenda in question, which for Ramus and Harvey was a kind of neo-Roman republicanism – whose major texts were Cicero's writings. This continued the civic humanism of such as Salutati and Bruni, and, closer in both time and place, Lefèvre and Erasmus. We will have more to say on this, but cannot pursue here the details of a strain of political thinking that might tie them as well, via Protestant political theorists like François Hotman and Philippe Duplessis-Mornay and polemicists of the Dutch Revolt and French Civil Wars, to a republican theorist such as Johannes Althusius (nominally drawing his 1603 *Politica methodice digesta* along Ramist lines) and thence to a path from Algernon Sidney and the abbé de Saint-Pierre to Jean-Jacques Rousseau and Immanuel Kant.
34. In the early 1500s several schools for the study of these languages were established in Western Europe. They included the Collegium Trilingue at the University of Louvain, founded in 1517 through a bequest from Jerome Busleiden, Erasmus' and More's friend; Corpus Christi, Oxford; Christ's and St John's Colleges, Cambridge; the trilingual college at the new University of Alcalá, founded earlier by Bovelles' friend, Jiménez de Cisneros; the College of St Nicholas at the University of Vienna; the Collège Royal in Paris (now the Collège de France). See Thompson, in Erasmus, *Colloquies*, 224.

that the sixteenth century saw so huge a production of rational and
normative Latin and vernacular grammars. [35] And meanwhile in
ambush, so to speak, lay the fear that rhetoric, the ground of education, public welfare and civic life, might be not just an ambivalent
expression and persuasion of knowledge and action, but their delib-
erate falsification.

Such was Method's general context. We now also need some immediate idea of what Method itself was thought to be. Ramus himself,
we know, began with a critique of Aristotle. He focused at once on
the philosopher's authority in the schools, impeding novelty of thought,
and on his characterizations of the human, of rationality and of knowledge. Simultaneously, Ramus examined the nature of the relation
between reason, knowledge and language in those analyses of Cicero's
theoretical rhetorical work and of Quintilian that we have seen. His
Method was elaborated from that thinking, in the ten years after his
1536 master's defence, and consolidated in the *Dialectici commentarii
tres* of 1546. Ramus himself then lay under royal ban against writing
or teaching philosophy (whose reasons will be of interest), and the title
appeared over the name of his colleague Omer Talon. There he gave
definitions of *Method*, *Genesis* and *Analysis*.

Method in general, he still wrote in the 1555 *Dialectique*, precisely
echoing its 1546 Latin predecessor, was 'a disposition by which
among several things the first noted is disposed in the first place, the
second in the second, the third in the third and so on'. [36] He divided
it into two kinds. The first was that of 'art' or 'nature', 'by which
whatever is absolutely most evident and clearest is set first'. Such
Method was 'of art' since it was traditional doctrine and 'corresponded

---

35. On these, see Padley's three *Grammatical Theory* volumes and the materials referred
to in chapters 1 and 2 above.
36. Ramus, *Dialectique*: 'méthode est disposition par laquelles entre plusieurs choses
la première de notice est disposée au premier lieu, la deuzième au deuzième, la
troizième au troizième et ainsi conséquemment'. I am quoting from the French
Dialectique (which does not differ greatly in substance from the Latin for the matter
being discussed here – see Vasoli, *Dialettica*, 333–589 for description of the developing Dialectic) because Ramus claimed in his preface that modern philosophy
written in Latin could only be a feeble imitation of the Ancients; written in the
'*vulgaire*' it could at last *rival* them. Like mathematics, as he elsewhere urged, it
could address and affect marketplace and workshop. Issuing his Dialectic in French
was thus a further stage in that refutation of authority whose earlier ones had
been writings against Aristotle, Cicero and Quintilian. One may note that in
their arithmetics, Peletier du Mans, Claude de Boissière and Pierre Forcadel made
the same point for their writing arithmetic in French (echoing Du Bellay's and
others' claims for poetry). In Forcadel's case he was perhaps making a virtue of
his avowed lack of Latin. (Compare N. Z. Davis, 'Sixteenth-Century French
Arithmetics', 31.)

in quality of judgment to necessary utterance and properly concluded syllogism'. [37] It was 'of nature' since it deployed principles of 'universal reason' to explain singular cases. It set a clear taxonomic relation between universals and particulars: from definition to rule, distribution of parts, and final explanation of singulars. The second kind of Method lacked such universality and clarity. Of 'prudence', it was constrained by communicative demands, dependent on contingent conditions, and substituted 'suitability' and 'probability' for certainty if teaching need required. [38] In practice it was more or less the same Method adjusted to the civic virtue of *prudentia* as notably explored in Cicero's *De officiis* (one of Ramus' favourite works). It replaced rhetoric with a logic whose 'loosening' was not thought to impede its embodying the same truths. [39]

Analysis entailed examining 'our own or others'' examples in which invention and composition are to be looked into. It was a technique through which 'the argument, enunciation, syllogism, method, in short ... the whole art of logic' were to be verified. The deployment of argument from universals to particulars was there thoroughly analyzed. It was a procedure common to all arts, wrote Ramus, not

---

37. Ramus, *Dialectique*, 145: 'Méthode de nature est par laquelle ce qui est du tout et absolument plus évident et plus notoire est préposé.' Also called 'méthode d'art parce qu'elle est gardée en la tradition des ars et doctrines et respond en qualité de jugement à l'énonciation nécessaire et syllogisme deüement conclu'.

38. Ibid., 150: 'en laquelle les choses précédentes non pas du tout et absolument notoires, mais néanmoins plus convenables à celluy qu'il faut enseigner, et plus probables à l'induire et amener où nous prétendons'.

39. Ramus' Method of nature seems to correspond to the compositive of the Aristotelian resolutive/compositive pair. The first of these analyzed particular effects to reach general causes, the second synthesized universals to explain effects. A mild overlap here with Jacopo Zabarella does not hide manifest differences (not the least being that the latter sought to re-establish Aristotelian authority, not undermine it). In his *De natura logicae*, Zabarella distinguished a natural from a conventional (*artificiosa*) logic. The first was

a certain natural instinct, a certain power obtained through no human study, by which even wholly untaught people make syllogisms and arguments, with no knowledge of the art of arguing: the first sages used this natural logic to philosophize, for before anyone had written or taught the art of logic, led by natural instinct itself they observed a certain method for the contemplation of things, and proceeded from certain known principles to unknown ones. (*Opera*, col. 27)

Artificial logic came later, providing readily repeatable rules for natural reason. *That* logic Zabarella discusses in his *De methodis* and *De regressu*, separating mere 'order' from 'method' as pedagogical disposition from structure having 'vis illatrix', force of inference (*Opera*, col. 223), and defining *regressive* logic as a path to practical validation of theoretical scientific inference (cols. 479–98). Ramus' 'Method' is more like Zabarella's loose 'order' (cf. Gilbert, *Renaissance Concepts*, 171). The Paduan had no place for anything so 'soft' as Ramus' method of 'prudence'. We shall see more of Zabarella and of these questions later on.

only logic. Genesis reversed this process: it explained the development of an argument from singular instance to its generalization. [40]
Analysis and genesis, then, belonged to what one might think of as
'metamethod'. They were an exegetic means of checking the Method
that 'was to govern all subjects' and let Ramus 'reorganize the entire
curriculum under the rule of *technologia* . . . the logic or science of the
arts themselves'. [41] They were a part of, but supplementary to, this goal
that Ramus did indeed try to achieve, 'himself undert[aking] to apply
his method to nearly all the academic fields of knowledge'. [42] Through
Method, Genesis, and Analysis, he said, Dialectic taught 'the art and
judgment of the syllogism, whether simple or complex, whose proposition normally belongs to a particular art: as Grammar, Rhetoric,
Logic, Mathematics, Mechanics, Physics, Ethics, Politics, those of divine
and human laws, and generally of all the arts'. [43] I will not urge any
similarity of these efforts, claims and procedures to a later more popu-
larly known *méthode*. Their novelty is anyway doubtful.

For so stated, and except for its taxonomies, little was new or even
complicated about this Method (the lack of complication was no doubt
a major reason for its becoming fashionable). Since Aristotle all agreed,
as he held in *Prior Analytics*, that while many principles were specific
to each discipline, 'method [was] the same in all cases, in philosophy
and in any art or study'. 'Dialectic', he insisted in *Topics*, 'is a process
of criticism wherein lies the path to the principles of all inquiries.'
Indeed, in the *Nichomachean Ethics* he virtually summarized Ramus'
triple device: 'the person who deliberates seems to inquire and analyse
in the way described as though he were analysing a geometrical
construction [Method] (not all inquiry appears to be deliberation – for
instance mathematical inquiries – but all deliberation is inquiry), and
what is last in the order of analysis seems to be first in the order of
becoming [Genesis, 'discovery'].' A change is that Aristotle did not
see analysis and becoming/discovery as meta-discussion of Method,
means of verification, but as two ways of understanding how a single
procedure worked. [44] On the other hand, Aristotle's use of geometry

---

40. Ong, *Ramus, Method*, 245–6, 263–4. See, too, Bruyère, *Méthode*, 205–310.
41. Ong, introduction to Ramus, *Scholae in liberales artes*, v.
42. Ong, introduction to Ramus and Talon, *Collectaneae*, viii.
43. Ramus, *Dialectique*, 142: 'Voylà l'art et jugement du syllogisme, tant simple que
    composé, duquel la proposition est ordinairement de quelque art, comme de
    Grammaire, Rhétorique, Logique, Mathématique, Méchanique, Physique, Ethique,
    Politique, des loix divines et humaines et génerallement de tous ars.'
44. Aristotle, *Prior Analytics*, rpt. in D. J. Jenkinson, trans., *Complete Works*, I. 73
    (46a3–18); *Topics*, rpt. in W. A. Pickard-Cambridge, trans., *Complete Works*, I. 168
    (101b3–4); *Nichomachean Ethics*, rpt. in W. D. Ross, trans., and. O. J. Urmson, rev.,
    Complete Works, II. 1756–7 (1112b19–24).

and mathematics as examples may have come to have considerable further significance. But even as Ramus had rather pulled in his horns after his vehement 1543 tracts, so the scandal and influence of Ramism stay inexplicable: setting aside its unoriginal reorganization into logic alone of *inventio* and *dispositio*, themselves corresponding to reason and heuristic display.

Ramus may have become something of a figure of scandal with his 1536 master's defence, the brashness of whose thesis, that everything Aristotle had written was wrong (maintaining both that the texts were forgeries and that they contained only errors), and his success in nonetheless defending it, themselves sufficed to grab attention. [45] But this was nothing at all compared to the outcry that greeted the two 1543 publications. To understand the scandal and the violence of the responses we need to look, then, not just inside the texts, but to outside circumstances as well. For, as to the first, Alsted's ambivalent criticism of 1609 virtually echoed reactions of Ramus' immediate opponents: that they were confronted with a curious combination of bombast and confusion, of mutilation and effective pedagogy. But if that was all there was, whence the outcry? One might think them matter for Scaligerian mockery, but hardly for legal proceedings and dire threats against Ramus' person. But his contemporaries claimed to see a revolutionary threat to educational manner and matter, hostility to religion, and an attack on public order: although Ong thinks that publicizing the university curriculum's flaws (as Ramus saw them) and trying to 'force' general change sufficed for the faculty to become 'panic stricken' and 'turn on Ramus'. [46]

That Ramus gave his two books highly visible protectors does suggest that he sought effect. One, the *Dialecticae partitiones ad Academiam Parisiensem*, was dedicated to the king, François I, the other, the *Aristotelicae animadversiones*, was offered to his erstwhile college companions, Charles de Lorraine and Charles de Bourbon. The first was a kind of logic breviary, presenting the art's elementary principles. It contained none of the analyses of Method we have seen, first made public in the 1546 *Dialectica*, and very little that could be thought at all controversial, far less scandalous. The second was an altogether different kettle of fish. Ramus gleefully and intemperately attacked and vilified Aristotle and his disciples, ridiculing them in terms not very different from those that had been used by earlier humanists against medieval and contemporary scholastic logicians. For good

45. Waddington, *Ramus*, 28–9. But see above note 14 for Ong's query about the thesis (and his reflections on *commentitia*'s meaning).
46. Ong, *Ramus, Method*, 23.

measure he attacked the professors of the university of Paris to whom he had 'addressed' the companion *Dialecticae partitiones*.

Right away, then, Ramus did associate pedagogy, dialectic, ancient authority, and a dismissal of all areas of knowledge as they were grounded in Aristotle's works and conceived by him and his followers: not just logic and rhetoric, but metaphysics, natural philosophy, ethics and politics. So to the extent that Ramus' rejection of the accepted grounds of education was avowed, and that, at least in the domain of ethics and politics, this included the acknowledged theoretical bases of contemporary analyses of public and private behaviour, one might indeed take the Paris professors' accusations as well-founded at least in two of their claims. And because Aristotelianism and Christianity had been co-mingled since St Thomas, hostility to religion was a natural addition. But one could anyway not separate religion from the political arena: especially not in Western Europe in 1543.

Supposedly prompted by the current rector of the university of Paris, Pierre Galland, principal of the college of Boncour, Joachim de Périon and António de Gouvea set out to refute Ramus. Their works appeared in November 1543. Périon dedicated his to the archbishop of Paris, Jean du Bellay, and argued that to sap Aristotle's authority was to make all philosophy insecure, that the philosopher's writings were indeed genuine, and that Ramus was philosophically impertinent, theologically impious and politically mischievous. [47] Gouvea's work appeared shortly before Périon's, and was dedicated to Jacques-Paul Spifame, chancellor of the university of Paris and a royal counsellor. As in Périon's case, its heatedness suggests he hardly needed Galland's urging: he is, he began, 'answering your slanders on behalf of Aristotle, whom I love, whom I admire, and to whom I willingly owe everything'. [48]

Gouvea accused Ramus of wrongly setting Aristotle against Plato, and of knowing neither of them well enough to claim that the pupil had corrupted his master's Dialectic. Quite apart from lacking the necessary mental capacity, Ramus, he urged, scarcely mastered Latin and had no Greek. It was Ramus, he asserted, who had muddled the

47. Waddington, *Ramus*, 39–40. Graves' presentation of these events (*Peter Ramus*, 30 ff.) plagiarizes this work, summarizing and translating (at least once seriously incorrectly) its pages on the matter, with no acknowledgement other than inclusion in the bibliography. I suspect this to be the case for much of Graves' book. It is thus not just 'sophomoric' in its account of the historical context and does not copy from Waddington only his words of 'moral indignation' at the treatment meted out to Ramus, as Ong more generously allows (*Ramus, Method*, 6).
48. Goveanus, *Opera iuridica*, 787: 'pro Aristotele, quem amo, quem admiror, cui debere plurimum volo, tuis calumniis respondeo'.

different arts, not his opponents. Furthermore, he had simply falsified Aristotle (to say nothing of Cicero and Quintilian). He spent most time on this last point, examining the Organon's parts as they were traditionally taught in the schools (including Porphyry's *Isagoge*). 'How', he concluded, 'do you dare to call a sophist him whom Plato himself, whose disciple you wish to be, called *the philosopher of truth*? the power of whose mind was so superior and so copious in philosophy that it spread out through Theologians, Physicians, Jurisconsults, and ultimately all writers, doctors, and masters of all arts and sciences?' Why did he elect to 'vomit [his] venom' on Aristotle, rather than on one of his own sort of ignorant [*imprudentem*] and linguistically inept contemporaries? 'Impudence', 'presumptuous dishonesty', and 'impiety' were the least of his sins. [49] Dismissing Aristotle, he undermined the truth of philosophy and the historically tested sureties that all the aforementioned experts represented.

Such abuse was not unusual, and answered Ramus more or less in kind. But most modern commentators agree that Gouvea was by and large correct both in his presentation of Aristotle and in his criticisms of Ramus. One of these indeed almost surely guided Ramus to his Method. For in the 1543 works, following Agricola (a constant reference) in dividing dialectic into invention and judgment, Ramus then split judgment into three kinds. The first dealt with propositions giving true assessments of *quaestiones* (syllogisms, of which Ramus claimed to identify three sorts: induction, enthymeme and example), the second treated the arrangement of series of propositions, the third concerned ascent from the (Platonic) cave to God. The odd third we may set aside: doubtless it most concerned the use of Plato as a cudgel for Aristotle, and Ramus henceforth dropped it. But Gouvea noted especially that the second was out of place in a treatise on discourse, since it had to do only with teaching:

I think you call *second judgment* the order of teaching the arts that the Greeks call *method*. Why would Aristotle teach it in his *Organon*, where only the rules for rational discourse are given? It is one thing to reason, another to teach

49. Goveanus, *Opera*, 815:

Tune sophistam appellare audes, quem Plato ipse, cuius te discipulum esse vis, *philosophum veritatis* nominabat? cuius ingenii tam excellens vis, tantaque in Philosophia ubertas fuit, ut in Theologos, Medicos, Iureconsultos, in omnes denique omnium artium & scientiarum scriptores, doctores, magistros redundarit? ... Cur Aristotelem, ac non ex hac potius aetate aliquem elegisti tui ordinis scriptorem imprudentem, indisertum, similem tui, in quem tuum virus omne evomeres? an id eo fecisti, ne tibi ad summam impudentiam, improbitatem, impietatem reliqui quicquam faceres?

any art: thus rules for the former are one kind, those of the latter another, nor is the ground of both things the same. [50]

Ramus heeded: as we have seen, in 1546 and 1555 first and second judgment became the two kinds of method, of art or nature and of prudence, dianoetic and axiomatic as they were in 1572. [51]

Whatever positive result Ramus may later have drawn from the dispute, in 1543 matters did not stop there. Gouvea's critique took on greater weight. Galland had been succeeded as rector in early October by Guillaume de Montuelle, principal of the college of Beauvais. He had Ramus' two books censored by the faculty of theology and then urged Parlement to take steps to suppress them. Ramus was cited as an 'ennemi de la religion et du repos public', as bruited in Périon's and Gouvea's published refutations. [52] The latter was to present the university's case before Parlement. [53] Before this procedure got under way, a friend of Galland's, the bishop of Mâcon, Pierre Du Chastel, who was François I's reader, was persuaded to bring the matter to the attention of the king. He removed jurisdiction from Parlement in favour of his Council and, on Du Chastel's advice, ordered that a dispute take place between Ramus and Gouvea before a jury of five, two each chosen by the disputants, the president by the king. For his judges, Ramus obtained Jean Quentin, dean of the law faculty, and the physician Jean de Beaumont, who had unusually been twice rector of the university of Paris. Gouvea had Francesco Vimercato (Vicomercatus),

---

50. Goveanus, *Opera*, 810:

   Secundum iudicium credo vocas rationem artium tradendarum, quam Graeci μέθοδον appellant: eam in suo *Organo*, ubi disserendi duntaxat praecepta dantur, cur doceat Aristoteles? Aliud *disserere* est, aliud *artem aliquam tradere*: alia itaque rei illius, alia huius praecepta sunt, neque eadem utriusque rei ratio est.

   On the judgments, this debate and Method, see too Ong, *Ramus, Method*, 182–90, 218; Vasoli, *Dialettica*, 380–422; and L. Jardine, *Francis Bacon*, 43–4.
51. See, for example, Ong, *Ramus, Method*, 224–69; Vasoli, *Dialettica*, 423–34, 474–519, 582–9 (including further adjustments); and Schüling, *Geschichte*, 103–9.
52. These details are from Waddington, *Ramus*, 42–3.
53. A member of a well-known Portuguese humanist family, whose brothers were also working in France, Gouvea had been trained at the college of Sainte-Barbe, obtaining his doctorate in arts in 1532. He taught there until 1534, when he went to Bordeaux's college of Guyenne, joining some of the foremost scholars of his day at the celebrated college, teachers like George Buchanan and Nicolas de Grouchy. In 1537 he undertook law studies at Toulouse and Avignon, where he perhaps became acquainted with the much younger future great jurist, Jacques Cujas. In 1541 he was back in Paris as a professor at Sainte-Barbe (see Carvalho, *António de Gouvea*, 27–44). Waddington wrote of his 'science remarquable' and commented that Cujas held him in the highest possible regard (*Ramus*, 42, 39). Although Gouvea also sought to return to the 'true Aristotle', one cleansed of medieval cavil and the later *imprudentiae* of contemporaries 'like Ramus', he was of the institution and shared his university colleagues' interests.

who had been a renowned Aristotelian at Pavia and Padua before becoming professor of Greek and Latin philosophy at the Collège Royal, and Pierre Danès, first professor at the same college in 1530. The king's nominee was the theologian Jean de Salignac. All three, Waddington scolded, were 'de zélés péripatéticiens'. [54] So in a sense was Ramus, deep-set as he was in Aristotelian thinking.

Ramus sought to make the debate public, but this was denied. For two days Ramus and Gouvea battled over Aristotle's Dialectic, at the end of which the Aristotelians, who seemed to be losing, interrupted the debate, eventually urging that it be renewed from scratch. Ramus refused, accusing his opponents of contradicting their own already signed opinions. The objective now seemed no longer to be to clarify Aristotle or reaffirm the university's curriculum, but indeed to condemn Ramus. The king then refused a requested change in the jury. Realizing the case to be prejudged, Quentin and Beaumont withdrew, both first writing their belief in philosophical freedom and refusal to be used to put an imprimatur on injustice. Ramus made an effort to find replacements before asking for the inevitable judgment. The three remaining judges condemned both books – even though the *Dialecticae institutiones* had not been formally in question – in an *arrêt* of 1 March 1544. Twenty-five days later, on 26 March, the king's sentence was published across Paris, with the aim, it began, to 'bien ordonner et establir la chose publique de nostre royaulme [to order and establish properly the public welfare of our kingdom]'. [55]

It was a text of surpassingly bad faith. After reviewing details of the debate's establishment, it gave a description of its end in which even the more or less correct fragments were bent out of recognition. It asserted that it was only recording a sentence whose justice Ramus admitted. It claimed the debate had ended when he had seen that he could not uphold his books, had said he no longer wished to go on debating, and accepted the judges' sentence, and when, once his

---

54. Some of these factual details are from Carvalho, *António de Gouvea* (33–44), most are from Waddington, *Ramus*, as are all those of the next paragraph (42–7). Ong discounts what he calls the 'cloak-and-dagger' view of the trial he sees as resulting from Waddington's 'passionate' but intellectually muddled moralized defence of Ramus (*Ramus, Method*, 5, 23–5). But, again, setting aside other matters, one must wonder whether a 'threat' to the curriculum posed by such universally agreed and 'demonstrated incompetence' really explains either the violence of reaction or the need for government intervention.

55. I give here Waddington's date, taken from its 1544 separate publication – a pamphlet of extreme rarity even in 1855 (49–52). But I cite the rather more correct text given in Launoy, *De varia, Opera*, IV. 1.206–7. Launoy gave a date of 10 May 1543 (which must be a misreading for March: '1543' would then be correct, since until 1568 the year ended on 31 March, and this would be our '1544').

representatives had chosen no longer to participate, he had refused to
replace them, agreeing to whatever decision the remaining three might
reach. [56] Before its announcement, the sentence was then justified in
terms drawn more or less exactly from Gouvea's book (and Périon's):

that the said Ramus had been ill-considered, arrogant, and insolent in reproving
and condemning the process and art of logic accepted by all peoples, of
which he himself was ignorant, and that, because in his book of *Animadversions*
he attacked Aristotle, his ignorance was visible and manifest. Further, he
showed his ill will by criticizing many things that are good and true, and by
accusing Aristotle of many things which he never discussed at all. In sum,
his said *Animadversions* contained nothing but complete lies and such slander
that it seemed to the entire welfare and profit of letters and sciences that the
said book be altogether suppressed; and likewise the other aforementioned
book, titled *Dialecticae institutiones*, as also containing many false and strange
things. [57]

Both books were thus 'condemned, suppressed and abolished', their
printing forbidden. Ramus was ordered 'not to read, write, copy,
publish or otherwise broadcast' them, and to teach 'no Dialectic or
Philosophy' without the king's express permission, and no more to use
such 'slanders and insults against Aristotle, other approved ancient
authors, or our above-mentioned daughter, the University [of Paris]
and its instruments'. Disobedience, it warned, would meet with 'confis-
cation of the books and corporal punishment'. [58] Parlement duly

56. 'Et voyant par iceluy Ramus lesdits Livres ne se pourroient soustenir, eust declaré
    n'en vouloir plus disputer, & qu'il les soûmettoit à la censure des dessusdits. Et
    comme l'on y vouloit proceder, lesdits Quentin et Beaumont l'un apres l'autre
    eussent declaré ne s'en vouloir plus entremettre. Au moyen de quoy eust iceluy
    Ramus esté sommé et requis d'en eslire & nommer deux aultres. Ce qu'il n'eust
    voulu faire et se fust du tout soûmis aux trois autres dessus nommés.' (206)

57. Launoy, *De varia, Opera* 206–7:

    que ledit Ramus avoit esté temeraire, arrogant & impudent, d'avoir reprouvé &
    condamné le train & art de Logique, receu de toutes les Nations, que luy mesme
    ignoroit, & que parce qu'en son Livre des Animadversions il reprenoit Aristotle,
    estoit évidemment connuë & manifeste son ignorance: Voire qu'il avoit mauvaise
    volonté, de tant qu'il blasmoit plusieurs choses qui sont bonnes & veritables, &
    mettoit sus à Aristotle plusieurs choses, à quoy il ne pensa oncques. Et en somme
    ne contenoit son dit Livre des Animadversions que tous mensonges, & une maniere
    de médire, tellement qu'il sembloit estre le grand bien & profit des Lettres & Sciences
    que ledit Livre fust du tout supprimé: Semblablement l'autre dessusdit intitulé:
    Dialecticae Institutiones, comme contenant aussi plusieurs choses fausses & estranges.

58. 'Et semblablement audit Ramus, de ne plus lire lesdits Livres, ne les faire écrire ou
    copier, publier, ne semer en aucune maniere, ne lire en Dialectique ne Philosophie,
    en quelque maniere que ce soit, sans nostre expresse permission: Aussi de ne plus
    user de telles médisances & invectives contre Aristote, ne autres anciens Autheurs,
    receus & approuvez, ne contre nostredite fille l'Université & Suppôts d'icelle, sous
    les peines que dessus [de confiscation desdits Livres et de punition corporelle].' (207)

registered the king's edict. The university greeted it with delight. Danès
publicly burned Ramus' two books. Anti-Ramus plays were performed
in the colleges. His lifelong enemy, Jacques Charpentier, thought
Ramus should have been exiled. Danès was said to have voted for such
a penalty. Du Chastel apparently had to prevent the king from acceding
to others' demands that he be condemned to the galleys. Waddington
views the condemnation as an inexplicable blot on François I's record,
interference in things 'that were none of his business' and with which
'public power had nothing to do'. [59]

What all this suggests, of course, including the savagery of the punishment and the reactions, is that government authority did indeed believe
that the stakes in the argument concerned it and had to be dealt with
by deployment of its legal powers. It was not accidental that the royal
edict began by talking about 'la chose publique', or that Gouvea
accused Ramus of lacking the prime Ciceronian civic virtue, *prudentia*.
Those grouped against Ramus (in this instance) were as convinced as
he and his predecessors were that in education, in law, in political life
and in religion the debates about grammar, rhetoric and logic were
fundamental. Changes in forms of intellectual analysis and public
debate, in understanding of what knowledge was and how it could be
obtained, and, perhaps above all, in the people who would be thought
authoritative in such affairs, meant fundamental reorganization of all
spheres of social and civic life. Ramus was in fact claiming a right to
participate in the kind of communal civic exchange that we saw urged
by Lefèvre d'Etaples (after, say, Salutati and Bruni), echoed in many
ways by a Fabri, and that would lead directly to late sixteenth-century
Protestant political argument against what was by then seen as abusive
authority (see note 33 above).

That is why Ramus and his colleagues in fact got straight back to
teaching, Talon putting the revised *Dialectica* under his name in 1546,
Ramus concentrating for the while on mathematics – an area more
esoteric to most of his contemporaries, but which he saw eventually as
having no less importance than those matters of the trivium that had
just now put him in such trouble: in the last version of the *Dialectica*
(1572) he was to equate the method of logic with geometry, extending
it to all the arts. [60] In this regard, his 1566–8 battle with Charpentier

59. Waddington, *Ramus*, 48–9. For the just preceding details, see 53–7. Of course, if we
    agree with Ong, much of the afore-going can be set at the door of Waddington's
    fevered moral Protestantism, but even Ong refers to 'the highhandedness of the
    government intervention' (*Ramus, Method*, 24), and Waddington does bring
    supporting evidence. Vasoli follows Ong in doubting tales about proposed banish-
    ment or condemnation to the galleys: *Dialettica*, 422.
60. Compare Sharratt, 'Peter Ramus', 14, and Vasoli, *Dialettica*, 587–8:

is notably revealing: against Charpentier, who, with the powerful help of the cardinal de Lorraine (both of them rabid anti-Protestants) had been given a mathematics chair at the Collège Royal, Ramus, by then dean, fought tooth and nail, finally telling the conseil privé that not only did Charpentier have neither mathematics nor Greek (hence no direct access to Euclid anyway), but that he boasted of intending to divert the chair towards (Aristotelian) philosophy and wholly away from mathematics. The implication was that mathematics then represented as strong a reforming instrument as logic had done – and that both Ramus and Charpentier recognized the fact. [61] Ramus indeed censured the absence of adequate university teaching in mathematics as bitterly as he had the abuse of Aristotelianism on an earlier occasion – and for similar reasons: that it deprived students of an effective instrument in the real world of business and manufacture, and, as he said in the *Prooemium mathematicum* of 1567, of its 'military and commercial' utility. [62]

We will, of course, be coming back to mathematics. But it matters to have some sense of the wide implications of these often violent quarrels. (Indeed, there has always been some suspicion that Ramus' death late in the Bartholomew's massacre had more to do with Charpentier than with Catholic/Protestant hatreds.) [63] Clearly education and

---

[In 1572] la struttura del metodo ramista resta cosí definita come un procedimento che muove, in ogni caso, dagli 'assiomi universali' per illuminare, con la loro assoluta evidenza e chiarezza, le nozioni 'piú oscure' e 'singolari', e che cosí può realizzare la 'disposizione' piú acconcia e funzionale di tutte le conoscenze. Il prototipo, il modello concreto di questo metodo è perciò indicato nei procedimenti tipici della geometria, la sola scienza che, a giudizio di Ramo, segua una via veramente rigorosa e necessaria, l'unica disciplina che possa offrire une guida sicura alla nuova logica e suggerire un criterio di 'chiarezza' valido in ogni campo del sapere. La fonte di ogni possibile verità sta nell'evidenza intrinseca dei primi postulati che forniscono la 'materia' e i 'fondamenti' propri di ciascuna disciplina; anche nei rapporti tra le diverse scienze può e deve essere attuata un'analoga connessione e ordinamento degli 'assiomi universali', al fine di ricondurre tutto il sapere alla 'luce comune' di un unico principio metodico.

61. Extensive extracts from Ramus' 1567 'Remonstrance au Conseil privé' are given in Waddington, *Ramus*, 411–17. For details of the fight, see 166–81. The Latin texts of Ramus' earlier complaints to the senate (March 1566, o.s.) can be found in *Scholae in liberales artes*, cols. 1117–44. Charpentier had been pursuing Ramus since he had been rector of the university in 1550/1 (73–80, 100–2). He had published a polemic against his dialectic in 1554. Ong suggests that we take the mathematics fight as told by Waddington with a pinch of salt (*Ramus, Method*, 33), but Ramus' published plea is telling, and see, too, Vasoli, *Dialettica*, 562–72.
62. Egmond, 'How Algebra', 132, 140. He cites Hooykaas, *Humanisme*, 84 *et passim*. The last quotation is from N. Jardine, *Birth*, 266 (*Prooemium*, 212–16).
63. The clearest presentation of the case against Charpentier, if distinctly biased, is still Waddington's (*Ramus*, 258–83), but Ong and others dismiss the accusation with little ado (Ong, *Ramus, Method*, 29).

pedagogy were understood to be major tools for change, while the possibility of a different logic of discovery was equally clearly seen as a *public* threat. Ramus and his colleagues and opponents were not alone in such feelings. Both sides had their supporters. In 1545 Ramus was named principal of the college of Presles. Then, when Henri II succeeded to the throne in 1547, he lifted the ban against Ramus at the request of the latter's two old school friends, Bourbon and Lorraine. Four years later he named him to a Collège Royal Chair in philosophy and eloquence. In later years Ramus would make frequent speeches on educational reforms in the university.

All these things are why, to begin to understand both the scandal and the influence of Ramus' work, we have needed to look behind Method itself: not only at the method's development (an altogether easier project since Nelly Bruyère's study tracing the movement of Ramus' thinking from the earliest manuscript and writings onwards), but at the relation between the contemporary work on meaning already discussed and those wider sociopolitical concerns I have named. Among these contemporaries, I will make Henri Estienne a principal. He was a friend of Ramus who fought many of the same battles. Further, because he set his thinking on these issues in both philosophical and political contexts, his writings emphasize the connections we have been indicating. For, as I noted, under the simplicity, even naïvety, of Method lay deep discomfort and unease about the very status of the elements essential to it – indeed, to any logical system at all.

Remarking this unease, I continue, then, to stress the first aspect of these chapters' threefold case about these explorations in Method, rhetoric and dialectic: social and conceptual context (the other two, I recall, being the matter of a supposed passage from a verbal to visual or spatial mentality, and that of Method, pedagogy and mathematics). This discomfort echoed, we have now more than begun to see, the general dread of dissolution and decay deplored by Erasmus in 1526:

King Christian of Denmark, a devout partisan of the gospel, is in exile. Francis, King of France, is a 'guest' of the Spaniards ... Charles is preparing to extend the boundaries of his realm. Ferdinand has his hands full in Germany. Bankruptcy threatens every court. The peasants raise dangerous riots and are not swayed from their purpose, despite so many massacres. The commons are bent on anarchy; the Church is shaken to its very foundations by menacing factions; on every side the seamless coat of Jesus is torn to shreds. The vineyard of the Lord is now laid waste not by a single boar but at one and the same time the authority of priests (together with their tithes), the dignity of theologians, the splendour of monks is imperiled; confession totters; vows reel; pontifical ordinances crumble away; the Eucharist is called in question; Antichrist is awaited; the whole earth is pregnant with I know not what calamity. [64]

In Erasmus' 1529 *Charon*, Alastor comments that the 'Furies' have set to work with a fine zeal: 'not a corner of the earth have they left unravaged by hellish disasters, dissensions, wars, robberies, plagues.' Yes, replies Charon: 'I've hopes of a splendid slaughter in the near future.' [65] The same concern with public welfare and political stability (and its contrary) we have already seen among such as Lefèvre and his group, not to mention the courtier humanists whose work part 1 explored. So one is not surprised that later in the century Henri Estienne (whose father and grandfather worked with the earlier humanists) explored the purity of the French language following and in conjunction with scathing attacks on current political and social conditions. The need for secure meaning and comprehension, one cannot repeat often enough, paralleled the demand for social and political stability.

We have seen how virtually all those working up to the 1530s on grammatical and rhetorical questions were facing difficulties in expressed meaning and truth. They found themselves multiplying what one might call 'places of meaning', even though some sought to turn that 'copiousness' to advantage. They still worked on the basis of a theory of the sign as a place of repeated 'readings', of continuing 'glosses', as it were. For them, words were signs of signs of signs ... So long as this process had been able to remain grounded in some authority, whether divine or secular (as in Bovelles' efforts), there was no very serious dilemma. The distanced relationships of God, humans and the world (matter of theology), of truth, concepts, and signs (matter of grammar and logic), and of knowledge, language and reference (matter of grammar, the whole trivium and of specific art and science) was assured. So long as the assumption survived that the structure and use of words had in some way been created from objects in nature, however mediated, one could rely on linguistic '*causas*' (as Scaliger still called them in 1540): explicable origins of language and confirmable meanings. [66] Once guarantees of such fixed relations between concept and linguistic sign, between referent and concept, and between denotatum and sign had been removed, then urgent and profound problems arose.

---

64. Erasmus, 'The New Mother', *Colloquies*, 269–70.
65. *Colloquies*, 390–1.
66. Breva-Claramonte, *Sanctius*, 73. Scaliger's *causas* were three of Aristotle's four: material (*littera*), formal (*significatio*) and efficient (inventors of language and historical development of it): Jensen, *Rhetorical Philosophy*, 111–84.

Without such certainties how was any knowledge or action, of whatever kind, possible? Lacking external guarantees, how could the queried relations be defined? How could they be stabilized? Who or what could be responsible for them? The indications of uncertainty multiplied. Fabri's and Palsgrave's remarkable accumulation of vocabulary seeking to define and fix 'places of meaning' were one such effort to introduce and grasp settled relations of meaning, enabling analysis, knowledge and finally action. In the end they could never affirm any last 'anchor' assuring conceptual surety or 'scientific' realism. Agricola's suasive language and Erasmus' *copia* marked the same 'failure'. And this inability produced a widespread feeling that no kind of truth could be expressed, so that social action was entirely contingent, disordered and indeed groundless. In the mid-1540s Buchanan wrote two tragedies exploring these very dilemmas. Montaigne recorded his performance in them at the college of Guyenne, and the essayist's own sense of the inconstancy and disorder of 'inner life' may have owed much to these debates. [67]

The dilemmas, that is to say, were to continue to be worried for some considerable time, and still very much in terms of a fundamental association between language and civil life, communication and political stability, the grounds of knowledge and discovery and the claims of public authority. Ramus' battle with king and university was perhaps between a 'humanist' civic ideal and its conceptual grounds and a quite different view of ruling authority. By appointing him to the Collège Royal, Henri II may have shown himself as politically conscious and careful as his father. By 1551 Ramus was an altogether more visible person than he had been in 1544. Once in the college, Ramus was, as it were, brought in from the cold. The college was closer to court than to university: as Ramus' 1567 plea against Charpentier, to the Royal Council, and his 1572 dedication to the queen show (see note 61 and chapter 2, note 45 above). Its professors came directly under royal authority. Alan Sinfield argues that in England during this period the crown gradually increased its 'social and intellectual control' over the universities (as to both curriculum and the social class of students attending: poor scholars being replaced by offspring of the gentry and nobility) and a potentially 'good' civic humanism yielded to a 'bad' 'court humanism', itself bowing the knee in servitude to government authority. [68]

No doubt this simplifies complex movements (what explanation does not?), but it is suggestive. One wonders whether the turn to an

---

67. Reiss, *Tragedy*, 40–77 *et passim*.
68. Sinfield, *Faultlines*, 145–6.

ever more specialized and technical mathematics did not have the initial effect – and benefit – of removing its practice from political control (at least for a while). In any case, how one area of debate was resolved was understood to be wholly dependent on and related to others. That is why the demands of pedagogy, claims of rhetoric and titles of discovery were no more thought indifferent to the conditions of state by François than they were by his successors.

Estienne still worried in 1562 that if words lost their meanings, however conventionally established, the processes of language and learning became nonsense, decaying into madness:

Similar absurdity (indeed, even more) is found in certain other locutions, which nonetheless please many, and for no other reason than that they are spoken against all reason. And it is the case that if this idiotic (indeed, insane) desire for novelty continues to gain ground, overturning everything wherever it goes, I fear that in the end we will have to call head foot and foot head. Especially will this be so once such a desire has entered the heads of ignorant people, be they courtiers or others. [1]

He tied this unreason directly to political conditions, arguing that bringing Machiavellian political practices into France had fatally undermined linguistic, and so conceptual, sureties. He blamed the matter on those who frequented the Medici-controlled court, and in this we may well see a continuation of that path of civic humanism to which I have already several times referred.

Like most others in France, as religious disturbances in the 1540s and fifties became increasingly vicious civil dynastic wars in the 1560s and seventies, Estienne grew warmer on the subject. By 1575, he had joined the Protestant polemicist Innocent Gentillet in directly attacking the queen: *Discours merveilleux de la vie, actions & deportemens de Catherine de Medicis royne mere.* [2] Three years later he published his

---

1. H. Estienne, *Conformité*, 27:

   Autant se trouve d'absurdité (voire encores plus) en quelques autres locutions, lesquelles touttefois plaisent à plusieurs non pour autre raison que pource qu'elles se disent contre toute raison. Et de faict, si ce sot (voire enragé) désir de novalité va tousjours gagnant pays, & renversant tout par où il passe, i'ay grand peur qu'en la fin il ne faille appeler la Teste le Pied, & le Pied la Teste: & principalement quand un tel désir sera entré au cerveau de gens ignorans, soyent courtisans, ou autres.

   There is not a lot on Estienne (although all books on the growth of printing include discussions of him and his relatives). The standard life remains Clément's now dated *Henri Estienne*.

2. It is not certain, but probable, that Estienne and Gentillet wrote this together.

Deux dialogues du nouveau langage françois italianizé et autrement desguizé, whose punning title itself again emphasized the association of politics and language: the Guises (foreigners from Lorraine, as the Medici were from Florence, and equally guilty of the wars) were responsible for debasing, indeed destroying the language as they had the country. His earlier *Apologie pour Hérodote* (1566) was a slashing satire on current circumstance, where again language and political conditions were brought keenly together.

For an Estienne, especially after the Saint Bartholomew's Day massacre, this foreign court was beyond the pale. By the late 1570s, while conditions showed small hope of improvement, for Protestants especially, the lack of a Valois successor at least created the hope of a French court sometime in the future. And, while he was a Protestant, Henri de Navarre was politically much more a *politique*, as his past activities and associations implied and his future ones would confirm. In many ways, *politique* ideals of civic stability and of sovereignty as an accord between prince and people itself carried on some aspects of civic humanism. The attacks of an Estienne on the dynastic and religious politics of the last Valois rulers and their Guise cousins manifestly carried on the tradition that came down to him from humanist predecessors like Salutati and Bruni, Lefèvre and Erasmus, and his friend Ramus, whose Calvinism went in hand with those ideas of a quasi-republican order often implied covertly in choice of reference but overtly in very many works.

The catastrophe of political instability Estienne blamed on foreign interests and interference in French civic life was still seen then as intimately embroiled with the linguistic chaos that was here also laid at the door of foreign interference. [3] The very form the language debate took, that is to say, was dependent on political conditions. We are far from Lemaire's *Concorde des deux languages* and equally so from the praises a successor French court would receive a century later as the

---

3. Estienne was not the first to assert the quality of his language by rejecting others. Bembo and Dolet had just done so; Dante and Machiavelli were among many eminent predecessors. Most important for sixteenth-century scholars was the scorn poured on Greek affectations by Cicero in *De finibus*. Bembo's and Dolet's anti-Ciceronianism came from Cicero himself (Meerhoff, *Rhétorique*, 6–8). Like Ramus, they were rejecting not a style *per se*, but a theory and a slavish aping of style. These might be needed while forging a new language. The end was to free the imitator and let the writer 'sound', depict and work out 'son naturel', as Du Bellay wrote. The poet was clear (in 1549) that proper language use inevitably accompanied individual 'jugement', as well as knowledge of one's 'forces' and abilities ('combien ses epaules peuvent porter'). He was approaching the idea that language and meaning involved the responsibility of a 'subject' – a notion perhaps beginning as early as Bovelles' *arbitrium* and *sapiens* (Du Bellay, *Deffence*, 107).

source of the most excellent language. [4] But it was the same debate
that continued, and which, as far as language was concerned, would
not come to any kind of end until very much later (marked by those
praises). Estienne's upside-down world of 'fantaisie', where people
acted 'sottement', 'à tort et à travers', where the 'fou' had annexed
language (to use just a few of the terms of the preface to his
Conformité) corresponded exactly to fear of political and social dissolution. The *Apologie* had already satirized much of this, and one may
read Ramus' own, otherwise mildly curious, 1559 treatise on the
'ancient Gauls' as inspired by similar concerns. [5]

By the 1570s and eighties they were no longer alone in relating civic
catastrophe to linguistic and conceptual incapacity. François de
Belleforest, Louis Le Roy, François de La Noüe, Montaigne, Etienne
Pasquier and Michel Hurault were a few of those who echoed and
embroidered Thucydides' well-known claim that linguistic decay was
largely responsible for civil war in Greece. [6] Most of these were high
in government council and one, La Noüe, was judged perhaps the most
considerable soldier of his time. Concerns of humanists associated with
court and Parlement circles had by then become embedded in the
thinking of those who ruled these circles.

Earlier in the century people were possibly less conscious of the
enormity of the *political* stakes, although we have seen by Ramus' trial
that such distinctions cannot really be made. Ramus certainly aimed
his 1555 French *Dialectique* as much at political and theological
concerns as at philosophical ones. [7] Yet we have seen that there was
no doubt, even well before, that the sense of philosophical discomfort
was already associated, however imprecisely, with a feeling of more
general disquiet. The Method publicized by Ramus was part of the
search to resolve an anxiety in one area of activity. But it depended
on ideas of universal reason, of the real, of particulars, of words and
meanings, of concepts and signs, that remained mostly unresolved,
far from clear, still less generally accepted. They needed redefining.
And they needed it without the primacy of the Word. Some new ground
was required. That was why Ramus argued the need to start afresh.

His dismissal of authority was partly a heuristic gesture in the case
of 'external guides', philosophers or others; it was wholly genuine

---

4. Reiss, *Meaning*, 81–3 *et passim* (to a degree the book's entire argument is tied to this), and 'Du système', 8–9 *et passim*.
5. Ramus, *Traitté des meurs et facons des ancien gavloys*. This reprinted the transla-tion published in 1559, when the first Latin edition was also published.
6. Reiss, *Meaning*, 45–60, and 'Montaigne' (now rewritten in this book's companion volume, *Mirages of the Self*).
7. See for example Dassonville, 'La "Dialectique"'.

where 'authoritative' concepts were concerned. He had proposed, he wrote, to use new principles, now derived from 'universal reason' and particular 'experience'. Only after 'finding out for [him]self such principles and rules' could he then arrange 'all this matter' according to Method. [8] He made no doubt that he saw Method as an ordering device secondary to the actual discovery of principles. But the novel purpose of those principles and their potential impact was clear to everyone, even if the nature of that impact could not be. It is this intimate connection between social and political anxieties and conceptual ones that explains the violent response to Ramus' *Aristotelicae animadversiones*, his coeval attempt to replace Aristotle with a new dialectic/hermeneutics, and his opponents' (momentarily successful) efforts to reaffirm lost linguistic and Aristotelian grounds. It also explains why the king's intervention was not an inexplicable interference in things not of his concern, and why Ramus was accused of *imprudentia*: an ignorance of right action in the civic sphere.

Although many of these questions will inevitably return, for the present they provoke the second part of my case: about the supposed passage, by dramatic Gutenbergian rupture, from a verbal to a spatial orientation of mind, from an oral to a pictorial acquisition and ordering of knowledge. They do so because what is much at issue here is the fact of cultural change, people's role in it and awareness of it and the manner of its occurrence. At stake, a bit more precisely, is our understanding of the nature of a supposed transformation in the mental life and practices of the West, which this familiar interpretation takes to have made vision and the privileged I/eye of the possessive subject crucial to a manipulative instrumental reason. They and this reason are understood to precede, accompany or respond to particular sorts of change in social, economic and political life. The order does not matter here, or agreement that *some* sort of change occurred. What does matter, firstly, is just what the change may have been, and how it was less abrupt and clear cut, more complicated and cumulative; secondly, why it happened; and thirdly, what – then – may have been its consequences.

Ramist Method, outside the battles we have just followed, has been seen as emblematic of the abruptness of such changes and illustra-

---

8. Ramus, *Dialectique*, 52–3: 'Certes, la voye mesme [to acquire knowledge] nous est proposée par laquelle ilz debvoyent tous cheminer et marcher, partie de principes, qui est la raison universelle, partie d'experience, qui est l'induction singuliere ... Et puis, après avoir faict ceste recherche et eslite, j'ai tasché à disposer toute ceste matière en manière et façon qui nous est monstrée par la méthode artificielle.'

tive of what they were. If the massive and wide impact of Method and the quarrels over it justify such an understanding of their historical role, then it is especially important to try and get *'right'* our interpretation of what Method was to its friends and enemies, as well as to situate it as exactly as possible in its social and conceptual context. It is not that changes did not occur, nor that we may not take these struggles as central to them. It is that they were not quite what they have been thought to have been, nor so unidimensional and unidirectional.

The pictorial presentation (on the page) of the Method's taxonomies clearly emphasized a visual dimension. This itself has helped enable, if not actually provoked, taking visualization for Ramus' solution to the lost conceptual foundation. Spatial dimensions, colour perceptions and so forth, could after all be thought to have offered ready closure for analysis, meaning and understanding in a way the accumulation of sign levels never did. At the same time, they corresponded to at least one important dimension of what *we* think of as 'scientific knowledge':

Ramism specialized in dichotomies, in 'distribution' and 'collocation' (*dispositio* rather than judgment or *judicium*), in 'systems' ... and in other diagrammatic concepts. This hints that Ramist dialectic represented a drive toward thinking not only of the universe but of thought itself in terms of spatial models apprehended by sight. In this context, the notion of knowledge as word, and the personalist orientation of cognition and of the universe which this notion implies, is due to atrophy.[9]

According to this argument, such visual models provided a firm distancing device, even that new ground whose lack posed such difficulties for Ramus' immediate predecessors. For the Ramists, thought itself had now become an object to be visually grasped. Words were no longer simply signs to be read under threat of an infinite regression, but were containers of such thoughts, themselves in turn containers of the reality to which they referred.[10] It is certainly the case that visualization played an important role in Ramist argument. Even its metaphors revealed such an impulse:

the truth of the things understood in our arts is thus naturally presented to the mind [in dialectics] as colours are to sight, and what we call teaching is not to inculcate knowledge but simply to turn and direct the mind to contemplate what it could itself have perceived had it turned and directed itself in that direction ... Just as the eyes of bats are blinded by daylight, so the point

---

9. Ong, *Ramus, Method*, 8–9.
10. Ong himself assigned the change to Agricola's work, but saw Ramus as his proximate successor (ibid., 121).

of our understanding blinks and closes before things whose nature is very clear and most evident. [11]

Rejecting Aristotle's demand for 'two logics', one for true knowledge, the other for opinion, Ramus couched the dispute in the same terms. 'As sight is the same for seeing all colours, whether immobile or changing,' he wrote, 'just so is the art of knowing, that is to say Dialectic or Logic, one and the same doctrine for perceiving all things.' Or, he said of Logic's very grounds: 'just as colours in themselves visible so principles in themselves intelligible are clearer the ones than the others.' [12] Antoine Fouquelin, in his 1555 translated version of Talon's Rhetoric, asserted that even the Philosopher yielded to such temptations: 'Aristotle praises above all others those metaphors that strike the eye by the clarity of their meaning.' [13] One can readily offer a myriad other examples. No one can question that the presence of visual metaphors, diagrams and similar devices in Ramist writings is massive. Yet we must beware.

Firstly, the implications of such metaphors are ambiguous at best, as juxtaposing the citations pro and con Aristotle shows. Secondly, even so convinced a Ramist as Fouquelin was ambivalent. The translation of the 1548 *Rhetorica* in the passage just cited was exact, but equally often Fouquelin changed Talon's visual metaphors into auditory ones. [14] That would suggest a return to discussions of the relation between *voces*, *notae* and *notiones*, between spoken words, written signs and denoted concepts, that had always been a part of the tradition. We will soon see that in fact they always remained essential in Ramism; as did their conceptual implications.

Here we might do well to recall Michael Irvine's observation that

---

11. Ramus, *Dialectique*, 61–2:

> la verité des choses comprises ès ars est ainsi naturellement proposée [in dialectic] à l'esprit comme est la couleur à la veüe, et ce que nous appellons enseigner n'est pas bailler la sapience ains seulement tourner et diriger l'esprit à contempler ce que de soy-mesme il eut peu apercevoir s'il se fut là tourné et dirigé ... Tout ainsi que les yeux des chauves souris s'eblouissent en la clarté du jour, semblablement que la poincte de nostre entendement se mouce et rebouche aux choses de leur nature trèsclaires et trèsmanifestes.

12. Ibid., 62, 124: 'tout ainsi que la veüe est commune à veoir toutes couleurs, soyent immuables, soyent muables, ainsi l'art de cognoistre, c'est-à-dire Dialectique ou Logique, est une et mesme doctrine pour apercevoir toutes choses.' '... comme les couleurs par soy visibles, ainsi les principes par soy intelligibles sont plus clers les uns que les autres.'
13. Fouquelin, *Rhétorique*, 15 v: 'Parquoy Aristote loüe entre toutes les autres, ces Metaphores, lesquelles frapent les yeus, pour la clarté de leur signification.' See, too, Ong, 'Fouquelin'.
14. Leake, 'Relationship', 101.

we saw before (chapter 1, note 28) of the importance of the visual in the manuscript tradition. While it is the case that every manuscript was/is unique, the visual organization of the page followed familiar if complex conventions as to colours, sizes and styles of script, decoration, layout, conjunction of scripts and so on. Such organization corresponded to specific cultural and conceptual expectations. [15] For such a manuscript tradition, one might then think of Llull's trees (for example) as a variant within a form of communication that was anyway heavily visual. (And of course, even if manuscripts were intended to be read aloud, writing is *also* a visual medium.) The earliest printed books copied many devices from the manuscript tradition, the principal difference being that each was no longer unique. It would be illuminating to know how (and if) contemporaries saw the connection between such books, with their manuscript-influenced design, and the 'trees' of Bovelles' Lullist volumes, say, or the illustrations and page design of the earliest emblem books (whose enormous output for a century and a half from the 1530s on needs the exploration it has only recently begun to receive).

Barring epistolary finds, the curiosity will be unsatisfied; but we would do well to remember that Ramus was writing not long after these incunabula, and virtually contemporaneously with the others. Lefèvre and his group, especially Bovelles, had been researching and publicizing Lullist trees since the beginning of the century, and their use for organizing and defining knowledge had always been readily available to Ramus, even though it was assuredly the case that his predecessors did not think they were merely using them to organize and define knowledge, but were actually discovering and producing it by their means. The issue, of course, is not one of originality, but of what such devices were being – and had long been – used for, how and why they were deployed.

Thirdly, visual devices of one kind or another had always been basic in *teaching* (hence Aristotle's remark on metaphors). Indeed, one could perhaps argue that most if not all manuscripts had been seen by their users as teaching and learning media. Early in the sixteenth century, some grammars and rhetorics for schoolchildren stressed visual devices as specific pedagogical aids. Mathias Ringmann's *Grammatica figurata* of 1509 and Thomas Murner's *Chartiludium logicae*, published in Warsaw in 1507 and Strasbourg in 1509, both taught grammar as a card game. [16] Tory's 1529 *Champ fleury* relied on its emblematic

---

15. Irvine, *Making*, 17, 371–93.
16. Margolin, 'Mathias Ringmann'; Ong, *Ramus, Method*, 83–91.

figurations and may have had as much place in the development of
the English anti-Ramist Everard Digby's emblematic theory of knowledge, published in his 1579 *Theoria analytica*, as anything drawn
from Ramus. We have already shown *Champ fleury*'s links to medieval
tradition.

All this suggests that at least until much later we need to distinguish
(as did Ramus himself and his humanist predecessors) between logic
as a teaching process, at least touching the domain of rhetoric, and
logic as a procedure for understanding reason and acquiring knowledge, as a process of discovery. The first made much of visual devices.
The second had little or nothing to do with them. And we do well to
see that it was as one approached activities traditionally assigned to
rhetoric that visual devices became more important. Joseph Scaliger
was right to remark that Ramist Method was just 'another path and
new road for teaching learning [aliud in disciplinis tradendis iter
novamque viam]'. [17] But Gouvea had made the same point from the
beginning, and when Ramus' English defender William Temple expli-
cated Ramus' system forty years later, he made it clear that '*methodus*
[was] a term only to be used in the context of teaching and laying out
material for clarity and comprehensiveness'. [18]

I hardly imagine these few comments to resolve the issue of visuality.
But they raise sufficient questions about the claims made for it as to
carry me on to the third and last part of the case: on mathematics and
discovery as opposed to Method and communication. And one may
hope that analyses here can indeed change the terms of discussion
about visuality and spatiality, and the nature of the change that is in
question.

Dialectic or logic as an instrument of rationality was first and foremost, Ramus insisted, a matter of understanding orders: both that of
rational elaboration of meaning within a given single level of argument
and that of the relation between diverse levels. More important for
this than any visual aid was the connection he eventually made between
dialectic and *mathematics*. I say 'eventually' because in his *Oratio de
studiis mathematicis* of 1544 he equated philosophy with logic and set
mathematics outside their (its) sphere of concern. Of course, at the
time he was forbidden from teaching philosophy on pain of 'corporal
punishment' and threat of worse. Evidently, as the schools felt and as
his trial had violently reaffirmed, Aristotelianism and logic were inseparable. Unable to take logic out of philosophy, he took philosophy, as

17. Scaliger, *Scaligerana*, 333.
18. We saw Gouvea's argument in the previous chapter. For Temple, see L. Jardine,
    Francis Bacon, 62.

it were, out of logic. In essence, he used the same tactic to teach Plato through the 'poetry' of Cicero's *Somnium Scipionis* in his first college lessons after his condemnation. Ramus' later affirmation of the relation between logic and mathematical arts suggests that the 'eventual' was not a matter of his thinking so much as of political realities. Real instrumental logic would eventually be geometrical (see chapter 3 note 60). Indeed, in his 1568–70 debate with the Swiss Aristotelian medical doctor Jacob Schegk, he urged the utter difference of geometrical method from the Aristotelian syllogism. [19]

Ramus was not alone in linking mathematics with lines coming from older logical arts. Many writers associated linguistic and mathematical questions and often wrote on both topics. Bovelles, reputed in his time as a mathematician, first published on its topics with his colleagues Lefèvre and Clichtove in 1500, and continued to do so into his very old age. We earlier saw that he published on linguistic matters in 1533, and that Tory linked the two areas of concern through particular reference to him. Claude de Boissière and Jacques Peletier du Mans also wrote on both (see bibliography). The association was wholly ordinary, and Catherine Dunn is not quite right to say that he 'turned to mathematics' in 1544–45 because he was no longer allowed to profess philosophy. [20] In fact, we have just seen, Ramus was simply finding another way to 'do' 'philosophy'. We may recall, too, his criticism of the universities' lack of mathematics teaching. Such 'disciplinary' boundaries were not very meaningful in a pedagogical system still partly based on trivium and quadrivium, the seven liberal arts – however little the full quadrivium may have featured in practice. But we may note that Ramus had earlier been a pupil of Fine. [21]

In 1555, Ramus published both his *Arithmetica* (defining its topic as the doctrine of reckoning well, *doctrina bene numerandi*) and the *Dialectique*, or 'art of disputing well' ('Dialectique est art de bien disputer'). [22] In the French text he went out of his way to relate them. Having declared in his preface that Euclid's ancient followers had been

19. Vasoli has detailed this quarrel: *Dialettica*, 573–9.
20. Dunn, introduction to Ramus, *Logike*, xii.
21. Waddington, *Ramus*, 107. The small attention paid to the quadrivium in humanist schooling is a constant theme of the authors of Sharratt's *French Renaissance Studies*, for example. Until the mid-seventeenth century, university texts confirm this absence: there was 'no intrinsic use of mathematics in textbook natural philosophy' (Reif, 'Textbook', 23). The issue will come up again especially in this book's fifth chapter. It did not apply to Ramus' teaching. The great humanist interest in mathematics that we have seen for long had little or no effect on general education. It was a concern of courts, armies and commerce. Melanchthon, Sturm and the Jesuits later were exceptions, but even they always justified it on grounds of practical utility.
22. *Arithmeticae*, 1; *Dialectique*, 61.

known as 'dialecticians', he later explained: 'So the first humans, who already knew Mathematics before the flood, also thought of Dialectic.'[23] In fact, neither he nor other writers were doing more than giving the Greek term *mathema* its etymological face value: that which is learned, or ordered knowledge itself (the mathematical sciences particularly, but as a special case). Nelly Bruyère shows how this mattered. In Ramus' earliest extant writings (all from 1543: a manuscript and the two now familiar printed works), she reveals how the terms *mathema* and *mathesis* were clearly derived from Plato (despite Gouvea's claims about Ramus' ignorance). Mathesis, she observes, retained its Greek sense of knowledge in process of acquisition. This dynamic mathesis 'constituted the fundamental definition of Ramist dialectic, inspiring the method and fulfilled within it'. Mathesis was a faculty of mind, a dynamic process somehow bound to the very sources of knowing. Mathema was knowledge ordered. As levels of rational judgment, they preceded those of Method itself and syllogistic (invention, the search for tropes and so on). [24]

A discussion of mathematics as simultaneously primary in reason and having some profound connection with the very order of things did not, however, require Plato as its source (whatever Ramus' own strategic needs may have been). These claims were so widespread that even in a practical arithmetic like Boissière's of 1554, its author instinctively told the reader that his 'art of arithmetic' was tied first to the regulatory ordering of 'this machine of the world' by the 'Creator'. [25] Estienne de La Roche had said the same over thirty years before, also in a practical arithmetic (drawn mostly from Chuquet, but I do not know whether such comments were found there). [26] A more sophisticated writer like Bovelles finally needed neither Christian Deity nor Platonic Idea as final source of ordered rational force, leaving unclear just what might be.

The earliest known printed (and vernacular) arithmetic book, the 1478 *Treviso Arithmetic*, had used the trope without claim of authoritative origin: 'all things which have existed since the beginning of time have owed their origin to number'. [27] Plato was not needed for

23. *Dialectique*, 50: 'Or doncques les premiers hommes, qui avoyent jà congneu les Mathématiques devant le déluge, ont pensé de Dialectique.'
24. Bruyère, *Méthode*, 55.
25. Boissière, *Art*, 4 v: 'ceste machine du monde'.
26. La Roche, *Arismethique*. For more than a century it has been known that La Roche copied most of his work from the manuscripts of the man who may have taught him at Lyon. He claimed no originality, and seems not to have understood Chuquet's more advanced mathematics (Flegg, Hay and Moss, eds., *Nicolas Chuquet*, 13, 15). On Chuquet see, especially, the essays in Hay, ed., *Mathematics*, 57–144.
27. Swetz, *Capitalism and Arithmetic*, 41 (text trans. D. E. Smith).

this sort of thing, derived directly or indirectly from Boethius, and intended in a work like the *Treviso Arithmetic* to support an essentially practical art, one of major utility in commerce, trade and divers 'mechanike' arts. Plato was in fact a major source of confusion between number mysticism and an idea of mathematical arts as rigorously denoting quantitative relations (a principal difference between Bovelles and his two colleagues). Between 1537 and 1554 Niccolò Tartaglia was stressing the last, with its *practical* applications (chiefly military in his case) and an idea of mathematics as a general method. Aristotle could not help, for he argued mathematics to be abstracted from matter: the objects and methods of natural philosophy and mathematics (and metaphysics) were mutually incommensurable and inapplicable. Ramus would not disagree with the epistemological consequences of this view, although matters were to get more complex for him and everyone else. Practical aspects of mathematics and those more strictly 'internal' to developments in the quadrivium are for part 3. For now, my concern is to examine the consequences of the felt need for something to replace a rhetoric/logic increasingly found inapt for discovery.

All agreed that arithmetic was the first of the mathematical disciplines (before music, geometry and astronomy, in varying orders). Arithmetic and geometry, wrote Bovelles conservatively, differed from one another 'as the soul from the body' ('pareille difference comme entre lame & le corps'). The first was 'devoted to numbers, which lie and are situated within the soul [lesquelz sont gisans & situez en lame]'. Thus arithmetic preceded 'in excellence of dignity and in natural perfection [en excellence de dignité & de naturelle perfection]', a point his friend Fine made at the outset of the four arithmetic books of his celebrated 1532 mathematical compendium, *Protomathesis*. [28] For arithmetic dealt with the concealed properties of things:

Arithmetic is comprised in but four principles: that is to say in one, two, three, and four which joined together make the number ten: according to Pythagoras'

28. The *Protomathesis* had four parts: arithmetic (four books), geometry (two books – a Euclidian exegesis and an instruction in practical measurement), cosmography (five books), and dialling (*De solaribus horologiis, et quadrantibus*: four books). The *Arithmetica practica* was published alone in 1535, 1542, 1544 and 1555. Several of the others were also issued apart (Heninger, 'Oronce Finé', 175). Only the arithmetic was of 1532, separate title pages for all the others indicate 1530 for the geometry and cosmography, 1531 for the dialling. Fine did the woodcuts and designs himself (often of great charm and humour). He did them for Bovelles' *Livre singulier* also, we learn from the latter's dedicatory epistle. Fine was best known as a cosmographer and astrologer/astronomer. He taught mathematics at the college of Navarre from 1516 to 1530/1, when he was named to the mathematics chair at the Collège Royal, staying there until his death in 1555. In 1536 he issued an important Latin commentary on the first six books of Euclid's *Elements*.

opinion, and that of all philosophers, this is most mystical and of great perfection. For in it as well, through the four numbers mentioned above, is based the whole science of Music, and all its consonances and harmonies. In imitation of Arithmetic, Geometry is also founded upon and contained by only four principles, in Latin called, *Punctum, Linea, Superficies, Corpus*: i.e., point, line, plane or surface, and body. And there is nothing to consider and contemplate other than these four, which are the measure of all things firm and solid, whether celestial or beneath the skies. [29]

Similar points were made by Fine in the proemium to his four arithmetic books. They were, in fact, quite standard, habitually being referred back to Plato and Pythagoras, who, said Fine, had taught that number grounded all 'things public and private', from 'administration of the laws' and right dispensation of justice to everything in life involving calculation. [30] Bovelles added that mathematical sciences echoed the Holy Trinity in having but three dimensions: length, width and depth (a thought nowhere shared by Fine). Only the point was exempt, resembling 'arithmetical unity, just as unity is not a number, but the beginning and principle of all numbers'. [31] Number itself had virtually replaced divinity as origin. Peletier would note in his 1552 *Aritmetique* that 'however much unity may be indivisible, inasmuch as it is the beginning of whole numbers ... yet we imagine it capable of infinite division'. In the 1554 *Algebre*, he added that 'One' was the

---

29. Bovelles, *Livre singulier*, 3 v–4 r:

L'arithmetique est comprise sur quatre principes seulement: cestascauoir sur vng, deux, trois, & quatre, lesquelz conioinctz ensemble font le nombre de dix: lequel selon lopinion de Pythagoras, & de tous philosophes, est fort mystique, & de grande perfection. Car aussi en luy par les quatre premiers nombres dessusdictz, est fondee toute la science de Musique, & toutes les consenances & harmonies dicelle. La Geometrie par limitation de Larithmetique est pareillement fondee & contenue sur quatre principes seulement, nommez en Latin, Punctum, Linea, Superficies, Corpus: Cestadire le poinct, la ligne, la plaine ou suffice, & le corps. Et na aultre chose à considerer & à contempler que ces quatre, lesquelles sont les mesures de toute chose ferme & solide, soit celeste, ou soit contenue soulz le ciel.

30. Orontius Finaeus, *Protomathesis*, fo. 1 r:

imperfecta relinquitur legum administratio, utpote quae iustitiam quibusuis pro dignitate dispensans, arithmetico semper videtur indigere suffragio. Ex humanae praeterea uitae, quàm sit amplexanda, cognoscitur usu: nam ad supputationes, ad rerum sumptus, permutationes, diuisiones, ad conuentiones, caeteraque eiusmodi discutienda, rationem sola praestat Arithmetica. Merito igitur Plato, primum numeros mandat pueros esse docendos: sine quibus nec priuatas, nec publicas res, satis commodè administrari posse confessus est, omnia in ipsorum numerorum (ueluti Pythagoras) cum dispositione, tum facta harmonia, mortalia uersari demonstrans.

31. Bovelles, *Livre singulier*, 5 r–v: 'Le poinct [qui 'ressemble à lunité en Arithmeticque. Car comme lunité nest pas nombre, mais est le commencement & principe de tous nombres ...'] de ces trois dimensions est du tout exempt.'

'true image of the divinity'. [32] More generally, Thomas Sebillet
wrote in his 1548 *Art poetique* of all the arts as referring to an ultimate order of things hidden in 'the profound celestial abyss where is
the divinity'. [33]

These things have, no doubt, a neoplatonic air to them, or at least
remnants of such. But looking more carefully, one sees that number
has become something like its own origin. 'Nam unitas', Bovelles' friend
Fine had written, 'omnium numerorum radix & origo, in se, á se, ac
circum seipsam unica uel impartibilis permanet . . .'. [34] One thinks of
nothing so much as of Bovelles' own *Liber de sapiente*, where the wise
man became 'the final cause of all things and as a god on earth'. [35] In
both respects, one has a strong sense that divine grounding was growing
less necessary. Something new was coming to be offered as a foundation replacing the absent ground of meaning, whether in the *arbitrium*
of human authority, or in the unitary *punctum* of rational search (the
former associated more with civic communication, the latter with
discovery). In the body of the *Livre singulier*, Bovelles asserted that
the need for mathematics lay simply in its coincidence with the order
of things and indeed of all practice. That order lay otherwise hidden
('occulté', as Peletier noted in the 'Proëme' to his *Algebre*). Where it
came from was indifferent to mathematics in particular or to the
certainty of knowledge in general:

Nor is it at all possible for the human mechanism to profit well in philosophy
and the science of natural things without the help of the mathematical arts.
These contain several mystical ones, upon which the ancient philosophers based
themselves and by which they were guided in finding and describing the hidden
properties of all natural things. For as the philosophical proverb says, *Species
rerum sunt, ut species magnitudinum & numerorum*. That is to say, the kinds
of natural things are like the kinds of quantities and of numbers. [36]

---

32. Peletier, *Aritmetique*, 28 v: 'Or est-il que l'Unité combien qu'elle soit indiuisible
    autant qu'elle est le commencement des Nombres Entiers, . . . nous imaginons aussi
    l'Unité se pouoir [*sic*] diuiser en infinies particules'; *Algebre*, 123: 'l'Un [est la] Vrey
    image de la Diuinite'.
33. Thomas Sebillet, *Art poétique françoys* 7–8: '. . . ce profond abyme celeste ou est la
    divinité'.
34. Fine, *Protomathesis*, fo. 1 r: 'For unity stands as root and origin of all numbers, in
    itself, from itself, around itself singular and indivisible . . .'.
35. Bovelles, *Livre du sage* 148: 'cap. 19: Quod sapiens omnium finis et ut terrenus
    quidam Deus.'
36. Bovelles, *Livre singulier*, 55 v:

    Et nest aulcunement possible, que lengin humain puist bien prouffiter en la philoso-
    phie & sciences des choses naturelles, sans laide des ars mathematiques: esquelles
    sont contenues plusieurs mystiques, sur lesquelles se sont fondez & reiglez les antiens
    philosophes, pour inuenter & descripre les occultes, proprietez de toutes choses
    naturelles. Car comme on dit en prouerbe philosophique. Species rerum sunt, ut

For 'What is there in the world', Peletier was to ask, 'that is not signified by numbers?' Denoting the true form of the material world, this 'delectable abyss and ordered confusion' of numbers 'represents the face and figure of the universe, wherein all Beings are in their order and hold an invariable place'. [37] Such words, surely derived from Sebillet's *Poétique* or the like, and however neoplatonic in inspiration, yet do little else than express assurance of a single and clear principle of order. In this way, wrote Fine in a verse epistle to François I on his appointment to the Collège Royal, mathematics was 'perfect, authentic, / And the mirror of all certainty.' [38]

Such statements came to have their counterparts in very many treatises having to do with linguistic questions as well, whether grammars, poetics, rhetorics or logics. Words and their order corresponded, wrote Louis Meigret in his 1550 grammatical work, to concepts and judgments. So thought Robert Estienne in his 1558 Latin grammar. [39] *Ratio* and *oratio*, we saw, were often identified with one another. In his 1555 *Art poétique*, Peletier compared words in language, numbers in arithmetic and stones in masonry. A year earlier he had opined that arithmetic provided the ground of all judgment, without which one was like a mason with stones, lime and sand, but no knowledge of how to combine them. Numbers, he wrote in his 1552 *Aritmetique*, were like an alphabet, a genuine language whose order signified and corresponded to mental concepts and judgments. [40] Three years later Ramus turned this equation around:

---

species magnitudinum & numerorum. Cestadire que les especes des choses naturelles, sont comme les especes des quantitez & des nombres.
37. Peletier, *Algebre* 124: 'Qui à il au Monde qui ne soèt sinifiè, voere conduìt par Nombres? ... cet abíme delectable [des nombres], e cete ordonnee confusion, represente la face e figure de l'Vniuers dedans lequel tous Etans, sont an leur ordre, e tient un ranc inuariable.' (Peletier, like Louis Meigret, was experimenting with a rationalized orthography, much of which I cannot repeat: mute e, for example, was shown by *e* with a / through it; at other times complex symbols were combined: ę with ´.) This is surely also linked with what is being explored here. The thought that a sound and the sense it communicated could be precisely represented by a combination of fully rationalized symbols shared much with the idea of an algebraic representation of concepts and their connections.
38. The French text of this epistle was reprinted at the end of Fine's 1551 translation of his *Cosmographia*, *La sphère du monde* P2 v: '... perfettes, authentiques, / Et le miroer de toute certitude' (cited by Heninger, 'Oronce Finé', 179).
39. Meigret, *Tretté de la grammere françoeze* [1550], 3. Estienne's Grammar was put in French by his son Henri: *Traicté de la grammaire françoise*, 14–15. See, too, Meigret, *Traité touchant le commun usage de l'escriture françoise*.
40. Peletier, *Art poétique* 116; *Algebre* 'Proëme'; *Aritmetique* 2 v–3 r (cf. 28 v).

These two words ['logism' and 'syllogism'] properly signify counting and enumerating. And from this signification arithmetic is called Logistic. It would seem that these words have been translated out of mathematics into dialectic because just as the good reckoner, in addition and subtraction, sees with certainty the remainder in closing the count, so dialecticians, adding the proposition and subtracting the supposition, see in their conclusion the truth or falsity of the question. [41]

Amidst the seeming confusions, what is at least evident is that clarities and systematic orders once thought to lie in and through natural language were increasingly being sought in mathematics, itself becoming as well a model for clear order of any sort. This relationship between language and mathematics does indeed, then, seem to show the beginnings of a passage from one to the other in certain areas of rationality. It is this *transfer* that I am trying to follow in this chapter, where the next treats developments within the mathematical disciplines. But if we must speak of '*seeming* confusions', it is because when Ramus connected 'logism' and 'syllogism' through 'counting and enumerating', he appeared to refer directly to a lively discussion in mathematics itself, and we need to take a quick look at it here.

We saw Ramus call Euclid and his followers 'dialecticians'. We also saw how he took Charpentier's inability to read Euclid in the original Greek as a principal reason for scorning him as a mathematician. Ramus himself had worked on the ancient geometer, with Archimedes and Ptolemy, for some ten years after 1544. [42] He had published a Latin *Euclid* for students in 1545 (reprinted in 1549 and 1558). [43] These claims and activities placed him in a mainstream of contemporary mathematical preoccupations, and he certainly knew the discussions focusing on Euclid's *Elements* and Proclus' commentary on their first book to which I refer. Around these, and with growing availability of editions and translations of other ancient Greek mathematicians due in particular by this time to the labours of Regiomontanus in the north and

---

41. Ramus, *Dialectique*, 126:

   tous ces deux motz ['logisme' et 'syllogisme'] signifient proprement compte et dénombrement. Et de ceste signification arithmétique est nommé Logistique. Et semble que ces vocables soyent traduictz de mathématique en dialectique car comme le bon compteur en adjoustant et déduisant veoit certainement en la closture du compte le reliqua, ainsi les dialecticiens en adjoustant la proposition et déduisant l'assomption, voyent en la conclusion la verité ou falseté de la question.

42. Ong, *Ramus, Method*, 33. Compare Vasoli, *Dialettica*, 436–7 and, more generally, 451–74. Apart from the Greek mathematicians, Ramus was also working at this time on Hippocrates and Galen, of whom the second was a major reference for debates on method, being the proximate source for notions of synthesis and analysis.

43. Ong, *Ramus and Talon*, 68–9.

Francesco Maurolico in the south, discussions of geometrical method had become widespread. [44]

The *Elements* themselves had been known in the Middle Ages, and in Latin they were among the earliest texts to be printed (Venice, 1482). This Latin edition was followed by others in new translations as well as by commentaries: among others, Lefèvre prefaced the older Henri Estienne's 1517 edition, Fine produced a commentary on the first six books in 1536. Then, in 1533, Simon Grynaeus published at Basel the Greek *editio princeps* of both Euclid and Proclus. Cardano's subsequent *Encomium geometriae* to the Milan Academia Platina in 1535 was followed by Melanchthon's 1537 introduction to another Basel *Euclid*. This, writes Schüling, 'with its praise of mathematics and above all of geometry, gained most influence in the course of the sixteenth century'. Inspired perhaps by these texts, a medical doctor, Justus Velsius, printed at Strasburg in 1544 a speech he had given at Leuven arguing 'the utility of exact knowledge of mathematics for understanding the other disciplines [*Wissenschaften*] (metaphysics, physics, ethics, politics, law, medicine, etc.). But according to Velsius, the mathematical disciplines were especially useful for the practice of scientific [*wissenschaftlichen*] demonstration, essential in all the disciplines.' Grynaeus, Melanchthon, Velsius, all held 'that the *ars demonstrandi*, taught in the *Posterior Analytics*, [was] applied practically in Euclid's *Geometry* and best acquired by studying this writing'. [45] They, like Fine in his commentary and Schegk in the quarrel with Ramus to which I referred, thus asserted that geometric demonstration was syllogistic.

We see why Ramus could assert identity between dialectic and arithmetic: in 1569 he claimed that *only* arithmetic and geometry were true mathematical arts, for only they were free of matter (a view supported by the insistence on them that we saw in Bovelles and Fine). [46] The syllogistic claim supposed 'that geometric proofs of the ancient authors counted as *demonstrationes propter quid*', as demonstrations, that is, of effects from true causes. [47] This raised the question of what was a 'true cause'. So when, in 1547, Piccolomini issued his *Commentarium*

44. See, for example, Gilbert, 'Galileo', 227; N. Jardine, 'Galileo's Road', 306–18 (although both, as their titles suggest, are more concerned with a later moment).
45. Schüling, *Geschichte*, 38, 41. The idea of applying mathematical means in non-mathematical disciplines was shared by many (72–5).
46. Ramus, *Scholae mathematicae* 113: 'Mathematics . . . is (I say) the doctrine of quantity: so that arithmetic is truly defined as the doctrine of reckoning well, geometry as that of measuring well' ('mathematica . . . est [inquam] doctrina quantitatis: ut vero definitur arithmetica bene numerandi, geometria bene metiendi doctrina'). Music and 'astrology' (i.e. astronomy), he added, were mathematics only insofar as their quantitative aspects could be reduced to arithmetic and geometry.
47. Schüling, *Geschichte*, 43.

de certitudine mathematicarum disciplinarum, he provoked wild debate by arguing that Proclus' analysis of Euclid provided a *'mathesis universalis'*, a *'scientia communis'*. [48] Mathematics, so understood, he wrote, gave absolute scientific certainty, for it gave full knowledge of the rational mental artifacts of which it treated, even though, not dealing with material causes, it could not give 'the most powerful demonstrations'. [49] Paduans like Federico Delfino, Pietro Catena and Barozzi, and Northerners like Dasypodius, as we saw in the introduction, all responded, the last three extending the thesis considerably. [50]

Ramus (and most others by this date) did not go so far. He certainly thought his two mathematical sciences could give sure knowledge of calculable concepts. So, for instance, he believed that the Babylonians, Egyptians and earliest Greeks had a non-hypothetical 'prisca astronomia' founded on 'the elements first of logic, then of arithmetic and geometry': 'it follows', he said in the 1567 *Prooemium mathematicum*, 'that first logic, as I have said, then the mathematical elements of geometry and arithmetic, would provide the greatest assistance in establishing the purity and dignity of this most excellent art'. [51] Given his equation of logic and 'enumeration', the order he asserted here was less than clear. What *is*, however, is that he considered the mathematical disciplines to provide 'the solution of practical problems in mensuration'. A 'geometrical theorem [was] a generalization about the results obtained in measurement of real bodies, not a truth about abstract geometrical entities'. In this sense, Ramus denied one could know 'real' causes, as they were in nature (or in God's mind). [52] What one *could* know *with utmost precision* was rational order itself. As for Aristotle and Proclus, 'the exactness and certainty of mathematical constructs result from their being the soul's own creation'. It was in this sense that Ramus dismissed Platonic 'Forms' by saying that with Idea 'nothing else was meant in Plato but logic'. [53]

---

48. Crapulli, *Mathesis*, 25, 31.
49. Ibid., 34. Compare N. Jardine, 'Epistemology', 693–4.
50. Crapulli, *Mathesis*, 33–91; N. Jardine, 'Epistemology', 695–7; Schüling, *Geschichte*, 41–60. It seems worth noting that in 1566 Dasypodius published his own commentary on the first six books of Euclid, intending it for students trained in dialectic.
51. *Prooemium mathematicum*, 211–16, as translated in N. Jardine, *Birth*, 213, 266–8.
52. N. Jardine, *Birth*, 234, 236. Here, Ramus was closer than most of his opponents to Aristotle, for whom the syllogism served didactic needs, not discovery (Barnes, 'Aristotle's Theory', and Gaukroger, *Cartesian Logic*, 20–1). The change in claim was due to Galen. Too, Aristotle held the mathematical disciplines quite separate from those of the Organon, as well as from those treating matter, society or metaphysics.
53. Ramus, *Dialectique* 93: 'ne fut entendu autre chose en Platon que le genre logicien'. Compare Reiss, *Discourse*, 32–3. The previous quotation is from Pérez-Ramos, *Francis Bacon*, 56.

If some kind of mathematical 'logic' was to offer a model and an underlying scheme for language (and indeed all order in reason), then the relation between language and rational concepts also took on new meaning. Much earlier, in his 1540 *De causis*, J. C. Scaliger was already thinking beyond the relations between 'languages' or the metaphorically inclined material comparisons suggested by several of those just quoted:

For things are as if double: either material or immaterial. And immaterial things are either outside the intellect, as God, or in the intellect, as concepts (I call concepts kinds of things understood in the mind) for as the hand acts on matter so the intellect acts on concepts ... and utterance is a sign of such notions as are in the soul. Utterances have three conditions: Formation, Composition, Truth. Truth is the adequation of a proposition to the thing of which it is the sign. [54]

Sebillet followed up on this eight years later by remarking that once 'a foundation has been laid by invention, and the project for the future building set by calculated order [*économie*], a search follows for the stones or bricks to build and shape it. These are propositions, words or vocables, among which as careful a choice and discretion exists as among things'. [55] Picking up on a constant simile in Aristotle, this recalls Bovelles' analogy between 'kinds of natural things' and 'kinds of quantities and of numbers', as it looks forward to Peletier's assumption of the same figure, whether intended to be a metaphor or to express an actual relationship.

Mathematics, words and things furnished three systems each able to refer to each other, 'adequate' in denotation (Scaliger's word was *aequatio*), and able to be grasped in reasoned judgment. Increasingly, though, mathematics was taking first place wherever discovery was at issue. Bovelles emphasized that numbers related to what ruled the *system* of things. They revealed, we saw in both Bovelles and Peletier,

---

54. J. C. Scaliger, *De causis*, 2:

Res autem quem duplices sint: aut materiales, aut immateriales: & immateriales, aut extra intellectum, vt Deus, aut in intellectu, vt notiones (notiones appello rerum species mente comprehensas) quod vtique manus agit in materiam, hoc intellectus in notiones. ...est enim vox nota earum notionum, quae in anima sunt. Vocis affectiones tres: Formatio, Compositio, Veritas. Veritas est orationis aequatio cum re cuius est nota.

The extensive meaning of *res* here is that which we saw before (chapter 1, notes 6 and 17).

55. Sebillet, *Art poétique françoys*, 29: 'Ce fondement jetté par invention, et le projet du tout le futur bastiment pris par l'economie, suit la queste des pierres ou briques pour l'élever et former. Celles sont les dictions, mos ou vocables: entre lesquelz a autant bien chois et élection, comme entre lés choses.'

the 'hidden properties of all natural things'. They guided one towards the true meaning of things, Fine and Ramus agreed. We must be clear, here however, that what was shown was not things themselves, as we have just seen at some length in Ramus and others, but what made them meaningful in conceptualization (a mode of understanding that did not await arguments between Descartes, Hobbes and others). Like everyone else, Bovelles evoked Pythagoras, Plato, Archimedes and Euclid among the ancients. Alone among moderns, he named the neoplatonic and politically ecumenical Nicholas of Cusa: 'a man inferior to none in all kinds of knowledge, [who] cultivated geometry so studiously that he found very many things unknown to geometers before him'. [56]

If the divine re-emerged, it was as *deus absconditus*, under whose benign rule humans had to take responsibility for their knowledge and actions. The first they could do through a slowly renewing notion of the grounds of rational discovery, the second through some version of Bovelles' *arbitrium sapientis* that might also develop and practise a more peaceful and stable political process. The ground of reason was not that of Idea, some Platonic realism or its equivalent, as Ramus had now made explicit. It lay, rather, in the actual practice of human reason, *as* human. The French idiom, wrote Meigret, was now so perfected that it could contain 'even high theology' ('cete tant haote theolojie'). It 'has in itself such order as enables us to distinguish the parts of which all languages are composed'. The language 'of human reason' ('de la rézon humeine') might differ from 'the authority of divine wisdom' ('l'aothorité de la sapience diuine'), but in its French version, at least, it could now *contain* such divinity – on the model, it may be, of the claim we saw that number now 'replaced' the divinity (above, pages 112–13). [57] This echoed claims made for poetry by Du Bellay, for philosophy by Ramus, and for mathematics by Peletier, Boissière and Forcadel (see chapter 3, note 36).

Such 'mathematizing' clearly had nothing at all to do with visual-

---

56. Bovelles, *Geometricum*, 3 v: 'Nicolaus Cusanus . . . uir in omni scientiae genere nulli inferior, tanto studio Geometriam excoluit, ut plurima ante eum Geometris ignota adinuenerit.' Tartaglia was among those making the same encomia. Cassirer agreed that Bovelles held this view, seeing rationalized representations and 'kinds' of perceived objects as 'variables' organized by his *ars oppositorum*: 'Nicht die an sich bestehenden Gegenstände, sondern die Bilder und "Spezies" in unserem Verstande sind es, bei denen von wahrhafter Gegensatzlichkeit gesprochen werden kann' (*Erkenntnisproblem*, I. 78). Such knowledge lies in 'intellectual functioning and operation', inseparable from the movement and creation of concepts.

57. Meigret, *Grammaire*, 3: 'ell' a en soe quelq'ordre, par le qel nou' pouuons distinger le' parties dont sont composez tou' langajes, e la reduir' a qelqes regles'.

ization, and very little to do – at least directly – with spatial figura-
tion. The 'mathematical' order discussed here did assure certain kinds
of conceptual elements, certain modes of representation, certain kinds
of reasoning processes. It had to do with some logic of rationality
(although it might not yet be 'ours'). But it stayed very much a 'verbal'
order. If arithmetic was the doctrine of reckoning well, dialectic was
the art of disputing well, and it was so because the one was developed
from the other (as we saw Ramus claim). In that sense, Ramus
continued his definition, dialectic 'is named logic, for both are derived
from *logos*, that is to say, reason'. [58] And we have just seen at some
length the much wider importance of the notion that logism and syllogism signified counting and enumerating, as he wrote later in the same
work (above, note 41).

'*Dialectica virtus est disserendi*', he had long since written in the 1543
Dialecticae institutiones: 'the force of dialectic is that of discoursing
precisely'. *Disserere* connoted a carefully analytical use of language. So
it is no surprise to see Ramus assert that *disserere* was the same as
reasoning. Dialectic had to show a process, as he put it clearly in the
1566 *Dialectica*, that 'continually proceeds from universals to singulars'
('ab universalibus ad singularia perpetuó progreditur'): the *propter quid*
of whose discovery Piccolomini and so many others sought to make
mathematics the instrument. [59] All this appears profoundly related to
the explorations in the mathematical disciplines that we have just been
following. Certainly, at least amongst the writers looked at here, these
still remained for long inseparable from debates in language – as the
question of the syllogism itself makes fully evident.

The *demonstratio propter quid* was the 'compositive' part of
Aristotle's pair, the way of reasoned judgment, not just of the language
bearing it. Ramus would thus write in the 1569 *Scholae* that reason
and 'discourse' were the same. He claimed to have found this in Plato:
'For I perceived from his Socratic dialogues the universal power of
human reason, that to discourse is the same as to use reason; I understood that the division into invention and disposition [syllogism

58. Ramus, *Dialectique*, 61: 'Et en même sens est nommée Logique, car ces deux noms
    sont dérivez de *logos*, c'est-à-dire raison.'
59. Ramus, *Dialecticae libri duo*, 367.
60. Ramus, *Scholae dialecticae*, book 4, chapter 16 (=13), in *Scholae in liberales artes*,
    col. 155: 'Ex Socratis enim sermonibus generalem illam rationis humanae facultatem,
    percepi idem esse disserere & ratione uti: partitionem inventionis & dispositionis,
    logicam esse cognovi.' Ramus' exact meaning is not very clear, and I have been as
    literal as possible. Ong's version of this passage is selective, not to say slanted
    (*Ramus, Method*, 42). He 'translates' the last clause (after the colon) as: 'and hence
    that the distribution of dialectic which I had come across applied to the whole mental
    apparatus (*logica*)'. This is to prejudge Ramus' argument.

and method for Ramus] was logic.' [60] Ramus seems to be saying that invention corresponded to syllogistic reasoning and disposition to rational methodical discourse, and that both together were a logic corresponding to universal human reason itself. Thus the art of '*bene disserendi*' was also one of thinking well.

Such an art depended on exact comprehension of how words and syntax meant and on fixing language as to terminology, grammar, and syntax. That was why mathematics seemed such a resource (and why so many sought a rational orthography: see note 37). It mattered, too, therefore, that the mathematical disciplines were not just a source of clear reasoning, but were also practical. Indeed, many have noted that what was to some degree original in Ramus himself was the extent to which he emphasized this aspect in his teaching (although the second book of Fine's geometry, published apart as *Liber de geometria practica* in 1544, dealt mostly with surveying techniques). [61] The sense of a need for such a sure rational art was counterpart to the fear of a kind of infinitely ungrounded regress that combined with so strong a fear of madness in the writings of so many who dealt with language – and why, too, such madness was associated with the social dissolution and political disarray of the age.

Logic, dialectic, the proper use of words did allow one to get at meaningful truths. But they were truths of relation and practical truths of manipulative action (of one area on another). A hidden origin of order might yet exist but discourses no longer had access to it or need of it. Alone among them, mathematics might suffice as its own origin. As for the rest, 'notation', wrote Ramus, showing (by etymology or otherwise) the meaning of a word (*nom, nota*) in a represented real – easy when languages were 'whole' (*en leur entier*, he often wrote) – could now be used only with great care. When one did so, it was not to find some outside origin, but the process of rational judgment itself:

---

61. Compared to the 'very conservative' Fine, Margolin sees Ramus as the real reformer, fundamentally 'positif et pratique', his work being continued notably by Pierre Forcadel ('Enseignement', 132). Verdonk also stresses the relation of Ramus' mathematical work to practice (*Petrus Ramus*). We have seen others do the same. The issue was the combining of abstract mathematics with a mathematics that had always had practical weight, whether for medieval stonemasons or early Renaissance financiers and traders. As we will see in chapter 5, Italy seems to have taken the lead. Forcadel, Arnaud d'Ossat and Jean Péna were all pupils of Ramus, whom Waddington (*Ramus*, 109) saw as potentially pursuing their teacher's reforms. D'Ossat, who long worked with Ramus on mathematical matters, and defended his Method against Charpentier in 1564 (ibid., 158–9) became a cardinal and statesman. Jean Péna was named to the Collège Royal in 1556 (aged twenty-five), but died in 1557 (ibid., 110–11). Forcadel was teaching arithmetic and geometry in French at the Collège less than ten years later: Waddington viewed this as a decadence (ibid., 56, 333).

as when, for instance, examining conjugate terms one found 'a symbol
of causes and effects to whose discovery we are often directed thanks
to this conjugation of substantives, for the primitive term contains the
cause of its conjugates, as Justice is the cause by which humans are
just and live justly'. [62] But a 'final origin' for all this had disappeared,
remaining, if at all, only as the distant God of Descartes' future
Meditations.

Words, thought Meigret (firmly in the Erasmian tradition here),
might once have shown their first cause, but if so they no longer did.
A word was but the 'image' of a sound and a concept, 'an assemblage
of letters [un assęmblemęnt de lęttres]' whose meaning came from its
relation to other such images. If this went far towards dispersing
the fear and dilemma of infinite regress, it also deprived language of
any bond with discovery. It involved only communication, a matter
of ordered but customary usage. To believe otherwise was to adopt
'a false principle' from which 'follows an abyss of errors and confusion: so much so that when I consider the mistakes and difficulties
suffered by these poor superstitious people, I am reminded of a proverb
common in Lyon, that "mal avizé a prou peine".' Such beliefs could
come only from 'great ignorance and superstition' ('d'vne grand'
iñoranç' ę superstiçíon'). [63] Bovelles had turned for security back to
Latin from the vernaculars in fear of just such an abyss of error and
confusion, '*hallucinationes*', but it was his reason for having done so –
the idea that language could itself provide firm ground for knowledge
– that Meigret was now dismissing with such scorn.

Henri Estienne was even rougher in rejecting such claims of this sort
as still appeared. In the 1562 issue of his *Conformité*, for example, he
included a strong attack on Périon's etymologies. He railed that most
were fully 'imaginary' ('phantastiques'), and anyway 'stupid and inept,
and so clumsy and asinine that had this poor monk left no other
evidence of clumsiness and asininity one might think this work to
be a forgery'. [64] Léon Feugère attributed Estienne's 'bad temper' to

---

62. Ramus, *Dialectique*, 89: 'un symbole des causes et effetz à l'inuention desquelz
souvent nous sommes conduitz par l'indice de ceste nominale conjugaison car le
nom primitif contient la cause de ses conjugués, comme Justice est cause par laquelle
l'homme est juste et qu'il vit justement'.
63. Meigret, *Grammaire*, 4, 6, 7: 'Voęla comęnt d'vn faos prinçip' il s'ęn ęnsuyt vn abime
d'ęrreurs ę confuzion': tęllemęnt qe qant je considere lę' faotes ę inconuenięns
q'ęncouret çę pouures superstiçieus, il me souuięnt d'vn comun dit dę' Lionoęs, qe
MAL AVIZE A PROU PEINE . . .'
64. H. Estienne, *Conformité*, 203 n. 1: 'sottes et ineptes, et si lourdes et asnières, que
n'estoyent les autres tesmoignages que ce pauvre moine nous a laissez de sa lour-
derie et asnerie, on pourroit penser cest [sic] oeuvre estre supposé'.

the fact that Périon was a monk. More to the point, of course, were the friendship and evident affinities between Ramus and Estienne. Ramus' dispute with Périon, we saw, dated back to 1543–47 and the battles over Aristotle and Cicero. But even if Estienne had other scores to settle, clearly most importantly in question here was the rejection of the very premises behind such etymologizing.

Language discourse no longer needed nor had, any more than the mathematical, a founding origin, Platonic or Christian. Even in 1598 a literary person like Lope de Vega might still echo such Platonic dicta as that arithmetic was the 'source and origin from which all good was born, which built all things', but his Arcadia was in any case a consciously archaic nostalgia. In 1573, the Jesuit Franciscus Toletus dismissed all such notions, while in 1597, Suárez rejected specifically and outright the idea that mathematics had any link with the 'good'. Its use lay elsewhere. These were now ideas long past. At the same time, other debates were deepening the 'Ramist' kind of ideas about mathematics: in his 1578 *De natura logicae*, Zabarella advanced complex arguments about logic as a kind of 'instrumental discipline' whose model still lay in the Aristotelian ambit, but whose detail was deeply affected by the debates about geometrical method. [65]

Ordered relations sufficed – plus judgment that a proposition was 'clear and manifest [clere et manifeste]'. 'If', said Ramus, 'a simple proposition is certain and credible, it is judged true, by a judgment of science if necessary, of opinion if contingent'. [66] The assertion seems comparable to the Cartesian axiom, and its proofs were no less nebulous: for how was one to make a *jugement de science*? Science and necessity, opinion and contingency were axiomatic, wrote Ramus. Certainly their proofs had nothing to do with dialectic or rhetoric, which merely used them as they were offered: one 'learns Dialectic to dispute well because it shows us the truth, and therefore the falsity of all reason, whether necessary, which is science, or contingent, i.e., what may both be and not be, which is opinion'; again: 'Judgment of absolutely true disjunction will be science, that of supposed or contingent disjunction will just be opinion.' [67] The argument was circular.

65. Lope de Vega, *Arcadia* 413, 406 n. 66; Toletus, *Commentaria*, 'Lectori' (unpaginated), and 6 v–9 v; Suárez, *Metaphysicae disputationes*, II. 171b–172a; Zabarella, *De natura logicae*, *Opera*, col. 21 *et passim*. Zabarella figures more in the next chapter. We have already seen (above, page 43) how he, too (with others), juggled old and new forms of thinking.

66. Ramus, *Dialectique*, 123, 117: 'Si l'enonciation simple nous est certaine et credible, elle est jugée vraye, par jugement de science si elle est necessaire, ou d'opinion si elle est contingente.'

67. Ibid., 61–2: 'apprendre la Dialectique pour bien disputer à cause qu'elle nous déclare la verité, et par conséquent la faulseté de toute raison, soit necessaire, dont est

It treated the internal coherence of a closed system of logic. Ramus claimed more, holding that such judgment was as natural to animals as to humans and defined *all* animate life. It followed, since animals do not verbalize, that the simple proposition *was* the order of phenomena received via the senses; or, at least, that it was an axiomatic ordering of 'sensible things':

Judgment of the simple proposition is wholly natural and indeed common in part to animals as for instance of sensible things in the proposition itself. . . . every animate being has in itself a natural power of judging that we call sense, also called, in [Aristotle's] second Topics, species of judgment. And certainly sense is the true judge of things properly subject to its jurisdiction, as the eye of colour, the ear of sound, the olfactory of smell. . . . Thus the judgment of the simple proposition is not wholly proper to humans, whereas the understanding of the universal proposition is, even though it appears that animals have some small part of reason. . . . Yet certainly this judgment is nothing else in animals than the phantasm of sensible notions, and animals do not have any conception of the universal. [68]

This argument implied not only that the word corresponded to the thing in some way beyond association of their ordered systems (as it did in Scaliger, in Sebillet, in Bovelles), but also that some relations were 'naturel', able to be known by some kind of innate 'sensible union' between '*fantasie*' and phenomenon. These relations were essential and in no way dependent on some symbolic system. Beyond them, however, lay the universal, approachable but by rational understanding: 'By so much as it knows the universal, by so much is it more excellent and honorable than sense, grasps better cause and principle, and is more scientific . . .'. To that extent, Method showed the divinity of humans, just as intellect, 'the syllogistic [enumerating] faculty', set them above animals. Such a supposition sought perhaps to 'justify' the entire

---

science, soit contingente, c'est-à-dire qui peult et estre et non estre, dont est opinion'; ibid., 123: 'Le jugement de la disjonction absolument vraye sera science, de la supposée et contingente sera seullement opinion.'

68. *Dialectique* 118:

Le jugement de la simple énonciation est fort naturel mais voyre commun de quelque part aux bestes comme des choses sensibles en l'énonciation propre. . . . tout animant a en soy une puissance naturelle de juger qu'on appelle sens, lequel est pareillement nommé, au deuziesme des Topiques, espèce de jugement. Et certainement le sens est vray juge des choses proprement subjectes à sa jurisdiction, comme l'oeil de la couleur, l'ouye du son, l'odorement de l'odeur. . . . Ainsi le jugement de l'énonciation simple n'est poinct propre de toute part à l'homme, mais bien l'entendement de l'énonciation universelle, combien toutesfois qu'il semble que les bestes ayent quelque petite parcelle de raison. . . . Mais certes ce jugement n'est autre chose aux bestes que la phantasie des notions sensibles et la beste ne conçoit poinct l'universel.

absence of any explanation as to how a coherence theory of truth might yet provide reliable knowledge of the world. [69]

Axiomatic knowledge was becoming, then, something like the origin and source of the 'mathematical' processes of a logic of discovery (they even seemed to lie somewhere in the background of a logic of communicative action). These immediately intelligible axioms of the universal principles were unique to human reason. They relied on those ordered systematic relations of mathematics, language, reason and things whose very interplay bore witness to their truth. This reliability made possible subsequent derivation of truths, 'theses', through those 'sensible notions' enabling propositions and judgments to be commensurable (*aequationes*) with the structures of phenomena. [70] These ordered relations allowing knowledge of material (and immaterial) *res* were thus *themselves* thought of as a coherent system of logic. Later, correspondence theories of truth and knowledge, increasingly dependent on visuality and spatialization, were not yet at all at issue.

Even when they were, one may query how much such dependence can be considered a transformation of the very ground of thought, operation of reason and nature of mentality. Yet these are the claims fervently made, not just in the wake of arguments about the effects, for example, of printing, but in their conflation with earlier 'Heideggerian' claims about 'conquest of the world as a picture', insofar as it was *made into* a picture. [71] At the moment moreover, the problem of what grounded mathematics still needed solution. The world and human reason were a logic, a precisely structured discourse – an arithmetic. And at the level of their teaching and learning, they were a rhetoric: both as the teacher *did* actually teach them, and as that – let us say, future – teacher learned such discourse from the world.

By the time he wrote the *Conformité* in 1562, Henri Estienne was thus very clear that what made for *linguistic* perfection was twofold. It consisted, firstly, in properly ordering the system in itself (as a *mathema*, we might say). In this, it was more than just analogous with arithmetic or any other mathematical system. Secondly, such perfection consisted in the number of clearly and separately defined

---

69. Ibid., 118: 'Et jà d'autant qu'il cognoist l'universel, d'autant est-il plus excellent et honorable que le sens, et comprend plus la cause et principe, et est plus scientifique'; ibid., 153, for the remark about intelligence as the 'syllogistic faculty'.
70. Ibid., 124.
71. Weimann, *Authority*, 2. Such claims ground this analysis of early modern works. He cites Heidegger ('Age'), who actually saw founding mathematical models as long preceding ideas of the world as *Bild*.

words that a language had to name *res*. [72] With the use of such a
language, Estienne wrote in his later *Précellence* (1579), humans
had the advantage 'above all other animals' of 'expressing their conceptions to one another through language', a rationally ordered and
mutually clear language. [73] One had at last eluded Bovelles' *hallucinationes*, Meigret's 'abyss of errors and confusion'. Such language
was itself fundamentally communicative, not probative – not of
discovery.

For Estienne, this was also a political claim, one advanced after his
savage attack on Catherine de' Medici (1575: just three years, we
recall, after the Saint Bartholomew's massacre, with Ramus' murder
and the directly connected death of Denis Lambin, both Estienne's
close scholar friends), and after his scathing satire on the distortion
of the French language in *Deux dialogues*. As such, it had to do with
stabilizing and clarifying a system polluted by foreign meddling.
Philosophically, it sounded an end to debate at least as it concerned
the connection of linguistic and conceptual order and knowledge.
But all this stayed far from that dependence on spatial and visual
ordering for which Ong and previous writers argued, and which is
still the accepted evaluation in the wake of McLuhanite and earlier
philosophico-historical convictions. Ong indeed seems to doubt the
fact of such change well after the time in question, saying of Digby's
and Murner's books, the emblematic theory of knowing advanced
in the one's 1579 *Theoria* and the 1629 reprinted *Chartiludium*:
'[both] reveal some of the stresses and strains which put in their
appearance as the spatialized world apprehended by vision came to
be more and more exploited to aid thinking. In both authors the
stresses were particularly great because spatial models were being
pressed into service to deal not merely with reality but with thought
itself.' [74]

The very tardiness of this insecurity, however, leads rather to thinking
that a visual and spatial reordering of thought had yet to occur
(or that it may never have done so to the extent and in the sense
claimed by Ong and his successors; and if we recall that Murner's book
dated from 1507, then its 'prematurity' poses no fewer problems).
One remained, here, in a world where reason was predicated upon
an interrelation of conceptual, 'linguistic' processes in which an as yet

---

72. H. Estienne, *Conformité*, 19–25.
73. H. Estienne *Précellence*, 10: 'Entre les beaux et grands auantages que Dieu a donnez
    aux hommes pardessus tous les autres animaux, cestuy-ci estant un, qu'ils peuvent
    s'entrexposer leurs conceptions par le moyen du langage.'
74. Ong, *Ramus, Method*, 91.

somewhat imprecise concept of (mathematical) 'order' had replaced any other notion of 'origin'. What was above all common to these texts of mid and late century was their authors' awareness of responding to a breakdown in the authority of language (whether then seen as error and confusion or persuasive copiousness), the ambivalence of their effort to ground reason and its judgment, their clear sense of discomfort with social, political and educational conditions, and their disquiet as to philosophical sureties. Ramist Method furnished a teaching device that started to simplify the issues, by allowing them to be readily ordered and set out. But security of rational definition, stability of linguistic order and asserted adequacy of conceptual reference had always been necessary before its very foundations could be at all defined. We begin to see this in later Ramist texts, in later writings such as Henri Estienne's *Précellence*, but above all in Zabarella and thinkers of science.

Even so, years would pass before a coherence theory of truth and knowledge was at all articulated on one of correspondence. Nor is it clear that such was needed for modern epistemologies and an instrumental science. The foundation remained certainly for a long time linguistic, or quasi-linguistic. In the first thirty years of the new century, Alsted, archetypal polymathic Protestant educator that he was, sought to combine Peripatetic and Ramist logics, and to bring together various mathematical traditions to establish a 'universal mathesis'. Both projects remained wholly verbal. Both entrusted their pedagogical success to Ramist visual trees. A sort of paroxysm was reached in the four folio volumes of his 1630 universal *Encyclopaedia*. [75] Ten years later, in 1640, Pierre Le Moyne's *Peintures morales*, a text I have suggested typified a sort of watershed just because of its indecision, used visual *devices* to underpin an ethics and a kind of metaphysics, while staying deeply and professedly embedded in rhetorical forms of argument. Albeit differently, one may say as much for Descartes' various sciences, versions of Method as he claimed they were: singulars of a universal mathesis.

The point here is that the spatial was not a way of thought, but a method of teaching. What it taught was inseparable from ordered language and ideas *about* such language. The ground of discovery – and what was increasingly thought of as knowledge – still lay in language, but in a different idea of language, one at whose core lay the signs and syntax of mathematics. Francis Bacon could still write of experimental knowledge of nature as needing to learn 'her letters',

---

75. I refer here particularly to Alsted's *Compendium*, *Methodus*, and his *Encylopaedia*.

letters that corresponded to the 'alphabet' and syntax of material phenomena. [76] At the same time, Galileo was already famously writing of the mathematical language of this same book of the world. The two went together because the second grounded the first. Robert Hooke, much later, could still write of the need for natural philosophers to learn the 'Orthography, Etymologia, Syntaxis and Prosodia of Nature's grammar', even while what he had in mind was the idea that 'a new code of symbolic, mathematical or algebraic ciphers must be applied' to the nature made available through such a grammar. [77] Mathematics, that is to say, was now conceived as a model for and a kind of distillation of natural language. Not only could such a mathematics discover – as it echoed – the world's (and the mind's) syntax, but language itself could ideally be perfected in accord with the mathematical syntax of God's language of nature and of rational judgment. Indeed, the idea that a mathematical logic was at the core of natural languages remained a phantasm of European thought at least until Gottlob Frege's 1879 *Begriffschrift*. [78]

In addition to this weight of evidence of a passage towards mathematics (answering a need whose desperate thrust had been felt by then for more than a century), two fundamental claims made in the early seventeenth century tell heavily against a spatial grounding being anything other than at most supplementary, and perhaps further underscore the real nature of the adjustment in course. The first claim was as widespread then as earlier. It was that true knowledge concerned our *conceptions* of things, not *res ipsas*. The second, Richard Tuck has argued, was the real ground of the dispute between Descartes and Hobbes between 1537 and the early 1640s. That dispute confirmed Hobbes at least in his assumption that the very *processes* of judgment echoed the *fact* (whether or not the form) of change in the world. [79] Neither claim impeded the development of a science of instrumental effect. Both might be held, however, to involve a 'rhetorical' or 'mathematical' view of epistemology. And both had been entirely familiar to Ramus and his contemporary explorers, as we saw at some length (above, pages 115–20).

The world was not a roomful of objects to be viewed and represented. It was not yet the plain deal table in the fork of a tree mocked

---

76. Reiss, *Discourse*, 201–11.
77. The first citation is from Hooke's *Discourse of Earthquakes* (in *The Posthumous Works of Robert Hooke*, ed. T. M. Brown (London, 1971), 338). It is quoted in De Grazia, 'Secularization', 320, whose summation is my second citation.
78. I have discussed some contextual dilemmas of this 'endpoint' in the first chapter of *Uncertainty*, 19–55.
79. Tuck, 'Hobbes', especially 38–41.

by Lily Briscoe. [80] It was still a volume of signs. But signs have many forms. Not for nothing was Galileo's overly celebrated trope of the world as a book for reading a cliché in the early decades of the seventeenth century (before ever he used it). Nor was it chance that Descartes wrote in his 1629 letter to Marin Mersenne of a universal *language* ultimately able to found true and full knowledge of the world – if as yet utopian (see chapter 1, note 24).

Such signs persuaded the mind, as it were, into holding certain concepts. Their dynamic relationships moved judgment to action amongst these concepts, to articulate them in some way. Such a 'rhetorical' epistemology helps explain why Descartes' argument in the *Monde*, about seeing the movement of particles in a flame, is both unconvincing (who could possibly 'see' such a motion?) and gratuitous: his discussion about conceiving material signs did not need it. Here the effort to give even a visual and spatial supplement (an echo, perhaps, of Aristotle's argument in the *Physics* about finding principles behind the sight of things) actually impeded Descartes' argument about knowledge: unless we understand it simply as a *pedagogical* device. [81]

All this suggests a very different history from the one that has grown familiar in the past forty years (and used to ground many other arguments and claims about historical change, and about the 'Western mind' and its instrumental action – to say nothing of its 'historical legitimacy' (or 'illegitimacy')). Speculative confusion as to just what *might* have happened dates of course from the very years when whatever it was was happening. That may explain the odd echo of Alsted's contradictory comments about Ramus in Pierre-Daniel Huet's remarks about Descartes (both made about fifty years after their subject's work had first been appearing). Where Alsted had noted Ramus' pedagogical clarity and mathematical acuity, but the 'mutilation' and 'confusion' of many aspects of its application, so Huet remarked on Descartes' simplicity, clarity and minimalism, even as he dismissed the *cogito*, the reliability of mind, the proofs of God, the mixture of efficient and necessary causes, arguments about body, origin of the world, cause of weight and just about everything else, accusing his philosophy finally both of *being* uncertain and of *producing* uncertainty (especially in matters of morality). [82]

Whatever the uncertainties, however, two things are clear. The first, again, is that there was no quick change from dialogue to sight, even

---

80. Woolf, *Lighthouse*, 38.
81. Reiss, '*Concevoir*'.
82. Huet, *Censura*. The accusation about scepticism concluded the book (222), whose chief grounds of censure I have otherwise paraphrased.

as mere metaphor of analytical reason, let alone as ground of rational analysis. Gutenberg and his colleagues may have transformed the circulation and communication of knowledge, the number and nature of participants, the quantity and variety of matter included. But printing did not suddenly change the foundations of understanding. Rhetoric did not instantly yield to visual and spatial certainties. A far more complicated and slower change in mental life took place, one that explains (if need be) why drastic cultural struggle and debate went on over at least the century and a half 'between' a Bovelles and a Hobbes.[83] When concluded, it had not rejected a rhetorical and linguistically oriented past but assimilated it in new ways. Those new ways then led from Zabarella's neoaristotelian 'method' to Descartes'.

For this is the second clear thing: that the dilemmas posed from the early sixteenth century by a far older idea of language as tool for discovery began, as it were from within the language debates themselves, to push people towards a mathematically directed solution. Cassirer was surely right to argue that Ramus marked 'the passage to the mathematico-scientific [der Uebergang zur mathematisch-naturwissenschaftlichen] Renaissance'. Himself neither an original nor, we have seen, even a clear mathematical thinker, he still gave huge impetus to mathematical education. 'Here, as in the struggle against Aristotle', Cassirer summed up, 'he was not the originator but rather the spokesperson of modern thought'. But that impetus is why John Schuster can also observe 'the tendency of late sixteenth-century Ramism to concern itself with problems of the practice and pedagogy of the mechanical arts and applied mathematics'. [84]

Certainly, a problem remained of which Ramus and many others among those we have seen were well aware, one to which they have already made us attend. Language may no longer have had a bond with discovery, but it was not clear how mathematics might have either (which was what the Piccolomini-sparked debate over Euclid and Proclus was for the most part all about). Still, here, there was also another history: the internal and transformative passage from trivial to quadrivial concern was strengthened, even urged perhaps (for this is a matter of chicken and egg), by continuities of debate within the quadrivium itself. Who can say whether the pressures within language

83. They make a nice metaphor of continuity and change: their lives missed overlapping by just twenty years, but from the birth of the one to the death of the other was exactly two centuries. The one saw the last remnants of medieval debates, the other lived deep into modern ones. Together, their lives covered the whole 'northern Renaissance' and more.
84. Cassirer, *Erkenntnisproblem*, I. x (table of contents) and 133 (also 129–34 as a whole); Schuster, *Descartes*, 56.

debates caused their turn, or whether developments already occurring in the quadrivium encouraged them? Who can say whether practical pressures – economic and political, but also such conceptual ones as we have already seen in areas of language – provoked movement in the quadrivium, or whether that, too, was the other way about? The only sensible answer is that a response to any such questions as these involves all and each of the others. In any case, it is to the quadrivial side of these continuities within change that we must now turn.

Part 3

Mathematics, music and rational aesthetics

5   Quadrivial pursuits

That there was a general reorganization of education and its disciplinary divisions from the late Middle Ages into the period we now call the 'Renaissance' has long been a historiographical commonplace, although the precise nature of the changes varied from place to place. In the Italian universities, for example, the *artes liberales* of trivium and quadrivium became a sort of propaedeutic to the advanced university faculties of law and medicine, while in Paris the faculties of arts, medicine and theology remained distinct. [1] Then, too, if these did not give way to the *studia humanitatis* of the humanist educational system – grammar, eloquence, poetry, history and moral philosophy – yet they did find themselves increasingly in competition with and affected by humanist schools and colleges from early in the sixteenth century (no doubt starting with Sturm in Strasbourg, and then reaching a peak on the Continent with the spread of the Jesuit colleges).

The situation of mathematical, logical and musical studies in schooling, as much in the Middle Ages as in the Renaissance, is for the most part rather unclear, although they did play a greater or lesser role after the *studia humanitatis* course (even if most advances happened, we have seen, outside the schools). [2] What I wish to address is surely connected to these shifts, but should not be confused with them. The early claims of humanist education, its emphasis on civic eloquence, moral responsibility and what one may call 'grammatical reason' finally proved unsatisfactory. [3] Like the trivium, if in rather different ways, humanist education took rhetoric/dialectic as the foundation of rational assertion. Increasingly, through the sixteenth century, such grounds were useful for pedagogy and communication

---

1. Giard, 'Aristotélisme', 287.
2. Rose's *Italian Renaissance* is largely about this. See, too, comments in Kristeller, *Italienischen Universitäten*, 18; N. Jardine, *Birth*, 247; and Reif's study of (later) textbooks.
3. Grafton and L. Jardine have argued that humanist goals in education were more successful ideologically than pedagogically: *From Humanism*.

alone, others being needed for the production of knowledge, for discovery.

The arguments of these last chapters are that sixteenth-century debates in logical and mathematical method, especially as they came together in music theory, eventually enabled the old foundation to be replaced by a new 'mathematical' one, probative for purposes of discovery. That this new foundation was indeed general is strongly implied by the case of what would much later be called 'aesthetics'; what I call the 'fictive imagination', its products, and its and their comprehension. In this context, and in that of new debates about catharsis and imitation, an agelong assumption of some 'sympathetic' relation between music and human passions/ affections was given fresh life by sixteenth- and early seventeenth-century thinkers. Those elements began to be worked into a rational conception of imagining whose eventual form has usually been thought an eighteenth-century development: what *did* happen, then, was that the 'aesthetic' was named and given a place separate from, subordinate to, that of logical reason, in a differently conceived relating of human activities. [4]

Here, it is incorrect to argue that the study of music, for example, moved from quadrivium to trivium (or equivalent). [5] We are, in any case, speaking about educational changes themselves also responsive (above all?) to pressures from elsewhere. We have been watching some of them. But even in the area of education, it is more accurate to assert a shift of *epistemological* emphasis in the other direction. Music in fact, like the other mathematical disciplines, now simply served a changing idea of knowledge: an idea that has itself, I think, not always been grasped with any precision.

Traditionally music had been one element in what Boethius had called the quadrivium, the others being arithmetic, geometry and astronomy. While 'music', *harmonia*, had once designated for the ancient Greeks a broadly conceived *paideia* of physical, intellectual and spiritual harmony, enabling a stable integrated polity of good citizens (as we learn most familiarly from Plato's *Republic*), in the quadrivium it named a mathematics of quantity – multitude – in relations. It made a pair with arithmetic, which analyzed quantity as such, multitude as composed of integral wholes. It was also related to astronomy (exploring magnitudes in motion – geometry treating magnitudes at

---

4. Reiss, *Meaning*, 224–5 *et passim*.
5. See, for example, Maniates, *Mannerism*, 115; Palisca, introduction to Girolamo Mei, *Letters*, 81; Moyer, *Musica*, 3; Palisca, *Humanism* 333, 338. It should be said that the last two are more nuanced.

rest) by virtue of the theory that the harmony of the universe was manifest in musical ways and able to be analyzed in its terms. [6]

Music was thus centrally important in the old quadrivium. It was so because of its broad application and because it brought to the quadrivium not only 'the task of searching for the truth' shared with the other mathematical arts, not only an association 'with speculation', but one 'with morality as well'. So Boethius had it. For his part, Martianus Capella described music as the culmination of the quadrivium, coming last, summing up and embracing the achievements of the other three arts. [7] Music's renewed importance in the sixteenth century, along with renewed interest in the mathematical disciplines more generally and ever more vital discoveries in their areas, marked a shift in the grounding of reason, whose mathematico-logical form has been little attended to by those other than philosophers and historians of science. As a result, the full implications of these adjustments have been much misapprehended.

I have just argued that the supposed shift from an oral to a visual/spatial culture – so much part of received wisdom over the past forty years – did not occur; or at least, did not occur how or when it is claimed to have done. Pedagogical device (Ramus' celebrated trees) has been taken for a new rational foundation. Ramist *Method* was actually 'just' a pedagogical step *towards* a foundation, itself to be mathematical – and logical, once logic had shifted the ground of its adherence towards mathematics and natural philosophy. Joseph Scaliger was then reputed to have held Ramus' method as simply 'aliud in disciplinis tradendis iter novamque viam [another way and a new path to impart learning]'. [8] One may agree: as he was with Gouvea's 1543 remarks and Temple's of the 1580s. I have further suggested that the components of the trivium, the basic and often only training of medieval schools, even made over into the *studia humanitatis* as they

---

6. Ramus' 1569 *Scholae mathematicae* was still marked by this sort of distinction: holding that arithmetic treated discontinuities of number, geometry continuities of extension (we saw that he wanted to remove music and astronomy from the mathematical arts). This is really not surprising, especially for a French academic treatise, set in a tradition for which Boethius remained the core reference probably until Viète's work, although we know the importance of the Euclid/Proclus debates. Developments in algebra were also making changes: Egmond cites the German Johann Scheubel, whose *Algebrae compendiosa facilisque descriptio* was printed in Paris in 1551, Peletier's 1554 *Algebre*, Jean Borrel's 1559 *Logistica*, Ramus' 1560 *Algebra*, and, later, Guillaume Gosselin's *De arte magna* (1577) and Simon Stevin's *Arithmetique*, printed at Leiden, but in French and with 'substantial treatment of algebra' (Egmond, 'How Algebra', 140).

7. Boethius, *Fundamentals*, 2 (I. 1); Martianus Capella, *Marriage*.

8. J. J. Scaliger, *Scaligerana*, 333.

were by the humanists, were exhausted as grounds for rational knowledge by the early sixteenth century. [9] I do not say that grammar and
rhetoric no longer mattered *educationally*, but that rational discovery
and argument were increasingly deemed to need other grounds. These
grounds were found in disciplines once bounded by the quadrivium.

Here I should observe that for most of the Middle Ages the
quadrivium was narrowly focused: based on the Boethian compendia,
supplemented by matter drawn from Cassiodorus, Martianus Capella,
Macrobius and Isidore of Seville, with some Aristotle, Euclid and
Ptolemy, and, by late thirteenth century, Sacrobosco's *Sphaera*. A
century on, Johannes de Muris' musical work was put to use. But even
by twelfth century Aristotle's scientific and philosophical works were
encroaching increasingly on the more familiar liberal arts. [10] The exact
constitution of the quadrivium anyway changed by place, time and
availability of manuscripts, whether ancient or new. Its matter had a
major part in the curriculum, but its formal place is still argued.

In Italian universities advanced chairs in astronomy existed in the
thirteenth century, but none in arithmetic until 1384/5, when, Alistair
Crombie tells us, one was established at Bologna. In 1405 there was
also a chair there in astrology, whose duties included teaching
Euclid and 'algorithm', and in 1443 chairs in arithmetic and geometry.
Domenico Maria Novara was lecturing on astronomy at that university from 1483 to 1504, as was Pacioli in mathematics more broadly.
When Leo X reformed the University of Rome in 1514, he created
two chairs in mathematics (one of them held by Pacioli), besides others
in philosophy, medicine and astronomy. Pisa had a mathematics chair
in 1484, but Padua had one only from 1520. [11] According to Claude
Palisca, the chairs in arithmetic and geometry were actually established
at Bologna in 1395, while Paul Oskar Kristeller says that Pope Nicholas
V had created 'four chairs for the mathematical sciences' in 1450. [12]
But whatever the details, two things are clear. The first is the evident
scarcity of separate chairs for quadrivial subjects. But the second is
that their number grew dramatically from the second half of the
fifteenth century.

Actual chairs in the universities, of course, are not the only standard of evidence, and we must recall three other facts. In the twelfth

---

9. For medieval emphasis on the trivium, see, for example, Ferruolo, *Origins*, 42, 94,
   141–52, 246–51, 307; and Murray, *Reason*, 10–11, 18–19, 178, 183–210, 213.
10. On this encroachment see Shelby, 'Geometry', 204–5, Dod, 'Aristoteles', and Lohr,
    'Medieval Interpretation'.
11. Crombie, 'Mathematics', 63. 'Algorithm' meant computation in arabic numerals.
12. Palisca, *Humanism*, 24; Kristeller, 'Music and Learning in the Early Italian
    Renaissance', in *Renaissance Thought*, II. 147.

century the Chartres school had been active in mathematical speculation, and Robert Grosseteste at Oxford. In the fourteenth, Jean Buridan and Nicole Oresme were teaching in Paris, Thomas Bradwardine and the Mertonians at Oxford. They wrote textbooks on the quadrivial topics, even though the general level of student mathematical work seems to have been well below that of the books such teachers produced. [13] In Italy, Paul of Mantua and Paul of Venice combined logic and natural philosophy in the late fourteenth century, linked directly to the Oxford school – whose fourteenth- and fifteenth-century influence in Italy, we saw in the introduction, was considerable.

In the meantime, in 1202 Leonardo of Pisa had written his *Liber abaci*, bringing Arabic algebra to the West. This work, it is true, appears to have been virtually unknown outside Italy, except by Muris, whose 1343 *Quadripartitum numerorum* drew from it its brief treatment of algebra. [14] In about 1470, Regiomontanus established his press in Nuremberg, printing 'astronomical and mathematical' works: Archimedes, Apollonius, Ptolemy. His project was cut short by his early death six years later. However, while some humanists may have neglected such thinkers, others did not. With the works of Boethius, those of Jordanus Nemorarius, Muris, Georg von Peurbach and Bradwardine, for example, were among the first printed books. More importantly, in Italy, Maurolico and a bit later Federico Commandino picked up where Regiomontanus left off, issuing their editions and translations of Greek mathematicians. Some of these editors, indeed, were serious mathematical thinkers in their own right. Regiomontanus wrote the earliest systematic trigonometric treatise, *De triangulis* (published only in 1533), while Maurolico has been called 'perhaps the greatest geometer of the sixteenth century'. [15]

In the long run, however, academic research and recovery of other traditions may not have been the most important strands in the developments being followed here. The third fact concerns the growth of trade and commerce mentioned in my introduction. It is as well to note things like the technical importance of geometry to the mason's craft in the Middle Ages. [16] The matter was recalled, we saw, in metaphors used by a Peletier in practical mathematics books of the mid-sixteenth century. But such facts have little to do with change (the contrary, if anything). What did have were the demographic changes and

---

13. See, for example, George Molland's introduction to Bradwardine, *Geometria*, 9–10.
14. Beaujouan, 'Place' 77; Egmond, 'How Algebra', 131.
15. For Regiomontanus, see Whitrow, 'Why Did?', 266; for Maurolico, Rose, *Italian Renaissance*, 159.
16. Shelby, 'Geometry', 209–12.

consequent commercial growth that were occurring in Italy from the twelfth century, which saw the notable flowering of four city states, in order, Pisa, Lucca, Siena and Florence. [17] (Rome and Venice were separate and special cases.) Commercial and financial interests led to the establishing of schools to prepare future business people. By 1338 in Florence, the chronicler Giovanni Villani famously recorded, a city of 90,000 inhabitants, 8 to 10,000 boys and girls were learning to read and write, 1,000 to 1,200 were going on to learn the sorts of calculation needed for business in six secondary schools called *scuole d'abbaco* and 550 to 600 to learn Latin and letters in four schools of humanist-type. [18] Villani's figures have been questioned, but their exactness matters less than the facts they indicate.

While not much is known about the earliest such schools, it is about those establishments of the fifteenth and sixteenth centuries. Many manuscript texts remain from as early as the fourteenth century, as do occasional contracts and descriptions of what was taught. While, no doubt, this was still being worked out in the schools' early days, it was sufficiently fixed later for there to be small difference of order or subject matter in texts of the next two centuries. Pupils apparently went to the *scuole d'abbaco* at the age of ten or eleven, staying for two or so years – at the age of thirteen or fourteen they would then go on to an apprenticeship in some particular business. [19] They began by learning the elementary arithmetical operations of addition, subtraction and multiplication. This was followed by division, which was often done in three stages (learning how to divide by one, then two, then three or more digits). Pupils then learned about fractions, and went on to the celebrated 'Rule of Three', the so-called Golden Rule of proportion (at its simplest it solved such questions as: 'If twelve sacks of wheat cost so many florins, how many will nine cost?'; at its more complicated it 'produced' the harmonic scale: 4, 6, 8, 9, 12, 16). They would also learn the rules of single and double false position (a way to discover unknowns by successive approximations), and certain elements of algebra, the *regola della cosa*, as it was often known, since the word

---

17. Franci and Rigatelli, *Introduzione*, 23. See Egmond's useful catalogue, *Practical Mathematics*. I mention here for reference, although I have been unable to obtain it, the same author's 1976 dissertation, 'Commercial Revolution'.
18. Franci and Rigatelli, *Introduzione*, 26. The 8 to 10,000 figure relates to boys and girls in primary schools (to the age of ten or so). Most ended their education at that point. Bec notes evidence that girls sometimes continued on. He also records the existence of a 1304 contract with one 'domina Clementia *doctrix puerorum*', for her to teach such elementary education (*Marchands*, 384).
19. These details and those of the curriculum immediately following are from Goldthwaite, 'Schools', 418, 425.

cosa ('thing') denoted the unknown in an equation. [20] They finished by learning about local money and weights and measures: whose local varieties and those from city to city were endless.

This order is followed fairly precisely by all the so-far known manuscripts. One sees it in Chuquet's of 1484 from Lyon and in Dionigi Gori's of 1544 and 1571 from Siena. You still see it, fundamentally, in writings by an academic like Fine in 1532, and in more directly practical arithmetics by Peletier and Boissière a quarter of a century later. Where academic writing differed from business–practical writings was in the latters' constant use, as one would expect, of instances drawn from commerce and trade: examples scorned by the academic writers. The curriculum we have just followed was actually drawn from a contract with an arithmetic teacher, and it by no means concluded the course taken by a *scuola d'abbaco*'s pupils. Beyond abilities to calculate rates of exchange (complex in the extreme in an age of no fixed coinage), tare allowance, barter, brokerage, commodity adulteration and the like, one had further to understand volumes, surveying, and other matters of 'extension' (to use Ramus' later term). So the arithmetic curriculum led directly to its geometric successor – again, the manuscripts all concur.

An example given by Michael Baxandall is useful here – for two reasons. It comes from Piero's *Trattato d'abaco*, dating from the third quarter of the fifteenth century and intended, like others such, 'a' mercantanti', wrote its author, so linking it up with the painterly debates to which we will come later. [21] But it also gives a good idea not just of the complexity of the questions treated, but of how they connect with more speculative branches, here, of geometry. Baxandall is observing that matters of gauging were especially important to merchants in an era (pre-nineteenth century) when standard-sized containers were not habitually used. Each barrel, sack or bale was unique. To be able to calculate its contents quickly and accurately was a skill essential for any merchant. Here is Piero more or less in Baxandall's translation:

There is a barrel, each of its ends being 2 bracci in diameter; the diameter at its bung is 2¼ bracci and halfway between bung and end it is 2⅔ bracci. The barrel is 2 bracci long. What is its cubic measure?

---

20. According to Franci and Rigatelli, in the fourteenth and fifteenth centuries almost all the extant texts 'employ[ed] the rhetorical style of abbacus treatises. Equations, formulae for solution, and all the operations used were written entirely in words; no symbols were used except those for natural numbers and fractions.' ('Fourteenth-Century', 15.) Although divers other writers in fact occasionally used bits of 'modern' notation, most of these came and went until the outburst of the late sixteenth century.
21. Piero della Francesca, *Trattato*, 39.

This is like a pair of truncated cones. Square the diameter at the ends: $2 \times 2 = 4$. Then square the median diameter $2\frac{2}{3} \times 2\frac{2}{3} = 4\frac{7}{9}$ı. Add them together: $8\frac{7}{9}$ı. Multiply $2 \times 2\frac{2}{3} = 4\frac{2}{3}$. Add this to $8\frac{7}{9}$ı $= 13\frac{31}{9}$ı. Divide by $3 = 4\frac{112}{243}$ ... [and keep this in your head] ... Now square $2\frac{1}{4} = 2\frac{1}{4} \times 2\frac{1}{4} = 5\frac{1}{16}$. Add it to the square of the median diameter: $5\frac{1}{16} + 4\frac{7}{9}$ı $= 10\frac{1}{29}$. Multiply $2\frac{2}{3} \times 2\frac{1}{4} = 5$. Add this to the previous sum: $15\frac{1}{29}$. Divide by 3: $5\frac{1}{888}$. Add it to the first result: $4\frac{112}{243} + 5\frac{1}{888} = 9\frac{1792}{888}$. Multiply this by 11 and then divide by 14 [i.e. multiply by $\frac{7}{4}$: the final result is $7\frac{2360}{44432}$. This is the cubic measure of the barrel. This method can be used when the measures are all equidistant from one another, not otherwise.

That merchants should be expected to be able to make calculations of this sort quickly (and at least in part mentally) attests to habits of attention that are very different from ones which are nowadays familiar. It was, Baxandall remarks, 'a special intellectual world'. [22] The same textbooks provide similar evidence with regard to the myriad surveying problems that they treated. Unlike the kind of trade-oriented gauging problem cited, the same sorts of surveying problems were in fact common to academic works (as the cases of Bovelles and Fine show) and to practical work aimed at merchants, no doubt because they were less directly aimed at business. Perhaps it goes without saying that the leading business teachers, *maestri d'abbaco*, are known to have had quadrivial expertise, and to have been adept in mathematics applicable both to architecture and optics (put to use in their presentations of surveying, in any case). [23] Pacioli may have consciously brought together practical and academic mathematics, but the same is evidenced in Chuquet's manuscripts, long before being claimed by Peletier in his *Aritmetique*. [24]

---

22. Baxandall, *Painting*, 86. The passage is from the *Trattato*, 233–4:

Egl'è una bocte che i suoi fondi è ciascuno per diametro 2 bracci; et al cochiume è 2¼, et tra i fondi e 'l cochiume è 2⅔, et è lunga 2 bracci. Domando quanto serà quadrata.

Questa è de spetie de piramide taglate, però fa' così. Montiplica il fondo in sè, ch'è 2, fa 4, poi montiplica 2⅔ in sè fa 4⁷⁄₉₁; giogni insiemi fa 8⁷⁄₉₁. Poi montiplica 2 via 2⅔ fa 4⅔, giogni con 8⁷⁄₉₁ fa 13³¹⁄₉₁, parti per 3 ne vene 4¹¹²⁄₂₄₃ cioè radici de 4¹¹²⁄₂₄₃ che in sè montiplicato fa 4¹¹²⁄₂₄₃: e questo tieni a mente. Tu ài che montiplicato 2⅔ in sè fa 4⁷⁄₉₁, hora montiplica 2¼ in sè fa 5¹⁄₁₆, giogni insiemi fa 10¹⁄₂₉₆, et montiplica 2⅔ via 2¼ fa 5 giogni insemi fa 15¹⁄₂₉₆; parti per 3 ne vene 5¹⁄₈₈₈, cioè la radici de 5¹⁄₈₈₈ che in sè montiplicato fa 5¹⁄₈₈₈. Giognilo chon quello de sopra ch'è 4¹¹²⁄₂₄₃ fa 9¹⁷⁹²⁄₈₈₈ il quale montiplica per 11 e parti per 14, ne vene 7²³⁶⁰⁰⁄₄₄₄₃₂: tanto è quadrata la dicta botte. Questo modo se po' tenere quando le mesure sono tucte eqidistante l'una da l'altra, none altramente.

The first bracketed phrase and last sentence are not translated by Baxandall.

23. On this last point, see Goldthwaite, 'Schools', 429–30. We may also remember that both architecture and optics fell under geometry in the quadrivium.

24. *Aritmetique*, 80 v–81 r. Peletier did not claim originality in doing so. I mention his remark further to suggest the very real connections.

I am interested not only in habits of mind that would impel people to look at solid objects in terms of measurable geometric forms, but also in rational habits that would familiarize them with, say, conic problems, as in the barrel instance, and more broadly with the idea of grounded rule underlying all observable reality. As Albrecht Dürer observed to the painter in his posthumously published work on human proportions, the painter's first task was to 'order the whole figure well' according to proportions known 'by Geometry', underlying visible differences, but nonetheless 'firmly fixed in Nature'. [25] This would seem a potentially more serious subversion of Aristotle than all the later clamour in Paris: 'The minute accuracy of mathematics is not to be demanded in all cases,' the Philosopher had said in *Metaphysics*, 'but only in the case of things which have no matter.' It could not explain 'perceptible and perishable magnitudes; for then it would have perished, when they perished'. Neither geometry nor astronomy measured real material things. [26] These 'artisans' were saying just the contrary. Aristotle's abstract and idealized magnitudes were joined here to material practice. When that junction found its way into speculative mathematical concerns, one could expect it to feed and magnify the changes already occurring.

What matters is the habit of seeing the relation between certain kinds of speculative questions and practical need, and, no less, the allied habit of seeing sure and clear mathematical rule under seeming vagary, of *discovering* universally applicable order in the real. For clearly enough, to take Piero's barrel example again, the 'equidistance' and other equalities that the problem assumed had to be *supposed* for the necessary purposes of speedy evaluation. The very uniqueness of each container in fact precluded the exactness that such practice demanded. But these calculations took for granted the validity of a 'systematic abstraction' and a certain spatial 'homogeneity' that assumed correspondence of some sort between 'mathematical space'

---

25. Dürer, *Four Books of Human Proportion*, as given from British Museum manuscripts in *Writings*, 245, 247: from book 3. (This anthology was originally published as *The Literary Remains of Albrecht Dürer* in 1889.) The thought – and perhaps much of the writing – of the books on human proportion was done in the earliest years of the century, and its theory seems not to have changed after 1504, when he drew Adam and Eve before the Fall: only they embodied fully perfect human forms – just as Bovelles (and others) depicted their language as alone perfect. Dürer had studied in Italy, and learned from Leonardo da Vinci and Pacioli, although he did most of his work on human proportion independently. Another minor but not indifferent connection is that in 1557 Meigret put the work on human proportion into French from a 1532 Latin translation (*Writings*, 229).

26. Aristotle, *Metaphysics*, rpt. in W. D. Ross, trans., *Complete Works*, II. 1572 (995a15–16), 1576 (997b34–998a6).

and material reality: universal rule underlying perceived difference. [27]
It also eventually assumed that the rules beneath appearance are, in
some serious and comprehensible way, *like* that appearance and that
that 'like-ness' lets them be *explanatory*.

A century after Dürer, Galileo caught the importance of the subversion, the connection between these commercial developments and a
'mathematically driven' natural *scientia*, and this relation between
underlying abstraction and material body with about as much precision as one could hope for. In the middle of the Second Day of his
1632 *Dialogue*, to Simplicio's again maintaining the Aristotelian assertion that 'mathematical subtleties' were inapplicable 'to sensible and
physical matters', Salviati replied in terms that could almost be
excerpted from the predecessors we have just seen:

> it would be novel indeed if computations and ratios made in abstract numbers
> should not thereafter correspond to gold and silver coins and concrete merchan-
> dise. Do you know what does happen, Simplicio? Just as the reckoner who
> wants his calculations to deal with sugars, silks and wools must discount the
> tares of the bins, bales and other packings, so the mathematical scientist
> (*filosofo geometra*) who wants to recognize in concrete the effects proved in
> abstract must deduct the hindrances of matter; and once he is able to do so,
> I assure you that things agree with one another no less exactly than the arith-
> metical calculations. [28]

The significance of the *scuole d'abbaco* and their mathematical education could hardly be more clearly expressed.

Perhaps even more than these (and assuredly by mid-sixteenth
century) music crossed between theory and practice, speculation and
everyday life. But it could also, we shall see, cross between the once
'separate' areas of trivium and quadrivium. In the Middle Ages music's
official academic place was as ambiguous as that of the other subjects
of the quadrivium, although it was certainly on the curriculum, whether
or not there were formal chairs. Kristeller says that the first such chair

---

27. The phrases in inverted commas are taken from Panofsky, *Perspective*, 30–1. In
chapter 7 of this book we will see the importance of this connection.
28. Galileo, *Dialogue*, 203, 207; *Opere*, VII. 229, 233–4:

> e sarebbe ben nuova cosa che i computi e le ragioni fatte in numeri astratti, non
> rispondessero poi alle monete d'oro e d'argento e alle mercanzie in concreto. Ma
> sapete, Sig. Simplicio, quel che accade? Si come a voler che i calcoli tornino sopra
> i zuccheri, le sete e le lane, bisogna che il computista faccia le sue tare di casse,
> invoglie ed altre bagaglie, così, quando il filosofo geometra vuol riconoscere in
> concreto gli effetti dimostrati in astratto, bisogna che difalchi gli impedimenti della
> materia; che se ciò saprà fare, io vi assicuro che le cose si riscontreranno non meno
> aggiustamente che i computi aritmetici.

> I have brought Stillman Drake's translation closer to the Italian and to vocabulary
> used earlier in my text.

was supposedly established in 1450 at Bologna, but with no occupant:
indeed Bartolomeo Ramos de Pareja is said to have left Bologna in
1482 just because he was *not* given it. Prosdocimus de Beldemandis
taught astronomy in Padua early in the century, but (Kristeller thinks)
almost surely not the music theory for which he was known. Franchino
Gaffurio held a chair at Pavia from 1494–99, but was not paid by the
university. It seems to have been a ducal favour. Music was taught at
divers universities in Italy, Spain, England, Scotland, Poland, Bohemia
and the German lands. [29]

By the fifteenth century music became ever more important outside
the universities, both in church and at court. Many of the principal
sixteenth-century theorists and practitioners held posts as church choir-
masters, while every princely court had its players. By 1528 Baldesar
Castiglione had Lodovico da Canossa opine: 'I am not satisfied with
our courtier unless he is also a musician and unless as well as understanding and being able to read music he can play several instruments.'
Music moves the affections, 'breed[s] good new habits and a virtuous
disposition and make[s] the soul more receptive to happiness'. Its enjoy-
ment is a sign of 'harmony in [the] soul'. [30] By the late sixteenth century,
for at least one German schoolmaster, Ramus' friend, biographer and
occasional editor, Johann Thomas Freig, music was to be the most
important subject by the fourth year of a child's education. [31] In the
course of the sixteenth century music was bound increasingly to poetry,
itself having become a vital part of the *studia humanitatis*. [32] The latter
had, we know, been rejected from *grammatica*, and by the late Middle
Ages was no longer in the trivium. Associating it with music, and so
placing it in the orbit of the mathematical arts and sciences, made for
various new possibilities. For at the same time new explorations in
mathematics, especially from the mid-sixteenth century, furthered the
quantifiable aspects of music theory.

---

29. Kristeller, 'Music', 147–9. He claims music was taught nowhere until the fifteenth
    century; then not in France or Italy (144, 147, 149) – but see his *Italienischen
    Universitäten*, 18–19. Academic chairs seem to be his measure. But a case like
    Prosdocimus' may be less clear. Carpenter's *Music* shows practice was less absolute
    (32–127). For the quadrivium in general I draw mainly here on essays in Masi,
    Boethius, and Wagner, *Seven*. See, too, Rashdall, *Universities*.
30. Castiglione, *Courtier*, 94–5. He constantly re-ran the theme: 82, 120–1, etc. For church
    posts, see Kristeller, 'Music', 150–1. Music (singing and dancing) had been 'an essen-
    tial element' in courtly life since the thirteenth century (Gallo, *Music*, 3, 5).
31. Freig, *Paedagogus* 27–30. See Waddington, *Ramus, passim*, for Freig's relations with
    Ramus. He edited Basel editions of Ramus' *Liber de Caesaris militia* (first published
    in 1559) and the *Liber de moribus veterum Gallorum*, both in 1574.
32. This is by now familiar, but see, for example, Kristeller, 'Modern System',
    Renaissance Thought, II. 178; Palisca, *Humanism*, 333, 401.

But before concentrating our attention on music, we should further emphasize how developments in mathematics as a whole were resulting in its growing in common intellectual and practical importance from before the early fifteenth century. Not by chance did the 1420s and thirties see Filippo Brunelleschi's and Alberti's mathematical work on pictorial perspective, unquestionably tied, as Piero's later *Trattato d'abaco* and *De prospectiva pingendi* show, with the grown concern for practical mathematics, its link with the speculative, and the place of both in everyday practical life. We also need to look further at those links with questions of method and discovery that we began to see in the previous chapters. My discussion will of necessity overlap chronologically both with them and with the discussion of music in chapters 6 and 7, although my immediate way into the last is through contemporaries of Ramus, his supporters and his enemies.

Long before Descartes made the point (probably nowadays, along with Galileo, the most familiarly known to have done so), Tartaglia wrote that 'no science or liberal art, they say, is more able to grasp the truth than the mathematical disciplines'. They improve the mind. No other science is needed to understand them, their operations are internal. Unlike natural philosophers, who 'examine things clothed', mathematicians examine 'them bare of any visible matter'. This may have been an Aristotelian point, but it was also Dürer's more practical one, derived from Piero via Pacioli. Unlike others, said Tartaglia, mathematicians do not draw on authority or opinion, but on demonstration. Mathematics are the ground for all other arts and sciences: just so had Cusa shown how theology needed geometry for proper comprehension.[33] Robert Recorde wrote in 1557 'that besides the Mathematicalle artes, there is noe vnfallible knoweledge, excepte it bee borowed of them'. In a famous 1570 text, John Dee likewise considered mathematics the source of universal learning and praxis: for 'the atteyning of knowledge incomparable, and Heavenly Wisedom: Mathematicall Speculations, both of Numbers and Magnitudes: are meanes, aydes, and guides: ready, certaine, and necessary'.[34]

Such claims did little other than codify assumptions coming directly from the sort of practical mathematical teaching we have seen. In a way, of course, they also lay behind the quadrivium, going back at least

---

33. Tartaglia, 'Lettione ... sopra tvtta la opera di Euclide', in *Euclide* 3 r–v ff, 5 r (for Cusa comment). Compare Bovelles, who we saw had made a similar point before, also through Cusa: *Geometricum* 3 v: 'Nicolaus Cusanus ... uir in omni scientiae genere nulli inferior, tanto studio Geometriam excoluit, ut plurima ante eum Geometris ignota adinuenerit.'
34. Recorde, *The Whetstone of Witte* (1557); Dee, 'Mathematicall Præface' to Henry Billingsley's translation of *Euclid* (1570), in Fauvel and Gray, eds., *History*, 281, 284.

as far as Plato and the Pythagoreans and living on through the Middle Ages, notably in Boethius' *Arithmetic* and his remark that God founded 'this first discipline [of the quadrivium] as the exemplar of his own thought and established all things in accord with it'. Roger Bacon, too, had asserted that of the 'four great sciences', mathematics was 'the gate and key'. He quoted Boethius that it was essential 'to discover truth'. For the discovery of categories, the first branch of Aristotle's logic, mathematics was unavoidable. Indeed, it was 'urgently ... needed for philosophy, theology, ... the Church of God, [and] for directing the commonwealth of the faithful.' [35] So, when Gaffurio strove in 1492 to update the 'totality' of earlier Greek and Western musical exploration, half of his first book on the topic, the *Theorica musice*, was devoted to numerical discussion. He echoed Boethius in writing: 'Since the rationality of numbers inheres in all things created by primeval nature, this principle was an idea in the mind of the creator ... The state of all things is governed by the ratios of numbers'. [36] We saw many remarks of this sort in the last chapter from the pens of early French writers, equally heavily influenced by Boethius.

However, arguing that the quadrivium takes us beyond sensual knowledge 'to the more certain things of the intellect' and to wisdom grounded in divine harmony was one thing. [37] This was still largely Gaffurio's effort, as it had been Boethius' and Bacon's, who understood God to have placed 'the rational soul' in humans 'in accordance with his eternal foresight' and divine plan. [38] *Pace* Crombie, this is actually a quite different sort of claim from the technical and practical ones of the early *maestri d'abbaco*, Piero and Dürer, of the later Tartaglia, Peletier, Recorde and Dee, or of Descartes' mastery and possession of nature (even though, as in other realms, Roger Bacon was before his time in arguing for practical knowledge). [39]

Tartaglia, we have seen, always drew his examples from and applied his calculations to gunnery, battle order, fortification, practical measurement and so forth. [40] Dee's list of applications was wholly practical.

---

35. Bacon, *Opus*, I. 116–17, 120 (Pt. IV. Chs. i–ii), 306 (IV. xvi).
36. *Boethian Number*, 74; Gaffurio, *Theorica* [cvi v]–di r (II. 6); Gaffurio, *Theory*, 69.
37. *Boethian Number*, 74.
38. Bacon, *Opus*, I. 412, 405 (IV. xvi).
39. Crombie, 'Experimental', 51–5. Otherwise, however, this essay (which I found late in my own researches) confirms the general argument of the present volume – often through the same authors.
40. See, for example, Tartaglia, *Noua scientia*. Of a later work, the whole title is revealing: *Qvesiti et inventioni diversi de Nicolo Tartaglia, di novo restampati con vna gionta al sesto libro, nella quale si mostra duoi modi di riduo una Città inespugnabile ...*: '... with an appendix to the sixth book in which are shown two ways to reduce an impregnable city'.

These correspond to the kind of practical business applications seen earlier. Nicholas Jardine avers that in his *Prooemium mathematicum* Ramus carried 'to an extreme the humanist concern with practical utility'. [41] But such claims on behalf of mathematics in general were commonplace (doubtless more than the particular debates in astronomy that Jardine is exploring), and what Ramus, Tartaglia and contemporaries now derived explicitly from such applications were 'abstraction of figure, generality of theorem, and logic of demonstration'. [42] These ideas, too, were widespread, as we saw in the last chapter. Indeed, in one form or another they were virtually universal. It was this that in the field of algebra allowed such developments as the solution of cubic and quartic equations by Del Ferro, Tartaglia, Cardano and Ferrari in mid-sixteenth century (the question of who originated the solutions provoked vehement quarrels).

These claims were now constitutive of mathematical sciences. But they also offered solutions to the kinds of epistemological and probative dilemmas earlier chapters have shown. And it was, in fact, from a century and a half or so earlier (in Italy) that the idea had begun to grow – via the sort of practical calculations we saw – that mathematics might provide a universal rule underlying perceived differences of material reality. James Ackerman opines that artists were first to work in terms of the 'submission of observed data to a rational and mathematically definable order', and to develop a 'perceptual attitude . . . of respect for empirical observation and a will to devise systematic and repeatable techniques for recording the results of observation'. [43] But people like Brunelleschi and Alberti (the latter a polymath with very wide interests) were part of a much wider movement of ideas and practice. For many others, as for them, mathematics showed its potential as a tool for creating and ordering knowledge and thought certainly by the second half of the fifteenth century – at the same time, that is to say, as those researches into language that were showing *its* limitations. A century later, thinking had moved far in the direction of making mathematics potentially foundational in various ways. One could give many examples other than those named of people expressing such views. The fact and form of the renewal seems hardly able to be doubted.

At the same time, as well, debate over the nature of logic itself, whether a separate science or a single instrument for organizing all the arts and sciences, was growing in vehemence and urgency – for the

41. N. Jardine, *Birth*, 266.
42. Strong, *Procedures*, 3.
43. Ackerman, 'Involvement', 94, 125.

same reasons we have been following. Some idea of a methodical logic, whether Ramus' or not, eventually grounded work in history, politics, ethics and the rest. [44] But however important grammar, rhetoric and even logic remained as tools for learning (one need only consider Descartes' Jesuit education or the kinds of emphasis approved by an educator like Alsted), increasingly logic was associated with the mathematical and natural sciences wherever discovery was in question: of this development a thinker like Jacopo Zabarella was not untypical, although he himself showed no direct interest in mathematics. [45] His 1578 *De natura logicae* urged that logic was the basic tool of natural scientific discovery. And while there were two logics, a natural and a conventional (*artificiosa*), they varied only by their stages of acquisition (compare above, chapter 3, note 39).

The first was a 'natural instinct': 'the first sages used this natural logic to philosophize, for before anyone had written or taught the art of logic, led by natural instinct itself they observed a certain method for the contemplation of things, and proceeded from certain known principles to unknown ones'. What we acquired when we *learned* (artificial) method, he added in the *De methodis*, was 'nothing but a logical *habitus*, or an instrumental intellectual *habitus* serving to acquire

---

44. For some sense of the difference between a 'methodical' and a 'humanist' thinker later in the century, one might compare (as I found myself doing through the accident of simultaneous library deliveries) Justus Lipsius' simple, even simplistic – so popular and influential – compilation of his six political books with Suárez's deeply thought methodical elucubrations on the 'same' topic. Lipsius almost parodied humanist ways of reading, glossing and compiling classics: he connected citations. François Ogier was humorous on the topic: 'Iuste-Lipse, qui n'a rien mis du sien dans ses Politiques que des adverbes & des conionctions' ('who put nothing of his own in his *Politics* save adverbs and conjunctions', *Apologie*, 23). Suárez's neoaristotelianism was imbued with the debates about the nature of logic and, no doubt too, with Jesuit education's emphasis on the teaching of mathematics.

45. Randall is best known for asserting the direct continuity of Zabarella's work with later mathematical sciences ('Development'), although Cassirer earlier argued that resolutive method 'clearly approached the empirical sciences', while the compositive 'attained its application in mathematics' (*Erkenntnisproblem*, I. 135). Both are weak claims – the second is wholly foreign to Cassirer's subject: 'the role that mathematics plays in "demonstrative induction" is nowhere understood by Zabarella' (137). Many writers feel Randall's mild disclaimer about the Paduan's lack of mathematics was also insufficient: for example, Gilbert, 'Galileo', 227; Schmitt, 'Experience and Experiment: a Comparison of Zabarella's View with Galileo's *De motu*', *Studies* VIII: 80–138; N. Jardine, 'Galileo's Road', 306–18. For now, my point is with shared problems, not their solutions. Against Zabarella and others though, and whatever the real practice of Jesuit education, the Society's 1586 *Ratio studiorum* emphasized the importance of mathematics. It

teaches poets about the rising and setting of the stars; teaches historians the situation and distances of various places; teaches logicians [*analytici*] examples of solid demonstrations; teaches politicians truly admirable methods for conducting affairs

knowledge of things'. [46] This method of discovery was what Zabarella called, in the 1578 *De regressu*, 'regressive'. It combined into a single process the Aristotelian resolutive/compositive. The largely unruled and more or less brute 'observational' knowledge derived from single cases (Aristotelian *demonstratio quia*) was then submitted to searching meditation, *negotiatio*, before being universalized by a *propter quid* demonstration setting it into a ruled structure of 'causes'.

Neither the term *regressus* nor the debates whence it came began with Zabarella. The word itself seems first to have been used in something like his sense by Pietro d'Abano in his 1310 *Conciliator differentiarum philosophorum, et praecipue mediorum*, where the relation between Aristotle's two ways of presentation, noted in the introduction to *Physics*, of particular to universal and universal to particular (which Averroes had already conflated with *quia* and *propter quid* demonstrations, and, respectively, with Galen's analysis and synthesis), was explained as *regressus*, a 'reversal'. [47] Over the next two centuries the debates became intricate, as commentators observed that among the problems with this notion were two major ones: that of circularity (one merely retraced the steps of the other), and that of *petitio principii* (both demonstrations were syllogisms involving only knowns). In 1508, Nicolò Leoniceno sought clarification by ways we have seen in other domains, distinguishing between methods of teaching and those of discovery, *modi docendi* and *modi doctrinae*. The latter he saw as Aristotelian syllogism and 'three Platonic methods for seeking definitions (*resolutio*, *divisio* and *definitio*)'. [48] In the same year, Agostino Nifo tried to offer more solid solutions.

In his commentary on Aristotle's *Physics*, Nifo noted agreement with those who 'are of the opinion that four modes of knowledge [*notitiae*] occur. The first is knowledge of the effect through the senses, or observation. The second is the discovery of the cause through the effect,

---

at home and during war; teaches physicists the manners and diversity of celestial movements, of light, of colours, of diaphanous bodies, of sounds ... not to speak of the services rendered by the work of mathematicians to the state, to medicine, to navigation and to agriculture. An effort must therefore be made so that mathematics will flourish in our colleges as well as the other disciplines. Quoted and trans. in Peter Dear, *Mersenne and the Learning of the Schools*, 44–5.

This echoes Dee's præface. I write of this mathematical education at much more length in chapter 5 of *Descartes, Philosophy, and the Public Sphere* (and about the debates over method in its chapter 4).

46. Zabarella, *Opera*: *De natura logicae*, col. 27: *De methodis*, col. 135.
47. Randall, 'Development', 225; N. Jardine, 'Galileo's Road', 285–6. Jardine's essay seems to me quite the best available analysis of *regressus*, as my many references will imply.
48. N. Jardine, 'Galileo's Road', 286.

which is obtained by *demonstratio quia*. The third is the *negotiatio* of that cause by the intellect, by which, in conjunction with the first, knowledge of the cause is increased so that it is worthy to be made the middle term of a *demonstratio simpliciter* [= *demonstratio propter quid*]. The last is knowledge of the reason for the same effect, through a cause [knowledge of which is] so grown that it may serve as the middle term [of the *demonstratio propter quid*]'. N. Jardine remarks that what Nifo meant by *negotiatio* was obscure. He later dropped the idea, stressing that *scientia* of nature was always *coniecturalis*: a word whose primary meaning here Jardine convincingly shows to refer to 'the peculiar characteristics of things', things that in nature cannot be otherwise: as smoke indicates fire. Of such, we can know, for example, their 'constant conjunction' but not with any certainty the 'proximate cause' of such conjunction. 'To put it in a nutshell,' Jardine ends, 'in a *syllogismus coniecturalis* only the *necessity* not the *truth* of the premises and conclusion is uncertain.' One could do no better in natural philosophy, and regressive *negotiatio* never gave necessary knowledge. One indeed used not Aristotle's *scientific* 'demonstration and conceptual induction', but the methods of *Topics*: 'contingent, probable, plausible, widely accepted' evidence founding 'sound belief'. [49]

As we saw in the previous chapter, the mid-sixteenth-century return to ancient geometrical sources was both provoked by and fed into these debates in the logic of natural inquiry. And as in the case of Parisian dialectic and rhetoric, so here it seemed to demand clear distinction between teaching and discovery. But we can now also, perhaps, better understand the contrary directions of reaction: one assimilating geometrical proof to the syllogism, one keeping them radically separate. Nifo's later argument seemed to invalidate the demonstrative syllogism as a method suitable in natural inquiry. Many others had already, in practice, restricted its utility to communication. But if both were so, then other grounds of discovery were needed: which may explain why Ramus' 1572 *Dialectica* emphasized what one may call a 'geometric turn'. It may also explain a difficulty in Zabarella's 'return' to Nifo (via, it would appear, a more immediate predecessor in Girolamo Balduino, an older colleague of Zabarella at Padua). [50]

Unlike Nifo's, we saw, Zabarella's regressive method relied on three, not four, steps. No special place was given to initial observation. And if Jardine deems Nifo's *negotiatio* obscure, he holds Zabarella's simply

---

49. Ibid., 290–5. The Nifo quotation is from his *Aristotelis physicarum acroasum ... liber, interprete atque expositore E. A. Nypho* (Venice, 1508), 7 v col. 2–8 r, col. 1: the bracketed interjections are Jardine's.
50. N. Jardine, 'Galileo's Road', 295–6; Pérez-Ramos, *Francis Bacon's*, 225.

'bizarre': he 'supposes that observation gives rise to images which merely serve to make the rational soul (*intellectus possibilis*) receptive to simulacra of the knowledge present in the mind of God. The vehicle for this inspiration of fragments of God's knowledge is *intellectus agens*, the Holy Ghost.' *Negotiatio* was the means by which the human mind worked through the relations between 'the simulacra of the ideas present in the mind of God which constitute the things of the external world' and the same ones 'inspired into the human mind through the agency of *intellectus agens*'. It was this that got us from a *quia* demonstration to a *propter quid* one. Such a notion is far from anything that Westerners today could recognize as 'scientific method'. It belongs in that mental world addressed in chapter 1 (see especially page 43 above).[51] Still, Zabarella held the natural knowledge produced by this process to be sure and to explain the universal ground of particular phenomena, to give us what Francis Bacon later named *experientia literata*, 'literate experience'.[52] This was clearly distinct from the knowledge expressed in the syllogisms of 'natural logic', while having nothing directly in common with a 'geometrical method'.

But in other ways Zabarella's distinction of a natural and an artifical logic corresponded to another distinction that would soon begin to be made: between experience and experiment. So, for example, the Jesuit mathematicians Christopher Scheiner (*Oculus*, 1619) and Josephus Blancanus (*Sphaera mundi*, 1620) distinguished, respectively, between 'phenomenon' and '*experientia*' and between 'phenomenon' and 'observation'. By observation and *experientia*, Blancanus and Scheiner meant Bacon's 'literate experience', the result of a ruled *experimenta*, a 'particular procedure whereby the experience may be instantiated'. For both, 'phenomenon' named something generally known, the second normally requiring specially devised rational instruments.[53] This was exactly the distinction Zabarella made between his two logics: while the first was made of untaught 'syllogisms and arguments', the second, regressive logic, was learned rule. It was certainly foreign to what Cesare Vasoli has in mind when calling the Euclid/Proclus discussions of the 1550s and 1560s 'so important to the final definition of the specifically logical character of mathematical demonstration, irreducible to syllogistic canons'.[54] But its own irreducibility to such canons echoed a parallel feeling of their insufficiency. Regressive method was ruled in the same sense (if not necessarily in the same way) as the natural

51. N. Jardine, 'Galileo's Road', 301–3; Skulsky, 'Paduan', 354–61.
52. Reiss, *Discourse*, 201–6.
53. Dear, *Discipline*, 47–57 (quotation on 56).
54. Vasoli, 'Introduction', xiv.

knowledge associated with it. To be sure, it *used* no element of Scheiner's, Blancanus' or Bacon's yet vague idea of contrived experiment. [55] But it was *itself* just such an artificial device for ordered rule.

Zabarelli was careful to separate both logics from 'ordo'. He used this word to name the simple systematic ordering required in teaching, and specifically rejected the idea that 'method' was for teaching, presumably with Ramists in mind and perhaps, too, its growing association with geometry. He was clear that the regressive method was for discovery: a 'functional, intellectual framework which serves in the acquisition of correct knowledge'. Scepticism as to humans' 'ability to obtain knowledge of causes' had disappeared – here, at least. [56] Zabarella, as Heikki Mikkeli observes, saw method as a way to reconfirm Aristotelian claim and argument. [57] To do so, though, he emphasized the distance between a 'natural' syllogistic reasoning and an 'artificial', contrived kind suitable to natural knowledge. His solution to the dilemmas we have been following is especially valuable precisely because of its sustained effort *not* to break with past habits of mind. His refusal of mathematical reason in discovery went against a deepening grain.

But if Zabarella and future 'scientific' thinkers differed on *what* and *how* one could know, they disagreed far less on claims about the obstacles that lay before knowing. And in the matter of the instrumental nature of method, as well as in that of two logics, Zabarella had the disputing company of Domingo de Soto, Pedro Fonseca, Toleto, the Coimbran commentators and others, including the Descartes of the *Regulae*. Whether one distinguished nature and artifice, 'intuition [intuitus]' and intellect, or even deduction and induction, the traditional play of compositive and resolutive had somehow been adjusted to a new organization of experience and reason. [58] 'History' and 'rule' needed somehow to be overlaid on one another, even as they were kept separate. Bacon's *historiae*, narrations of phenomena, had to be able to be known as the effects of a universal rule able to be manipulated by a mind in which it was native, although the term itself was

---

55. N. Jardine, 'Galileo's Road', 304.
56. The first citation is from Vasoli, 'Introduction', xxi, the next from N. Jardine, 'Epistemology', 690. On Zabarella, see Cassirer, *Erkenntnisproblem*, I. 134–41; Gaukroger, *Explanatory*, 167–9; L. Jardine, *Francis Bacon*, 54–8; Wallace, *Galileo, the Jesuits* especially chapters 2 and 5; and the essays by Edwards, Papuli and Risse, and books by Edwards, Mikkeli and Poppi indicated in my bibliography.
57. Mikkeli, *Aristotelian Response*, 174–6.
58. This, again, is discussed in *Descartes, Philosophy, and the Public Sphere* especially chapters. 4 and 8, and in Reiss, 'NeoAristotle and Method'.

assuredly drawn from Aristotle's once more non-committal ἰστορία: inquiry and/or account of inquiry. [59]

In this exact regard, it is not indifferent that Zabarella, even while he allowed rhetoric and poetry to be elements in a logical instrument of practical and civil philosophy (as opposed to the theoretical *artes* served by logic proper), yet rejected history as mere narration, not art and certainly not part of logic. Where later writers in a 'Baconian' tradition could even imagine a regulated 'science' of history, Zabarella retained the Aristotelian's distrust of any knowledge of material nature as ruled by abstract order. [60] The relation between experience, our perception of a material history, and mathematical rule that others were seeking and forging remained foreign to Zabarella, even though he was not less conscious than others of the seeming insuperability of the obstacles set before natural knowledge in their inherited ways of thought. To ever more thinkers, their solution was increasingly understood to be found in mathematics. And as it was, so the 'mathematical idea' was brought to areas of attention for which it had not originally been envisaged.

---

59. The changing meaning of ἰστορία/*historia* from Aristotle to late antiquity has been analyzed – or anyway catalogued – by Roger French in *Ancient Natural History*. Changes in 'history' drew concomitant ones in both 'nature' and 'knowledge': no interpretation of which last, he argues, lets it be interpreted as in any way akin to what is now meant by 'science'.
60. Edwards, 'Jacopo Zabarella', for his views about history and the rest; Reiss, *Meaning*, 179–80, for the 'science' of history.

6   Bridging effects

For the relation and distinction of experience and history, rule and method were surely *not* foreign, for instance, to what Henry Wotton had in mind when he distinguished, presumably in the 1620s, between two ways of conceiving architecture or any art, 'the one historicall', the other 'Logicall, by casting the rules and cautions of this Art into some comportable Method'.[1] It is not that a person like Wotton intended by this second anything *stricto sensu* 'mathematical', but we certainly find here a clear distinction between a method of pedagogy and one of discovery. Equally to the point, what a Wotton meant by 'Method' was the result of debates for which, by 1620, the arts that had been of the quadrivium now offered the firmest ground. We can already see how this distinction adopted conclusions of a nearly two-century-long discussion. But the issues I want to dwell on in the last three chapters lie in the fact that for the traditional reasons suggested, the early stress on mathematics (arithmetic, geometry, trigonometry, algebra), as well as new discoveries in astronomy, were directly bound to debate in music, the fourth mathematical art (the case of the Galileis, father and son, being exemplary).

In turn – and this will be of increasing importance to my discussion – the bond linked matters right away to debates over the nature of the passions, the functioning of the senses, what is and is not beautiful, moving, attractive, and why and how. These links, not any vague philosophical influence, justify the phrase 'Cartesian aesthetics' that I have used elsewhere, and my setting Descartes as the end point of the present study, as I shall. It may matter, as well, that someone like Wotton was an almost archetypal representative of a particular notion of state, one that he sought to further as an extremely activist English

---

1. Wotton, *The Elements of Architecture*, in *Reliquiae*, 199. Wotton died in 1639. He was ambassador, scholar, provost of Eton, friend of John Donne, Paolo Sarpi, Isaac Casaubon, the mathematician and lawyer Alberico Gentili and the mathematician Viète. He was, that is, deeply acquainted with many of those involved in the tail-end of the debates that this book is following.

ambassador to the Venetian Republic and the United Provinces in the first two decades of the seventeenth century. He never hesitated to intervene in the domestic and foreign affairs of these states, always pushing things in the direction of what one might call 'Protestant Republicanism'. This, despite James I's absolutist tendencies, was the image England projected of itself, that was largely accepted in diplomatic circles and that ruled the country's alliances. Its connection with the kinds of civic humanism we saw associated in the first two sections with so many of these developments is clear enough, and the issue will return especially in the last chapter.

Now, whether or not we agree that Descartes was 'the chief author of the [mathematizing] mechanistic hypothesis as a total characterization of the relationship between the perceiving organism and the world perceived', it is certainly the case that subsequent thought has taken him to be such a starting point. [2] But our discussion so far suggests, rather, that the hypothesis in question was a clarification, extreme form, and summarizing statement of a much longer developing thinking about perception, discovery and knowledge. Descartes was no less an end point than an originating one. And every bit as much – or more – to my purpose is the fact that his first theoretical work was on the very topics we have begun to discuss: music, those effects we now call 'aesthetic', and mathematics: the 1618 *Compendium musicae*. It was directly linked to the debates we have been following.

Over the years, interest in Descartes' earliest theoretical treatise has been sparse, compared to the industries others of his writings have spawned: a book, some scattered essays. All at once, in 1987–90, two editions appeared, the historical emphasis of the one supplementing the theoretical weight of the other. [3] This reflects an ever wider growing attention to music theory and practice in early modern Europe. In the anglophone world, it is manifest in various projects to translate classical, medieval and Renaissance texts, as well as in an impressive series of works by H. F. Cohen, Ann E. Moyer, Claude Palisca, Gary Tomlinson, D. P. Walker and others. Kristeller's plea for work on medieval and Renaissance music has assuredly begun to be answered. [4] This work shows among other things that Descartes' early

---

2. Crombie, *Science*, 239.
3. Descartes, *Abrégé de musique*, trans. and ed. Buzon; *Abrégé de musique*, trans. and ed. Dumont.
4. Kristeller, 'Music and Learning' 142–62. More recently the same plea has been made to historians of science in Kassler, 'Music'. The mutual ignorance of such areas of study and interest is always startling. For the other writers mentioned, see bibliography.

choice of field in which to exercise his theoretical genius was neither aberrant nor unfamiliar.[5] Music focused discussion of mathematical method and practice, and crossed over into many other areas of concern, psychological, civil, aesthetic, to name only some of those on which we have already touched.

The *Compendium* represented thinking Descartes completed between his Jesuit and legal education and the writing of the *Regulae* and the *Geometry* (neither of which can be accurately dated, but the first were certainly started by 1619), between his liberal studies and later scientific explorations. In the 1616 dedication of his law theses, Descartes wrote of forsaking liberal studies – grammar, history, rhetoric and poetry – in favour of law. He had, he told his lawyer uncle, set his lips to the *'nectareis liberalium artium fontibus'*. 'Rather than quenching [his] thirst, they made [him] thirsty to know more', so he had searched 'the vast lake of the sciences [*scientiarum aequor vastissimum*] and the rivers that flow from it'. At last, only in the 'pure fountains of [his uncle's] virtues and [law] learning' had he found satisfaction.[6] By 1618, less than two years later, his views of jurisprudence had clearly changed. Music was, in fact, the perfect bridge to go from letters to the 'marvellous science' whose discovery he foresaw in winter 1619. The passage typifies the major change, I am suggesting, in what were thought the sources of rational knowledge.

For by the late sixteenth century, music theory in general sat neatly in the midst of the arts and sciences. On this fundamental development hangs the further part of my tale. Since antiquity, although a member of the mathematical arts, music had been held to lie athwart them and ethics, pedagogy and natural philosophy, all training of body and mind. No one could be considered educated who lacked music. Indeed, for one ancient tradition, the *polis* itself would decay in the absence of such *harmonia*. Throughout the Middle Ages, both church and court maintained a tradition of music, but with considerable changes: neither any longer involved the old *paideia*. For the one, music was a source and form of prayer and praise, for the other, much a matter of entertainment. At the same time, as far as education was concerned, music now lay well within the quadrivium, in many ways connecting *its* arts, but not extending outside them.

---

5. Pirro (*Descartes*, 1–2) has noted how the very title, *Compendium musicae*, was common from the fifteenth century. He gives eight or so samples between 1415 and 1609, mostly instructional manuals in singing. A 1588 *Compendio della musica* by Oratio Tigrini summarized Gioseffo Zarlino's teachings. It sums up developments, we will see, and leads neatly into Descartes' and later discussion.
6. Descartes, 'Licence', 126–7.

Slowly this changed again as old texts were rediscovered, reinter-
preted and eventually put to wider service. Music came to traverse the
arts in new ways and to new purpose. In the modern era, not only
Descartes interested himself in music theory, played instruments, eval-
uated music's effects and read the ever-growing library of its
commentators. Music, as Castiglione had asserted a century before him,
was an essential civilizing accoutrement of gentle men and women. It
became very much more.

From the fifteenth century and the rediscovery of many ancient
writers on music, several issues had become central. Principal were the
efforts to understand the nature of Greek music and to elaborate a
mathematics enabling a rational comprehension of modes, harmony,
pitch, tunings and the rest. In this area, music thus overlapped many
of the preoccupations we have been seeing as now basic to mathematical study and instruction. Beyond these, three further issues were
of fundamental concern. Ancient writers were unanimous that music
had manipulatable effects on its recipients. Although sixteenth-century
writers agreed that modern music gave no clear evidence of such
miraculous effects as had been claimed for ancient music (even as they
endlessly reiterated them), they became obsessed with finding, again
mathematically if possible, just how music affected its hearers: both in
what way and by what means it did so. This was the second issue. But
the affecting, thirdly, was not at all casual. It involved the motion of
the passions or affections of the soul, themselves related to the humours
and their associated temperaments. So the obsession was tied in with
debates about catharsis and imitation. They wondered, indeed, what it
meant to call music mimetic, what kind of 'representing' was in question. Fourthly, but incorporating all these issues, they fought anxiously
over the relation between words and music.

This last question deeply involved both theory and practice. Since
public music (whether in church, school or court) was mainly singing,
the relation between poetry and the music to which it was set was
much debated. Should music capture rhythm and rhyme? Should it just
follow its own patterns more or less indifferently to the words, such
that words would, as it were, be adapted to the music rather than vice
versa? Should it be subordinate to words? Were they somehow, in
source, meaning or effect, coincident? Ancient theorists argued that
the different modes had different effects on listeners, and their analyses
assumed verbal accompaniment. Greek tragic *choroi* were said, for
instance, to use the solemnity of the Dorian and Mixolydian modes
further to arouse feelings of pity and fear, and although modern inter-
preters had no way of knowing what relationship was supposed to hold

between words and music, debate about that was central to the discussion of tragedy and the creation of opera (for explanation of Greek modes, see below, pages 190–1). Theoretical claim and practical concern combined. By the late sixteenth century it was widely agreed that music should affect its public by capturing the mood and temper of the verse it set. Claudio Monteverdi became famous for his achievement in this regard.

If music did affect its hearers in some explicable way, and if, at the same time, the relations called notes, tuning, pitch, rhythm and so on could be expressed in mathematical terms, should this not mean that the affecting itself was not just rational, but quantifiable? The emotional effect of the work of art, that is to say, should be able to be understood in some kind of mathematical terms: both because music itself followed mathematical rule and because human affections/passions belonged in a material world itself increasingly thought subject to such rule. There was thus no disjunction, *pace* most commentators, in Descartes' starting a scientific treatise on music theory by writing: 'Finis, vt delectet, variosque in nobis moveat affectus' ('its aim is to give pleasure and move in us divers affections'). We will actually find this to be a revised version of Horatian *delectare* and *prodesse*. Nor was it odd, again despite critics, that he went on to write of sympathetic vibrations and arousal of passions, of senses and their pleasure, of proportionality between an object and the sense to which it 'corresponded', and the like. [7] These concerns clearly picked up on late sixteenth-century preoccupations. They did so in another way. Introducing his science, we have just seen Descartes choose to echo a very familiar comment on art: 'Ars enim cum a natura profecta sit, nisi naturam moveat ac delectet nihil sane egisse videatur.' [8] Cicero was speaking chiefly of eloquence, but had already generalized the issue. Descartes would appear deliberately to have been placing his *Compendium* between 'art' and 'science'.

Twenty years after his law theses, in the *Discours de la méthode*, he would famously say that he had rejected letters for mathematics. Music theory was a basic step on that path. But in its context, the rejection was considerably more ambivalent than it appears today. I suggested that debates about singing had brought poetry and music together. Both were held powerfully to affect the passions, and so behaviour. Further, both could be seen to depend on number. They 'operate',

---

7. Descartes, *Abrégé*, ed. Buzon, 54–7.
8. Cicero, *De oratore*, II. 156 (III. line 197): 'As art came from nature, it would rightly be held to have done nothing if it neither moved nature nor gave pleasure' (my translation). Compare Pirro, *Descartes*, 3.

remarks Palisca, 'in the temporal realm, with recurrent rhythms, meters and pauses. Three parameters of sound – pitch, vocal timbre, stress – are common to the two media.' On these bases one might hope to be able to establish a rule of quantity. In 1501 Georgio Valla was writing in his *De expetendis ac fugiendis rebus* that music was an essential ground for all the liberal arts. He placed his analysis of the subject in the mathematical section of his encyclopedia, but stressed that even a grammarian must know music, because poetry is based on number and oratory on accent: 'therefore a knowledge of music is necessary, without a doubt, to learning the liberal arts, which are all dependent on speech'. [9]

In his 1525 *Prose della volgar lingua*, Pietro Bembo wrote of poetry very much in musical terms and again with reference to its effect. Having concluded that the sound of poetry was at least as important as its thought or image, he urged, as Palisca puts it, 'a new sensitivity to the sonic values of poetry'. Verse, he wrote, could be characterized by its gravity (*gravità*) or by its pleasingness (*piacevolezza*). These were themselves dependent on three elements: 'il suono, il numero, la variazione' ('sound, number, variation'). According to their nature, these elements gave to gravity its 'qualities of modesty, dignity, majesty, magnificence and grandeur', to pleasingness its qualities of 'grace, sweetness, charm, smoothness, playfulness and wit'. As Palisca adds: 'the rhythm, rhyme, number of syllables, accents, combinations of long and short syllables, the feeling of particular vowels and consonants, as well as the sonorous qualities ... all affect the gravity and pleasingness of a line of poetry or a sentence of prose.' [10]

Palisca points out the similarity of this analysis to later theories of how tonic accent or pitch in music directly communicate by, as it were, playing on the strings of the soul. His own example is that of Girolamo Mei, but such writers as Louis Le Caron, Pontus de Tyard and Francesco Patrizi would all echo the same or a similar view. In a letter of 1541, Giovanni del Lago likewise spoke of a relation between music and poetry in terms of rhythm and metre, asserting that musical cadences have to match exactly the movement of the verse: 'to mark the distinction of the comma, the colon, and the period ... Because the cadence in music is like a mark of punctuation', and so forth. [11]

9. G. Valla, *De expetendis* (Venice, 1501), 'De musica', I. 1. Quoted in Palisca, *Humanism*, 70. The previous quotation is from 396.
10. Bembo, *Prose*, 146; Palisca, *Humanism*, 355–6.
11. Lago, letter to Fra Seraphin, 26 August 1541, from Moyer, *Musica*, 137. Some elements of this section are drawn from my long review of this book (see bibliography).

We readily begin to see here how the mathematization of rhythm and metre could be conceived to have a relation to the understanding of poetic and musical effect on the passions of the soul wholly analogous to that implied in the mathematics of pitch and consonance. We also see how Descartes' supposed 'rejection' of letters was considerably more ambiguous, and ambivalent, than we are now likely or inclined to notice. Indeed, it was not at all strange that he would remain, we shall see, deeply interested in the fictive imagination and its writing 'of art'.

This series of associations opened the way for a new kind of theory. One could hope for a rational mathematical method to ground expressive arts, whose impact on the affections through the senses was held to give pleasure, change behaviour and thereby teach us something of the effects and implications of human action. Valla's comment and Bembo's analysis were, of course, a long way from the idea of any such method. But they do mark a shift, and Valla himself was careful, in following Aristotle's definition of the mathematical sciences as both related to and outside material things, to insist that they, with music among them, held 'medium quondam locum' ('a certain middle place') in the disciplines. This was said, again, in the *De expetendis*, a work that Crombie has been able to characterize as 'much the most important [piece of new scholarship] for the mathematical sciences and arts' of its age. [12]

At a time when those such as Bovelles were still struggling with a natural-language foundation for rational statement and discovery, and themselves turning away from grammar and rhetoric towards mathematics, but also when the latter sciences were themselves being deeply changed by practice-oriented research, such remarks indicate pressure on the same consensual division from the side of the mathematical sciences. The division of trivium and quadrivium, of language and mathematical sciences, seemed ever-less able to answer epistemological need. More to my point is that at the very time when mathematics was coming to be seen, in both practice and speculation, as grounding and grounded in universal rational rule, it was equally clearly being offered here, via music, as a way towards resolving the consequences of these and other pressures and tensions.

Perhaps, too, we should recall here that Lefèvre d'Étaples, like many of the others around him, had travelled in Italy and knew these late fifteenth-century thinkers not only through print and correspondence,

---

12. Crombie, *Science*, 165. The previous quotation is from Valla, *De expetendis* I.14, as quoted in Moyer, *Musica*, 98.

but in person. We should recall that he and his associates, too, were publishing and writing on music as well as on other areas of mathematics. Valla's *De expetendis* was an encyclopedic work treating all the arts and sciences; the French group's total output was encyclopedic in the same sort of way and with many of the same matters. Beyond those named in chapter 1, I do not know what the extent of personal acquaintance may have been, but there was certainly extensive intellectual cross-fertilization and sufficient acquaintance to mean that the same names we saw earlier will occur importantly as I discuss music further in the next chapter. They worked, it may be, in different ways and with different emphases, but their preoccupations and directions coincided.

In one sense, to be sure, tradition had always observed a relation between music and poetry – which last, we may again remember, was no longer in the trivium, however still linked to it as subject of a 'second rhetoric'. The historical claim had always been accepted that at least in Greece poetry and music had originally been a single art: 'the art of letters and that of music', Quintilian had written, 'were once united'. For his part, Isidore had related that 'the first, harmonic, division of music' pertained to vocal/verbal singing. [13] In this respect, the implications of the surviving six books of St Augustine's *De musica* could hardly have escaped anyone's notice, almost wholly restricted as they were to poetic metrics. Martianus Capella had also written that Harmonia's 'province comprises the knowledge of the proper regulation of measures applying to both rhythmic and melodic compositions', poetry and music. [14] In the course of the sixteenth century this historical claim was to acquire ever more argumentative importance. At the start of that century, however, it was altogether less interesting than a very different kind of argument based in mathematical reason.

Together these two arguments eventually gave the two ways to understand the arts, *historicall* and *logicall*, of which Wotton was to write in his *Elements of Architecture*, the division into teaching or communication and making or discovery: Zabarella's *ordo* and *methodus*. The function of *ordo* corresponded somehow, it would seem, to that of rhetoric. It ruled the delivery of the known, whether traditional or novel. *Methodus*, though (Zabarella's or not, but Ramus'

---

13. Quintilian, *Institutio* I. 169 (I. x. 17): music is the first art needed by the orator. Isidore, *Etymologiae*, III. xx: he contrasted harmonic to rhythmic, pertaining to wind instruments, and metric, concerning percussion.
14. Martianus Capella, *Marriage*, II. 359. The ninth book, 'Harmonia' (345–82), gave equal space to music – melody (359–72) and poetry – rhythm (372–81).

'geometric logic' rather than what *he* called 'Method'), structured rational discovery, production of the new.

In the bridging science and art of music, not surprisingly, such historical order and logical method began in elaborations on Boethius and recovery of various ancients, when Gaffurio printed his *Theorica musice* in 1492. Musically speaking, they continued in his 1496 *Practica musice*, a work that became renowned and deeply influential across Europe. It composed the middle volume of a trilogy, much of which was something of an update, we saw, of the Boethian/Pythagorean tradition. But in one area of his researches Gaffurio advanced arguments that seemed, if not quite new, at least sufficiently expanded to offer novel insight and fruitful directions. The second and fourth books of the *Practica* discussed mensural music and rhythmic notation. The first chapter of book 2 in fact analyzed poetic metres and rhythms, for 'poets and musicians', he insisted, both assign time values and give symbols for them. [15] Rhythm, he quoted Aristides Quintilianus as saying, 'consists of times in space' ('temporum spatio constat'), and according to Bede was to be understood as 'measured composition grasped not by metrical theory but by the number of syllables as judged by the ear ... Rhythm, indeed, seems quite similar to metre. And yet it cannot exist by itself without metre. For metre is theory with measure, rhythm is measure without theory.' [16]

So when musicians, like poets, assigned 'certain figures to the quantities of voices as proper and suitable names, by which they thus compose every piece in a conceived diversity of the measures of time (just as poetry in many feet)', they were, knowingly or not, incorporating theory in practice. [17] The theory (*ratio*) they were incorporating was not just that of rhythm and its notation – which was long-familiar. Gaffurio's expression of that idea was in some ways novel: metrics as both theoretical and practical; rhythm as both rational measure *and* its understanding – conception. But even newer was his extension of the

---

15. Gaffurio, *Practica mvsice*, aai r (II. 1).
16. Ibid., aaii r (II. 1): 'Rythmum interpretatus est modulatam compositionem non metrica ratione sed numero syllabarum ad aurium examinatam ... videtur autem rythmus metris esse consimilis. Et quidem per se sine metro esse non potest. Est.n. metrum ratio cum modulatione Rythmus modulatio sine ratione.' Palisca has noted the difficulty of *modulatio* (or its Italian transcription, *modulatione*) and its cognates, although they clearly refer to horizontal motion, not vertical relations: introduction to Zarlino, *Art*, xxiii.
17. *Practica* aai v (II. 1): 'Verum figuras quasdam veluti propria & congrua nomina: quibus concepta inde mensuratorum temporum diuersitate omnem conficerent cantilenam (nec secus que omne pluribus pedibus carmen) musici ipsi vocum quantitatibus ascripserunt.' As for Zarlino later on, *cantilena* here means a vocal composition: Palisca, introduction to Zarlino, *Art*, xxiii.

analysis of rhythm and its notation. In book 4, authorizing himself by reference to various ancient and modern mathematicians – Euclid, Campanus, Albert of Saxony and Giovanni Marliani – he elaborated on the rules of proportion. [18] But traditionally these rules had been confined to pitch. Gaffurio expanded them to measurement and notation of rhythm: 'Thus we propose a double understanding of musical proportion: first in the disposition of sound by consonant intervals (which is matter for the theorist), the other in the temporal quantity of those same sounds by the numbers of notation: which is held an active or practical question.' [19]

As Moyer observes, Gaffurio had systematically based rhythmic notation on the mathematical study of proportions: first putting it into the context of a Pythagorean tradition previously restricted to pitch alone, then into that of contemporary mathematical scholarship. He sought to subject the proportions of musical rhythm to the same rules as those of pitch. The rest of book 4 was then given 'to a detailed original exposition of Boethian proportion as applied to rhythm'. [20] Of course, Gaffurio did not downplay the importance of pitch – nor could he, since it was his model for the mathematical rationalization of rhythm. It indeed enabled him forcefully to present the more than familiar issue of the relation between music and the human passions. I must mention this here because it, too, as we saw when I wrote of Valla and Bembo (pages 159–60 above), was to be central not so much to the search for a new ground of reason *per se*, as to the effort to extend it towards a rational aesthetics.

In the tradition of the *laus musicae*, Gaffurio had begun his work by asserting the utility of music for training youth:

According to Marcus Tullius Cicero in the first book of the *Tusculan Disputations*, the musician and philosopher Aristoxenus claimed that a tension existed within the body itself just like that in vocal and instrumental music

---

18. Campanus de Novara was a thirteenth-century mathematican noted for a commentary on Euclid. Albert, first rector of the University of Paris, was a mathematician whose *De proportionibus* had just been printed at Venice (1487: it was reprinted at Bologna in 1502). Marliani, a contemporary Milanese mathematician and professor of medicine and astronomy at the university of Pavia (where Gaffurio also held a chair, we saw), was 'revered by his contemporaries as "a marvel of scientific attainments"': *Practica musicae of Franchinus Gafurius*, trans. and ed. Young, 165–6 notes 4–5.

19. *Practica*, eevi v (IV. 1): 'Inde duplicem proponimus musicae proportionis effectum: primum in sonorum dispositione per consona interualla (quod theorici est) alterum in ipsorum temporali quantitate sonorum per notularum numeros: qui activae seu practicae ascribitur consyderationi.'

20. Moyer, *Musica*, 77. I agree here with Moyer, though my examples are different or retranslated. For her entire analysis, see 75–8.

which is called 'harmony'; so from the nature and configuration of the whole body various modes [proportional vibrations] are caused like sounds in music. [21]

That music moved human affections was standard fare among Greek speculators. The idea was essential to the education of Plato's legislators in the *Republic* and to his exploration of music in *Timaeus*. Ptolemy explored in detail the 'harmonic' organization of the soul and its relation to music. Aristides did likewise. [22] But my interest is not just that of giving some sense of how the idea was taken over by everyone. It is, rather, that the kind of change assayed by Gaffurio suggested, however vaguely as yet, that some mathematization might potentially be involved. Such a view would be furthered by the practical and theoretical efforts to calculate rational temperament. These efforts to reduce the effects of variations of pitch from one scale to another by mathematical rationalization will be explored in chapter 8, because they were not finalized until two centuries later. But they may be borne in mind as another ingredient in these changes. The old was being transformed into something new in virtue not just of internal elaborations, but of a more general change in mentality, a habit of seeing a certain kind of rational order in the world.

To be sure, when Lefèvre's friend Ficino explored the notion of the relation between music and human nature at length in his 1489 *De triplici vita*, he stayed away from any such forms of rationalization, writing of the harmonies between music and the soul in familiarly vague terms: 'While therefore you temper the strings and the sounds in the lyre and the tones in your voice, consider your spirit to be tempered similarly within.' This took place by some sympathetic emanation or vibration. [23] These views would be echoed in the 1550s by a Le Caron and a Tyard. But long before, in his 1482 *Musica practica*, Ramos de Pareja was implying that the counterpoint rules generated exact rational effects in the 'souls of listeners', even though one might not be able to explain them or their generation in words. [24]

---

21. *Practica*, ai r (I. 1):

   quum Aristoxenus musicus atque Philosophus teste Marcho Tullio primo tusculanarum questionum: ipsius corporis intensionem quandam velut in cantu & fidibus: quae harmonia dicitur: sic ex totius corporis natura & figura varios modos fieri tanquam in cantu sonos affermauerit.

22. Ptolemy, *Harmonics*, 375–81; Aristides Quintilianus, *De musica*, 460–71, 489–94, 516–17.

23. Ficino, *Three Books*, 215 (II. xv).

24. Ramos de Pareja, *Musica practica* (Bologna, 1682), II. 1. 2, quoted and paraphrased by Moyer, *Musica*, 57.

Gaffurio, too, emphasized the relation between music and the passions – again citing ancient practice. 'Socrates, Plato and the Pythagoreans', he wrote at the beginning of the *Theorica*, ordered general musical education 'for moderating the motions of the soul under rule and reason [sub regula rationeque]'. Only those 'motus animi . . . qui rationi conueniunt ad rectam uitae pertinent harmoniam [which agree with reason belong to the right harmony of life]'. He went on: 'Every use of the musical voice is bestowed by the grace of harmony, and harmony, which has motions congruent and inborn to the courses of our soul, is useful to a man who uses the arts prudently [prudenter], not for pleasure devoid of reason [ad uoluptatem rationis expertem], as now seems the case.'[25] In the 1507 *Proemium* to his translation of Plutarch's *De musica*, Carlo Valgulio stressed how 'reason' could be 'tuned' to 'moral harmonies' of the 'divine', as 'the string mese to another string', and how such tuning was subject to mathematical analysis. He repeated the arguments two years later in his *Contra vituperatorem musicae*: 'we shall be able to tune, almost like strings, the contrary and diverse motions of our souls, and we shall always be able to make them consonant among themselves so that those who are lacking in reason by nature always would obey reason [rationem semper obtemperunt].'[26]

As one might expect, when Gaffurio further pursued the idea in his 1518 *De harmonia* (written by 1500), he sought to grasp harmonies as rational numerical proportions. He noted how Ptolemy (*Harmonics*, III. 5) had spoken of an exact relation, comparing

three simple intervals to the first three parts of the mind, namely, intellectual, sensitive and habitual. He gave the octave to the intellectual, the fifth to the sensitive, and the fourth to the habitual, because the fifth is closer to the equisonant octave than the fourth and is more consonant, as it were.

The correspondence further 'works' in that while habit does not suppose sense nor sense intellect, intellect subsumes the others if one reverses the order, and sense habit; just as the fourth does not involve the fifth, nor the fifth the octave, but the octave always supposes the fifth as the fifth does the fourth. Gaffurio detailed the relations by various applications of consonance species and various divisions of the mind or soul. He concluded his first chapter on these issues by remarking:

---

25. Gaffurio, *Theorica*, a[v] r (I. 1), *Theory*, 21–2 (I have slightly changed Kreyszig's translation).
26. Valgulio, 'Proem on Plutarch's *Musica* to Titus Pyrrhinus', in Palisca, ed., *Florentine* 31–44 (citations on 31); *Contra vituperatorem* as quoted and translated in Palisca, *Humanism*, 103.

For melody is an ornament of the mind and the intellect. Nor are those wrong who assert that parts of the mind are mutually joined according to arithmetic of an identical size and an increased equality; a corporeal magnitude is joined to geometric division because the parts of the magnitude are different. A living being arises from both, namely mind and body, according to which a harmonic division is appropriate. [27]

The 'emanations' or vibrations impacting upon the bodily senses and through them the mind therefore naturally affected the passions or affections marking that relation of mind and body. Some modern commentators incline to view these connections as 'simply' metaphors. [28] For reasons already evident, I disagree. They may seem so to us, but Gaffurio and the others intended them as nothing of the sort. What they were seeking was the same kind of rational mathematical order in music and the soul as Alberti or Piero could show in painting and in human vision, and as the practical mathematicians assumed lay under the material world more generally. Clearly enough, a field ripe for exploitation was presented here.

In his 1523 *Thoscanello de la musica*, Pietro Aaron took up many of these elements, putting music and poetry together, using much of the Pythagorean tradition, but echoing Gaffurio in giving about half of the work over to rhythm and its notation. Indeed, he followed Gaffurio far more closely than he acknowledged, in some places virtually simply putting him into Italian. Apart from the emphasis on rhythm, he also repeated the strong connection between poets and musicians. In this connection, he did, though, add an element absent from Gaffurio, if not from Ficino and many other contemporaries. For just as the listeners' emotions were affected and tuned by musical (and world) harmonies, so too were the musicians' and poets'. Indeed, without some such sympathetic emotion, people who held these views asserted, music would not achieve its effect. They connected them with another ancient idea: the poet's divine *furor*. With this, I think we can say that the last element of sixteenth-century discussion was in place – and of the solution to the language problem in the one area of human endeavour where language had always been thought to hold primary sway: that of the fictive imagination.

While ancient, the notion of *furor* had not been part of the Boethian tradition, and indeed it was much debated. Although, *qua furor*, it will

---

27. Gaffurio, *De harmonia*, 206–7 (IV. 17): chapters 17–20 (206–11) discuss these questions. He acknowledges Aristides as a source (207), who was indeed longer than Gaffurio on the subject. He and Ptolemy, recently discovered and translated, were of major importance in this Renaissance development.
28. For example, Moyer, *Musica*, 83.

not finally be of major importance for the precise development I am
tracing, it matters for the early stages as one more sign of the impact
of these discoveries and efforts. But in the long run it mattered
especially because it was tied to debate about mimesis and catharsis.
So by 1513 Raffaele Brandolini gave a public oration entitled 'De
musica et poetica' where he argued their similarity – unity – not through
any Gaffurian mathematical relation but through that of divine *furor*.
Poets and musicians transmitted divinely inspired truths, civilizing
influence, rewards of virtue and vice, and moral power. For him, in
fact, poetry and music were not just similar. They coincided. Poetry
and music were one (he was himself a performer of poetry). [29]

Earlier than this, though, and in a preface to Terence that all these
writers must certainly have known, Lefèvre's colleague Josse Bade had
made the same connection: 'we must be aware that the true poet is he
who is seized by a *furor* of a musical order, consisting in the consonance of sounds, which leads us to say that poets are inspired by the
Muses [who dwell in regions of cosmic harmony], whose priests they
are'. [30] Here the debate about words and music was urgently important. For Brandolini and Badius it had to do with the *effect* of music
and poetry on the passions or affections of their listeners. And we can
also see how they were claiming that *furor* functioned essentially for
purposes not so much of pleasure as of utility: *prodesse* rather than
delectare. *Furor* was not some kind of vague madness. It was *ruled* by
a harmonic order, and it aimed to create the same in its hearers. It,
too, was *explained* by the likeness of its effects to the rule underlying
its action (compare above pages 143–4).

---

29. This text presently exists only in manuscript, although Moyer's edition and transla-
    tion should soon appear (Binghamton, NY: Medieval and Renaissance Texts and
    Studies). For these comments, I am indebted to her *Musica*, 107–13.
30. [Badius,] *Josse Bade*: 'sachons que le vrai poète est celui qui est saisi d'une frénésie
    d'ordre musical consistant dans l'accord des sons, ce qui fait dire que les poètes sont
    inspirés par les Muses, dont ils sont les prêtres' (61: this is from chapter 1 of the
    Preface to Terence's comedies, which (49–119) discussed the origins of Greek and
    Latin theatre, compared comedy and tragedy, examined other commentators and
    considered the effects of drama and poetry).

One begins to see that by the early years of the sixteenth century Hans Keller's modern – contemporary – dictum that 'music is more a mode of thought than an art' was for many people literally true.[1] Lying as it did across spheres of knowledge, across theory and practice, and over the world and the human, some even saw in it something like access to a total mode of being; or at least, a vision of its ideal possibility. These elements – rhythm and metrics, pitch and consonance, relation between words and music, effects on the passions, purposes of such effects, matters of creativity and reception, historicization and of rational order – now remained central to discussion about music and poetry and their place among human activities in general and among the disciplines more particularly.

But issues concerning the effects of music and poetry on the affections and how such effects might operate or be achieved tended towards a repetitive impasse absent the aid of mathematics – an aid, as we will soon see again, that was, in the event, further urged by its primary use in another area of art, that of painting. Despite evident possibilities, such as Bembo and del Lago did not seem to get anything very exact from Gaffurio, no doubt because Gaffurio's own use of proportionality in discussing *affectus animi* and indeed the soul itself betrayed too much its origins in 'Pythagorean' mysticism and speculative numerology. So it mattered that by mid-century several major mathematicians had written at some length on music: Pacioli, Tartaglia, Cardano and others. Of course, mathematicians had always written on music in the quadrivium. But most of those who had done so were, exactly, 'quadrivialists', closer to what we would now think of as encyclopedists – most recently Giorgio Valla and Gregor Reisch, whose 1503 *Margarita philosophica* had made him, said Erasmus, an 'oracle among Germans'.[2] Pacioli and Tartaglia, at least, were

1. As reported in Harvey, 'Keller's Question', 12.
2. Various entries in Schmitt and Skinner, eds., *Cambridge History*, speak to aspects of Reisch's moral philosophy and psychology. De Morgan evaluates some 'peculiar' (as he calls them) aspects of his mathematics (*Arithmetical Books*, 4–8). His *Margarita*

foremost practical mathematicians (even though the former held university chairs): no one would call them 'oracles'. Cardano was evidently something else, but he prided himself above all on his mathematical abilities and discoveries.

One of the earliest was especially interesting, however, for combining non-mathematical arguments with mathematical ones. This was Lodovico Fogliano, who, in his 1529 *Musica theorica*, rejected Pythagorean tradition in favour of Aristotle (and Aristoxenus). [3]

Aaron had downplayed mathematical analysis of pitch and consonance, though not that of rhythm, in favour of expression. Fogliano tied mathematics to sense perception itself. He defined consonance less by ratio than by hearing: 'Consonance is a mingling of two sounds distant by height and depth pleasing to the ears; and dissonance, the contrary of consonance, is the mingling of two sounds distant by height and depth displeasing to the ears.' [4] Sound was generated by the vibrating motion of air, as Pietro d'Abano had long since taught. But as he had also held, like Themistius before him and Gaffurio in the 1492 *Theorica* later, the air striking the ear was not the same as that where the 'sound' originated. [5] This created a (properly Aristotelian) problem of continuity. To resolve it, Fogliano argued that what we called 'sound' was not coincident with the air, nor with the body moving the air, nor with the motion itself. Rather was it an affective quality existing as sound only in and for the ear. He proved this by Aristotelian syllogism and a claim of experienced effect:

Sound is an affective quality coming from the violent and rapid motion of the air, having its being in equal measure with it. It is called 'affective quality' because whatever has power to move sense is an affective quality: sound can move sense; therefore it is an affective quality. It is said to come from 'violent and rapid' motion because not any motion causes or can cause sound, but only if it is violent and rapid – as we learn from experience. [6]

Gaffurio had discussed the nature of sound at length in his *Theorica*. Comparing ancient views, he left the issue undecided and approved

had been edited by Oronce Fine in Paris in 1523 (rpt. Basel, 1535 and 1583): see Crapulli, *Mathesis*, 10 n. 3.

3. Palisca, *Humanism*, 20–21.
4. Fogliano, *Musica* XVro (section 2. 2): 'consonantia est duorum sonorum secundum acutum & graue distantium: auribus amica commixtio: & que dissonantia consonantiae contraria: est duorum sonorum secundum acutum & graue distantium: auribus inimica commixtio'.
5. Palisca, 'Science', 61–3.
6. Fogliano, *Musica*, XV v (section 2. 2):

sonus est passibilis qualitas proueniens ex motu aeris uiolento ac praecipiti habens esse in aequali mensura cum illo: dicitur autem passibilis qualitas: quoniam:

Boethius' compromise that whatever sound was, sense and reason were the *judges* of its effect. But he made no doubt that reason was superior: 'For, indeed, in the same manner as the ear is affected by sounds or the eye by sight, so is judgment of the mind affected by numbers or by continuous quantity.' [7] Forty years on, going beyond Gaffurio's proportional *analogy* of senses to their objects as reason to numerical quantity, Fogliano urged the primacy of sense experience even as he assimilated numerical ratios and Euclidian geometry to it. By doing so, he said, he wanted to divide the monochord 'in a new way, as it were by sense and materially [*nouo modo quasi secundum sensum: & materialiter*]': one that will function 'by art and science [*arte & scientia*]'. [8] Sound was *not* number, but its motion and rational effect might be described *by* number.

One wonders, here, whether the problem of discontinuity that seemed to have brought Fogliano to this 'solution', to somehow integrating matter, senses and rational calculation, did not belong to a thought pattern that European historians habitually claim differs from – indeed, not seldom opposes – that now taken as marking the 'Renaissance'. Erwin Panofsky suggested, for example, that such discontinuities characterized spatial perception and understanding *before* the Renaissance, and he argued that the 'development' summed up in Brunelleschi's and Alberti's work was 'the great evolution from aggregate space to systematic space'. In antiquity, he wrote, space was not 'a homogeneous and infinite system of dimensional relationships', but was composed of 'the juxtaposed contents of a finite vessel'; and while the Middle Ages had gone some way to reorganizing the 'succession of forms' ordering space, producing 'superposition and juxtaposition', making its elements 'partly the contents, partly the components of a coherent spatial system', no post-Aristotelian space yet existed such as could be the object of a single homogeneous and systematic measurement. [9]

---

quicquid potens est: immutare sensum est passibilis qualitas: sonus potest immutare sensum: ergo sonus est passibilis qualitas: Dicitur: proueniens ex motu aeris uiolento ac praecipiti: quia non quilibet motus causat aut causare potest sonum: sed tantum violentus & praeceps: ut patet per experientiam:...
Compare Moyer, *Musica*, 144.

7. Gaffurio, *Theorica*, c[v] v (II. 4), *Theory*, 66. In full: *Theorica* b[vi] v-cii v (II. 1–2), c[v] r-v (II. 4), *Theory*, 50–5, 63–6.
8. Fogliano, *Musica*, XXXIII r (Sect. III. 1).
9. Panofsky, *Perspective*, 65, 44, 48. No single-point linear projection was – or could be – conceived in Graeco-Roman Antiquity, he argued: Euclid explicitly denied it and a contested passage in Vitruvius cannot be read to do otherwise (35–45). Both claims have been proven inaccurate: Decio Gioseffi long ago threw doubt on the second (in *Perspectiva artificialis*, a work I have yet to see but must indicate). Richard

Fogliano (in a different area of attention) would complicate this linear evolutionary view: spatial discontinuities became the foundation of a 'rationalization' of the senses that otherwise seemed to be treading a path not dissimilar to that proposed by Panofsky in pictorial art. These pretty traces of 'one damn thing after another' would yield to complex swirls, interminglings, and overlappings. Fogliano's 'rationalized' sense perception actually depended on much 'older' conceptions and perceptions of the world and its material organization. And even in the directly spatial picture, we will need to complicate matters. We may come to see that Alberti's much controverted *historia* marked exactly the same dilemma (a disturbance in the neatness of a commonly accepted chronology that goes far to explain the controversy). [10] This would be another case of old structures of thought being turned to renewed purposes, incorporated into new ways of analysis and practice. Patterns of the mind, patterns of the world, patterns of social action meld and change and adjust one another.

A similar view to Fogliano's was adopted later by Cardano, who urged that the effect of music on the emotions did not depend on proportions, but on the way proportions were perceived: 'it is sufficiently clear from our discussions of beauty', he wrote in the 1574 *De Musica*, 'that the simplest proportion is the most pleasing to the ears'. [11] For this pleasingness Cardano referred to his analysis of the *De subtilitate*, where he had written:

Truly, every sense especially enjoys things which are recognized; those recognized things are called consonance when heard, beauty when seen. Therefore, what is beauty? A thing perfectly recognized; for we cannot love things which are not recognized. Vision perceives those things that stand in simple proportions: duple, triple, quadruple, sesquialtera, sesquitertia ... Certainly there is

---

Tobin has shown how Panofsky misread Euclid and that fourth-century BC Greek practitioners of perspective had access to both curved and plane projection methods ('Ancient'). I owe these references to Ernst Gombrich ('Icon', 30, cols. 3–4). They do not undermine my argument. Gombrich himself took Gioseffi's (and now Tobin's) point while noting perspective as neither natural nor universal but cultural (*Art*, 243–87). My concern is the simultaneity of diverse ways of conceiving and just what diversities become thus simultaneous, but no less their ways of mingling, their relative weight in cultural organization at a given historical moment, and their relation to other processes in that organization.

10. Damisch argues that the idea of such a uni-directional and singular chronology is anyway fundamentally inexact (*Origine*, 17–20: for example, but the whole work is partly intended to demonstrate this inexactness, replacing a familiar tale of perspective with a new one; 34–43 directly discuss this side of the argument). For allied criticisms of Panofsky's essay, see Wood's introduction to his English translation, 15–24, and its references, 74–5, targeting the theoretical coherence of Panofsky's argument more than its historical accuracy.

11. Cardanus, *On Music*, in *Writings*, 73 (chapter 1).

delight in recognition, sadness in non-recognition. Further, things are not recognized when they are imperfect and obscure; they are boundless, confused, and indeterminate. Those things are boundless that cannot be known; therefore the imperfect cannot delight, nor be beautiful. Thus, whatever is commensurate is beautiful, and wont to delight. [12]

All depended on perception, on *knowing* and *how* one knew: nor did Cardano accidentally use as his standard of beauty simple musical proportions: octave (2:1), octave and a fifth (3:1), double octave (4:1), fifth (3:2) and fourth (4:3). 'We find beautiful only what we know,' as André Pirro summed up Cardano's discussion, and 'we know only what we perceive as ordered.' [13] Here is yet another firm echo of an idea of knowledge shared, for example, by Ramus.

Setting Fogliano's views with Cardano's, one could hope to find a way mathematically to describe such sense perception of proportions. Inasmuch as proportions might be experimentally measured in the motion of air, and as the perception at issue *was* Fogliano's *passibilis qualitas* – quality affecting the passions, a quality inasmuch as it *was* associated with the passions – one might hope to achieve a measurement of emotive affect, of that proportionality between an object and the sense it affects to which I referred in regard to Descartes earlier (page 159 above). Cardano further justified his claim about proportions by recalling the common argument of antiquity that all perception, not just that of the beautiful, depended on a recognition of order. [14] Because mind was imprinted with the divine order, it recognized sounds (here) imprinted with the same order: the simpler they were the 'better' they were and, as we saw, even the more beautiful, because they were easier to perceive. One might thus hope to attain a mathematization of beauty.

It is at this point that questions of the relation of mathematics to the 'good' might enter, and not anywhere in regard to 'pure' mathematics – from whence, we saw at the end of chapter 4, any such eclectic connection had been explicitly rejected by the late sixteenth century. And we shall see towards the end of chapter 8 that such questions did indeed come back into account, precisely in regard of and by

---

12. *De subtilitate libri XXI* (Paris: Gulielmus Rovillius, 1559), 494: quoted and trans. Moyer, *Musica*, 161–2.

13. Pirro, *Descartes*, 26–7: 'On ne trouve beau que ce que l'on connaît, on ne connaît que ce que l'on appréhende ordonnément.'

14. Pirro (ibid., 26) cites Plato, Quintilian and Augustine: 'Nihil est inordinatum quod sit pulchrum', wrote the latter in the *De pulchro et apto*. The same claim had been echoed by Dürer in his book on human proportion: 'Things that agree in symmetry together are considered beautiful' (*Writings*, 246). Here, too, a 'geometry' was taken to underlie such symmetry.

reference to a concept of 'rationalized music', itself then directly associated with ideas of right moral order and legitimate political society, just as 'literature' was.

Years before, Gaffurio had already placed simplicity of beauty in the context of a discussion of pitch and rhythm, concluding of the former: 'When you consider the parts of the body, those which impart beauty seem to fit a proportion of consonant intervals.' [15] Mathematics certainly had little to do with his more historically inclined *De harmonia*, which would relate more, once again, to issues of communication and teaching than to discovery. But they had much to do with painting, that other activity of the fictive imagination already mentioned where the hope for a rational mathematical method to ground expression, to explain and indeed achieve affective impact, and to calculate pleasure, effect on behaviour, and didactic expectation, was by then in fact rather farther advanced. And here, too, a growing importance was being placed on the *perceiver* as the locus for understanding how a work of art might mean and have beauty.

For even before the changes in musical thinking, painting had faced similar pressures. The slow development of perspective effects throughout the thirteenth and fourteenth centuries, in the work of Cimabue, Giotto and the Lorenzetti brothers, with Jan van Eyck's painting and Brunelleschi's experiments early in the fifteenth century, had culminated in Alberti's *De pictura* (*c.* 1435). This set out those mathematical and geometrical rules of perspective that have been too much analyzed, discussed and adjudged a defining moment in the Renaissance rationalization of space and its establishment of the subjective individual – who perceived and manipulated, it has been endlessly asserted, from a self-organized single centre of will and attention. Alberti also argued, however, that neither proportional size nor geometric satisfaction but '*historia*' most 'satisfied the intellect'.

What was *historia*? It named a pleasing ordering of planes rendering bodies and their relations so as to communicate story and emotion. This way of putting things may well remind us more of what Fogliano later drew from spatial discontinuities than of notions about homogeneity. And their purpose was an effect on the senses and on the passions: ordered planes, that is to say, like sound, were a *passibilis qualitas*. The best *historia* 'captivates the eye of the learned or unlearned spectator with delight and motion of the soul [cum voluptate et animi motu]'. It must have abundance and variety, yet such simplicity and clarity as tragic and comic poets achieve with their few

15. Gaffurio, *De harmonia*, 208 (IV. 18).

characters. When those painted show most clearly the 'motion of the soul [animi motum], then will the *historia* move the spectators' souls [animos deinde spectantium movebit historia] . . . These motions of the soul are known from motions of the body'. [16]

The geometrical rules of perspective, then, were established here specifically to formulate a *narrative* whose order, however systematic and systematizing, was explicitly based on difference, just as would be Fogliano's music (and Piero's mathematical works may be no less multiple). [17] At the same time, its aim was that of moving the passions of the soul: those 'motions of the soul, that the learned call affections, such as anger, grief, joy, fear, desire, and others of the sort'. Painters would learn these from experience and by associating with 'poets and orators'. [18] They expressed these passions in perspective painting, whose *historia* conformed to the rules of pleasing beauty that Alberti noted elsewhere as 'a form of sympathy and consonance of the parts within a body, according to definite number, outline and position, as dictated by *concinnitas*, the absolute and fundamental rule of Nature'. [19] The likeness of this definition to Cardano's later one can hardly be missed – nor can the fact that perspective gave priority to the fixed place of the *observer*'s eye as music theory eventually emphasized the listener's role, and as poetics not seldom picked out the reader's (Bembo) or also the listener's (Brandolini). But the priority in question was that of a mediator, not an operator: the ultimate purpose was to tune the passions and organize the imagination of the *public* in a fundamentally public sphere.

Alberti's work was followed by Leonardo's and by Piero's *De prospectiva pingendi* (1470–80), which specified this spectator's eye as the first element in perspective. We have already seen one of the two mathematical treatises that Piero also wrote. They had wide influence thanks to their unacknowledged inclusion in two books by Pacioli, himself credited with introducing Alberti's and Piero's perspective ideas to Dürer – who issued his own writing on the topic in 1525. [20] When Pacioli printed his *Divina proportione* in 1509, his title page

---

16. Alberti, *On Painting*, 72, 78, 80. I translate more literally, checking, too, Alberti's 1436 Italian text: *Della pittura*.
17. On Piero, here, see Damisch, *Origine*, 18–19.
18. Alberti, *On Painting*, 82 ('motus . . . animorum, quos docti affectiones noncupant, ut ira, dolor, gaudium, timor, desiderium et eiusmodi'), 94.
19. Alberti, *Art of Building*, 303 (IX. v). I treat *historia* at more length, especially as it relates to affections of the soul and to ideas of human being, in this book's companion, *Mirages of the Self*.
20. Dürer, *Painter's Manual*. For Pacioli, introduction 12–13, 21–4, 27–31. On Piero and Pacioli, see M. D. Davis, *Piero della Francesca*, 98–123. See also pages 141–3 above.

dedicated it to 'students of philosophy, perspective, painting, sculpture, architecture, music and other mathematical matters'. Indeed, Pacioli also made contributions to the mathematics of music. All these connections clearly matter. Painting, music, and to a lesser degree poetry, were now held to have mathematically analyzable effects on spectator and listener.

At a nearly anecdotal level, consciousness of such relations is borne out in the fact that the earliest imitations of Giorgio Vasari's *Lives of the Artists* (1550) would be Bernardino Baldi's biographies of mathematicians (written mostly in the 1580s but not published – and then only in part – until the 1870s and eighties). [21] Strict mathematical analyses of perspective would gradually move towards and into optics. [22] In much the same way, mathematical analyses of music would create the science of acoustics. As far as the *affective* impact of music and painting were concerned, *mathematical* rule would tend towards the metaphorical: but that development still lay very far in the future. For the present, Leonardo expressed a widespread view when he began his manuscript treatise on painting as a science by saying:

Science is that mental analysis which has its origin in ultimate principles beyond which nothing in nature can be found which is part of that science ... no human investigation can be termed true science if it is not capable of mathematical demonstration. If you say that sciences which begin and end in the mind are true, this is not to be conceded, but is denied for many reasons, and chiefly the fact that the test of experience is absent from these exercises of the mind, and without it nothing can be certain. [23]

But now, caught up in this mathematico-logical approach, and no less important than it, was a historical use of Aristotle and others. For by the late fifteenth century, and even more by the 1540s, it was inevitable that these arguments would be linked to debates over 'Aristotelian' mimesis and catharsis. [24]

No less than painting or poetry, music achieved its effect by 'imitation'. Already in 1489, Ficino urged his readers to 'remember that song is a most powerful imitator of all things. It imitates the intentions and passions of the soul as well as words; it represents also people's

21. Hay, introduction to her *Mathematics*, 2–3; and Jayawardene, 'Renaissance', 190–3.
22. See, for example, Field, 'Perspective'.
23. Leonardo, *Treatise*, no. 1.
24. The *Poetics* was known from 1258 through Hermann the German's Latin translation of Averroës' Arabic commentary. Giorgio Valla's 1498 Latin translation of the Greek was largely ignored. It was Alessandro Pazzi's 1536 translation that became the basis for the flood of commentary during the second half of the century. On this, see, for example, Reiss, 'Renaissance Theatre', and, in the same volume, Javitch, 'On the Assimilation'.

physical gestures, motions, and actions as well as their characters
[*mores*] and imitates all these and acts them out so forcibly that it
immediately provokes both the singer and the audience to imitate and
act out the same things.' [25] This sort of argument could lead to Badius',
Aaron's and Brandolini's view of poetic *furor*. More importantly, it
tended to complicate the idea of music's effect.

Aristides had explained that, unlike poetry, music created its *mimesis*
'by words and by images of actions, and through agents that are not
static or fixed in a single pattern, but are alive, and alter their form
and their movement to fit every detail of what the words express'.
These agents were melody, rhythm and harmony. [26] The argument came
from Plato rather than Aristotle, but one can easily see how the two
could be reconciled – or anyway their differences elided. Just so, in a
January 1560 letter to Piero Vettori, just then finishing his commentary on the *Poetics*, Gioseffo Zarlino's sometime opponent and
Vincenzo Galilei's friend, Girolamo Mei first tried to clarify the matters
of imitation and purgation by elaborating on Aristotle's distinction of
the former in terms of medium, object and manner. [27] Melody, rhythm
and harmony were medium; intentions, passions, gestures, actions and
so on were objects; the alteration of form and movement was
manner. Cardano also drew on the *Poetics* for the kinds of mimesis
of 'artistic music' – 'manner (*modus*), sense (*sensus*) and sound (*sonus*)':
the last two corresponding to object and medium. But his claims, too,
about the 'expiative and purgative force' of music through its arousal
of 'strong emotions' and passions ('humility and pride, excitement and
calm, joy and sorrow, and cruelty and tenderness') could equally have
come from Aristides or Ficino. [28]

The discussions on imitation, we begin to see, easily shaded into
those about catharsis, especially where music was concerned.
Arguments about *what* was being imitated and *how* merged with those
about effect. Music, painting and poetry moved by affecting the human
passions, as almost all now agreed. Music, Le Caron wrote, 'educates
manners, softens anger, calms irritations, and tempers ill-ordered
passions'. It had the 'virtue of tempering and tuning *les afections de
l'ame*'. The 'wondrous effects of music' were such, added Tyard, that

25. Ficino, *Three Books*, 358–9 (III. xxi): 'Memento vero cantum esse imitatorem
    omnium potentissimum. Hic enim intentiones affectionesque animi imitatur et verba,
    refert quoque gestus motusque et actus hominum atque mores; tamque vehementer
    omnia imitatur et agit, ut ad eadem imitanda vel agenda tum cantantem, tum audi-
    entes subito provocet.'
26. Aristides, *De musica*, 460–1 (II. 4).
27. Palisca, introduction to Mei, *Letters*, 44–5.
28. Cardanus, *On Music*, 142 (chapter 36), 105 (chapter 18), 150 (chapter 39).

'the passions are moved and calmed by its sweet ravishments [les passions par ces doux ravissemens esmuës et appaisées]'. It 'tunes the affections, passions and corporeal and intellectual powers one with another, and does for the Soul's dissonances what purgation or correction of superfluous humours does for the restitution of health' (shades here still of old Deschamps). [29]

Like everyone else, Le Caron and Tyard emphasized that such effects were attained by 'number and measure'. The passions were tuned by the 'numbers, measures, rhythms and proportions of [the poet's] verse' as well as by the 'well-proportioned harmony of the measures and consonances' of a piece of music, Le Caron insisted, while Tyard noted how mathematicians could discover 'the numbers, weights and measures thanks to which the slightest [musical] differences are apparent'. [30] Galilei fulminated in his 1581 *Dialogo della musica antica et moderna* against modern music just because it had lost its ability to provoke such effects, deserting all hope of achieving the sympathies that everyone spoke about. Ancient music, he wrote, worked on the passions through the simple consonances of monodic song and its manifest melody. Modern music had set such consonances ajangle and confused them by its polyphonic mixing of modes, where effects merely cancelled one another out. The simplicity of mathematical rule had been undercut, true and exact proportion indistinctly muddled. [31]

Others, Cardano sometimes amongst them, thought that reason could not always hope to grasp such effects. 'It is necessary', he averred, 'to consider why a connection of tones which is pleasing to the ears does not have a rational explanation.' The triple usefulness of music – 'instruction and study, ... cleansing of the spirit, ... spending time pleasurable in leisure' – operates by affecting those 'emotions ... appropriate to action and ... those almost divine virtues suitable for intellectual endeavour'. [32] The idea that purgation was not a *logically* explicable effect, however it might be comprehensible medically or otherwise, was not uncommon among many of those who discussed catharsis.

Girolamo Fracastoro even apparently dismissed the notion of rational mimesis: a much rarer argument even quite early in the sixteenth

---

29. Le Caron, *Dialogues*, 255 ('Valton', dialogue 3), 278 ('Ronsard', dialogue 4); Tyard, *Solitaire second*, 171, 238.
30. Le Caron, 'Ronsard', dialogue 4, 278; Tyard, *Solitaire second*, 171.
31. Galilei, *Dialogo, passim*. Bits of this text are in Strunk, ed., *Source Readings: Renaissance*, 112–32. Palisca has shown that Galilei got these particular ideas from Mei: *Letters, passim; Florentine Camerata*, 45–77.
32. Cardanus, *On Music*, 104–5 (chapter 18).

century. In his 1540 *Naugerius, sive de poetica dialogus*, he proposed 'beauty of expression as the distinctive end of poetry and criticize[d] the theory of imitation'. In 1586, Patrizi wrote that neither poet nor musician imitated in any of Aristotle's ways: a bard expressed 'ideas but no imitation or resemblance whatever'. Sound bore 'ideas' directly from a poet's imagination through a listener's ears to the soul, moving the same faculties and emotions as those from which they arose, 'with all the knowledge, fantasies, opinions and discourses associated with them'. In Palisca's words, he reduced 'communication from poet [or musician] to listener ... to intellectual, emotional and spiritual faculties addressing each other directly through the medium of sound'.[33] Here, we again find something akin to the thought we saw before as commonplace amongst such as Piccolomini and Ramus around the same time, to the effect that mathematical truths had to do with rational order and conceptual 'causes' rather than with 'real' material ones (dooming Zabarella a few years later to an Aristotelian cul-de-sac, having elected to 'choose' between syllogistic and mathematical truths).

I do not think there is deep disagreement, however, between those assured of mathematical rule and those seemingly less sure; and the same issue would recur in Descartes. For mimesis had been retuned by the debates about catharsis and redefined in terms of an expressive relation between artist, artwork and recipient. Effects were achieved because well-ordered music (for instance) 'imitated' or, more accurately, recapitulated the consonances of soul and mind. What was expressed and what gave pleasure was the sympathetic vibration of the affections, the soul's passions. Gaffurio had begun his *Theorica* with a pretty play on *corda*, the string of an instrument, and *concordia*, the agreement of pitches made up from a diversity of sounds. He was noting the phenomenon of sympathetic vibration. But there was a play, too, on *cor*, the heart and its emotions.[34] All agreed that to give pleasure of this sort and in these ways was an essential part of mimesis and catharsis. The pleasure lay in the tempering of body and soul.

In many ways, then, mimesis was less important than catharsis. What was 'imitated' might be actions and feelings, but only insofar as they *moved* similar affects in the recipient. The tempering in question did not simply *have*, but *was* a moral effect – Cardano's virtue. *Prodesse* and *delectare* in a real way now coincided. To say that the purpose of music and poetry was to please presupposed both beneficent effect and

---

33. Palisca, *Humanism*, 255, 405.
34. Gaffurio, *Theorica*, aiii v (I. 1), *Theory*, 14, and see Kreyszig's note 78 (which misses *cor*).

the ruled order of rhythmic and consonant proportions that made such pleasing and effect possible. The tuning of the soul thus corresponded to all those claims of reason earlier traced out: from Alberti, Piero, Gaffurio and Bovelles, to Fabri, Dürer, Fogliano and Tartaglia, to Ramus, Estienne, Cardano, Peletier, Le Caron, Jean-Antoine du Baïf, Galilei and so many others. Rhythm, metre, pause, pitch, timbre, stress, planes, angles, colour and passions were subject to a calculus of proportionality that should be able to tell us how effective an artwork was and how, indeed, it affected.

Reason and emotion (not to mention morality) came together, where music was concerned, in the work of Gioseffo Zarlino, whose status in the seventeenth century was akin to that of Gaffurio in the sixteenth. Insisting always on the rationality of music, his 1558 *Istitutioni harmoniche* set a level of scholarly musicianship that was widely influential: including, as many have observed, on Descartes. The text was printed four times during his lifetime, and more after his death in 1590. Like others, he divided music into method and history. Under the first was the study of sounding bodies, using mathematics and ideas of sense perception drawn from Aristotle and Aristoxenus. This would eventually, as Moyer points out and as we saw before, become the science of acoustics (just as the mathematical study of perspective moved increasingly back to optics). Under the second was the use of these principles in the study of music at different times and places, but also the study of the meanings people give to sounds. Once again we find the link between sound and language, more particularly, between music and poetry. Indeed, Zarlino made an immediate connection between music, language and rhetoric and between music, poetry and metrics.

Zarlino asserted that full emotional effect (accomplished by Fogliano's *passibiles qualitates*?) was attained by a necessary combination of harmony, metre and proper accompanying text. The precise effect was, however, no less dependent on the listener, since the passions and their motion had to do with the humours. These last elements allowed for a notion of changes in musical style (listeners were socially determined) and consequent changes in effect: although Zarlino still sought to balance eternal Pythagorean verities against such change. As he put it in the 1588 *Supplementi musicali*, music was still fundamentally mathematical – still 'in' the quadrivium – but 'history' had to balance 'reason and good method'. [35]

---

35. Moyer, *Musica*, 200–23. Compare Palisca, *Humanism*, 244–50, and, for the often acid debate with Galilei, 268–75.

Others emphasized Zarlino's historical and cultural aspects. Whatever their other disagreements with him, Mei and Galilei both urged that to grasp music's functioning demanded historical research and understanding, a study of music in relation to history and culture. They argued that music and poetry were inseparable both because their parts were theoretically similar and because they were *historically* bound together. Patrizi, too, asserted that music was wholly a part of poetics, and that the text had therefore to be given primacy: in varied sound the text carried those ideas of which we saw him write. Poetic texts carried rational thought and were able to be 'mathematically' analyzed into rhythm, stress and metre. In these ways poetry further guaranteed musical reason against that lack of rational explanation feared by Cardano. Combined with music, it confirmed both meaning and logical order. It enabled one to talk of a culture-bound phenomenon *at the same time* as urging its more general rationality: a combination basic to what I am terming 'Cartesian aesthetics' (not to mention later Enlightened reason) and whose development and importance we glimpsed at the end of chapter 5 and beginning of chapter 6.

That is another reason why the debate about the relation of words to music was so fraught throughout the century. That Nicola Vincentino should have devoted a chapter of his 1955 *Antica musica ridotta alla moderna prattica* to instruction in the proper placing of words beneath the music seems rather anodyne to us. [36] In fact it signalled a theoretical change in the relation between the two that had major consequences for practice. Indeed, this chapter was preceded immediately by one discussing the need for composers to heed the accent and stress of words in whatever language they were setting and make their music match them in pitch and rhythm of melody and in the harmonies they used. The aim, he insisted, was that music express the ideas, passions and affections uttered in the words. [37] Vincentino was urging a polyphonic music wholly at odds with the simpler monodic music later sought by Mei, Galilei and the *Camerata* of Giovanni Bardi. But he justified it on just the same grounds: faithfulness to history (here, Greek), adjustment of that history to contemporary conditions

---

36. Vincentino, *Antica*, 86 v–87 r (IV. 30). I think this case was first noted by Jeppersen; *Counterpoint*, 21.
37. Vincentino, *Antica*, 85 v–86 v (IV. 29). The last sentence is from 86 r. Michael Chanan (*Musica*, 111–15) avers that new precision of word placement had to do with music's spread into amateur hands because of print. When polyphony was the preserve of trained singers able to calculate placement themselves (anyway often working with the composer), imprecision hardly mattered. This suggests not that my claim is wrong, but that print and its commerce were complexly related to other debates and practices (not an unusual thought).

and needs, and primacy of rational understanding. At the same time, he would also be at odds with the gradual decrease in importance of the polyphonic madrigal that would occur for similar reasons. [38]

When Monteverdi issued his *Fourth Book of Madrigals* in 1603, his further 'development of a declamatory musical speech' angered purists. He replied in the preface to his 1605 *Fifth Book* that one should now quit Zarlino's *prima pratica*, 'in which harmony is "mistress of the words"' and adopt a new *seconda pratica*, ' "where words are the mistress of the harmony"'. [39] As his work grew more theatrical, so affective intent of words and music grew closer. A short anecdote may give a further idea of the importance of the issue. In 1589, soon after succeeding his brother in Florence, Duke Ferdinand de' Medici and Christine de Lorraine celebrated their marriage. The ex-cardinal had brought with him from Rome Emilio de' Cavalieri, who was to take over the organization of court culture from Bardi. Cavalieri composed the final ballet for the *intermedi*. In what one can only interpret as a piece of sarcasm at Bardi's expense, he made a point of having the poet Laura Guidiccioni write her words only after he had composed the music. [40] Even so, no more than the others did Cavalieri dispute the grounding of music and poetry in historical and cultural argument on the one hand, and in physical behaviour and mathematical calculation on the other. When du Baïf founded his *Académie de Poésie et de Musique* in 1570, its avowed aims were firstly to assure the union of music and poetry, secondly to rediscover the ethical effects of ancient music, and thirdly to institute a kind of university whose scientific ground would also be assured by virtue of music's mathematical core. [41]

Zarlino had begun the *Istitutioni* by writing of the invention and history of music. Simultaneously, he emphasized the 'certezza' and 'primo grado di verità' it possessed because of its place among the mathematical sciences. He further urged that music's centrality came from its rational accord with human and natural harmonies: 'And it is in truth a reasonable/rational thing; because nature consists in such proportion and temper that every like rejoices in its like, and desires it.' Music's purpose was to 'dar solazzo & dilettatione all'Vdito [to give pleasure and delight to hearing]' for no other reason than to perfect

38. Bianconi, *Music*, 21–5.
39. Ibid., 25; Chanan, *Musica* 116. The quotations are from the second.
40. Pirrotta, *Music*, 224.
41. Walker, 'The Aims of Baïf's *Académie de Poésie et de Musique*', in *Music, Spirit*; Yates, *French Academies*, gives the letters patent of the academy in an appendix (319–22).

that sense, as sight is perfected when it perceives 'vna cosa bella & proportionata [a beautiful and proportionate thing]'. Still, if music's first aim was to please (a claim destined to be a deeply misunderstood cliché of later aesthetic debate), its rational rule 'dispone l'animo alla virtù, & regola le sue passioni [disposes the soul to virtue and rules its passions]'. It further 'accustoms [the soul] to rejoice and grieve virtuously and disposes it to virtuous habits'. [42] To this end, he repeated Gaffurio's wordplay: tones and sounds, he said, arise from the 'chorde, which, as Aurelius Cassiodorus supposed, are so named because they move our hearts; a fact he shows very elegantly with the two Latin words chordae and corda'. [43]

Just as objects are pleasing (grati) and smooth (suavi) to their 'proper sense [propio sentimento]' according as they are 'proportionate [proportionati]' to it, so 'Musical science ... treats sounds and tones [voices?], which are objects proper to hearing. It examines only the harmony (as Ammonius says) that is born from pitches and tones [strings and voices?]; and considers nothing else at all.' These produce the now combined (and sole) purposes of music and other arts: 'per dilettare [delectare], & per giouare [prodesse]'. [44] Whether or not Zarlino was making a vague play on propio and proportionati, he was assuredly connecting the proportionality of object to sense with those mathematico-musical proportions that his treatise was discussing at length. Descartes took up these two proportionalities in the guiding 'Praenotanda' that began his treatise on music: 'the object in which the difference of parts is least is more easily perceived by a sense'. And 'we say that the parts of a whole object differ less among themselves according as the proportion between them is greater'. [45] His treatise as a whole analyzed the latter as they concern rhythm and consonance.

---

42. Zarlino, *Istitvtioni*, 4 (I. 1): 'Et è in vero cosa ragioneuole; poi che la natura consiste in tale proportione & temperamento, che ogni simile se diletta del suo simile, & quello apetisce'; 8 (I. 3): 'auezzarlo a rallegrarsi, & a dolersi virtuosamente, disponendolo alli buoni costumi' – 'non altramente', he went on, 'che fa la Ginnastica il corpo a qualche buona dispositione & habitudine; & anche a fine di potere con tal mezo peruenire alla speculatione di diuerse sorti di harmonia: poi che per essa l'intelletto conosce la natura delle musicali consonanze'.

43. Ibid., 279 (III. 71): '... chorde; lequali (como s'imaginò Aurelio Cassiodoro) sono in tal maniera nominate; percioche muoueno i Cuori; come lo dimostra con molta gratia con queste due parole latine Chordae, et Corda'. The reference is to Cassiodorus' *Variae*, II. xl.: 'Ad Boetium patricium', a.507.12.

44. Zarlino, *Istitvtioni*, 278 (III. 71): 'La musica scienza ... tratta de i Suoni, & delle Voci, que sono Oggetti propii dell' Vdito; và speculando solamente il concento (come dice Ammonio) che nasce dalle chorde, & dalle voci; & non considera tante altre cose.' For translations see Zarlino, *Art*, 264, and Strunk, *Source Readings: Renaissance*, 60.

45. Descartes, *Abrégé*, ed. Buzon, 57 (Praenotanda 4 and 5).

But he also insisted on the 'proportionality' between a sense and its proper object from the start.

'All the senses', he wrote, 'are capable of some pleasure [*delectatio*].' 'For this pleasure a certain proportion [*proportio quaedam*] is needed of the object with the sense in question. It follows, for instance, that the crashing of muskets or of thunder seems unfit for music, since it evidently damages the ears just as the excessive brightness of the sun looked at directly damages the eyes.' In fact, Descartes also drew this last example from Zarlino, who had followed his remark about objects being *grati* and *suavi* to the *propio sentimento* with the contrary case, that of 'our eye, which is damaged by looking at the sun, because such an object is not proportionate to it'. (Both could have got it, however, from Cicero, for example, who with others remarked that the music of the spheres was inaudible to human ears by the same incommensurability as made it impossible to 'look straight at the sun, your sense of sight being overpowered by its radiance'.) [46] Descartes added in his third Praenotandum that 'an object must be such as to fall on the sense with neither too much difficulty nor confusedly'. That the 'lines' of an object be more 'equal' is better than that they be overly complex. Simplicity and clarity of visible line applied no less to the musical organization of sound: arithmetical rather than geometrical proportions, because the differences are everywhere equal and tire the senses less (Praenotandum 6).

This insistence on proportionality and 'properness' recalls not only the claims made for mathematical discovery and ordered foundation in both music and painting, but also the researches in language with which we started. And we should remember, at the same time, that the need was not simply for an assured process of knowledge but also for secure public (and private) behaviour, some moral standard. We have already seen how the rational, 'mathematical', tuning of passions and mind more than touched on questions of moral effect. Terms we have been meeting, such as Zarlino's *costumi*, Le Caron's *moeurs*, Ficino's *mores*, others' *consuetudines*, were a humanist translation of Aristotle's *ethos* – 'character' – considered as public *presence*, with particular kinds of ethical responsibility and obligation. [47] A longish quotation from a work by a later writer than these,

---

46. Ibid., 56–7 (Praenotanda 1 and 2); Zarlino, *Istitvtioni*, 278: 'come si vede dell'Occhio nostro, ilquale riguardando nel Sole è offeso: perche tale Oggetto non è a lui proportionato'; Cicero, *De re publica* 272/3 (VI. xviii. 19). Aristotle had also observed the loss or blunting of hearing, sight and smell by stimuli too violent: *On the Soul*, rpt. in J. A. Smith, trans. *Complete Works*, I. 682 (429a31–b2).
47. Reiss, 'Renaissance Theatre'.

but who was already past thirty by century's end, can give us some idea both of how the concept of morality in question could be put in such rational terms, and of how seriously its *mathematical* (and musical) character was taken.

In 1610 Scipion Dupleix wrote a section of his *Éthique* on 'Virtue, and how moral virtue was not inborn but acquired by practice' – rational practice. His third chapter discussed whether '*la mediocrité*' of moral virtue (the fact of its being defined as a mean) 'corresponds to arithmetic or geometric proportion'. It is, he writes, the second. For it

is founded on the equality of reason [as 4 is ⅔ of 6 and 6 of 9, even though one is a difference of 2 and the other of 3], and on the fact that by reason and prudence one must fix the right mean for each of us by weighing properly all circumstances of persons, places, and times: it is by this proportion that one must fix it and not at all by an arithmetic proportion. Which must be chiefly observed and practised in distributive justice, obligated to measure rewards and punishments, taking into account the above-named circumstances. [48]

This may strike us as odd, and not very meaningful, but Dupleix was evidently assured that the mathematical claim would give his argument more weight. He had more than a century of thinking to back him up, and that the *Ethique* had been printed separately or as part of his *Corps de philosophie* more than twenty times by mid-seventeenth century indicates that such views were indeed still very much alive. So, too, do Marin Cureau de la Chambre's 1634 'Thoughts' on '*amour d'inclination*', that the passion of love was caused by motions in the body just like those of a lute's strings, ruled by proportion of length and vibration, as 'la Mathematique demontre' ('as Mathematics demonstrates'). Each passion, furthermore, was composed of specific movements and proportions. This was why different music provoked different passions. [49] Cureau's 'psychological' argument corresponded to Dupleix's social one. As the soul could be tuned according to harmonic proportions, so too could moral virtue and social (and

48. Dupleix, *Ethique*, 106–7 (the bracketed insert is from 106):

la mediocrité de la Vertu morale ... est fondée sur l'égalité de la raison, & que par raison & auec prudence il faut determiner la mediocrité qui nous regarde en balançant iustement toutes les circonstances des personnes, des lieux & des temps: c'est suivant ceste proportion qu'il la faut establir & nullement selon la proportion arithmetique. Ce qu'il faut principalement obseruer & pratiquer en la iustice distributive, laquelle doit mesurer les recompenses & les peines auec les sudictes circonstances.

49. Cureau de la Chambre, *Nouvelles pensees*, 69–79. These views, as far as I have looked, do not seem to be repeated in Cureau's later work on the passions, on human nature and on animal reason.

economic) justice. Indeed, this 'tuning' also served to *discover* what such justice and virtue *were*.

Zarlino singled out Fogliano as alone having truly grasped and analyzed right musical proportion. [50] Like others, he urged that the rational, mathematically analyzable relationship enabling music to affect the humours and move the human passions was so by virtue of the proportional relations *within* the object (sound) and of the similarly 'proportional' relations *between* the object and the sense (ear). These proportionalities were what made music pleasing, what made it an imitation (of nature and the passions), and what made it affect the recipient. *Of* nature, the passions could easily be aligned with the 'uniformity, wisdom, and rationality of nature' in which he believed so strongly. [51] As he summarized Zarlino's *Istitvtioni* in 1588, Orazio Tigrini also reviewed the entire tradition we have been following, and virtually urged people further:

Those who are of the opinion that musical composition is nothing other than a certain practice and that harmony is measured only by hearing are very wrong. While it surely seems that the whole origin of this science lies in the sense of hearing – it being clear, as Boethius says, that were there no hearing, there would be no way of talking about sounds [tones] – nonetheless all the rest of its perfection and power of knowledge lies in reason, which, founded on true and certain rules, can in no way be wrong. This is not so for the senses, since the same power of hearing is not given to all, nor is it always found to be uniform in one person. And so when Aristoxenes relies only on sense and denies reason, he commits many errors. Hence the Pythagoreans prefer the middle way: they did not give all judgment to the ears; even without them they discovered many things. That is why, even if harmonies are measured by hearing, despite that, [the judgment] by what distances they may differ between one another is certainly not enabled by the ears, whose judgment is blurred, but by rules and by reason. So sensation is like a slave, and reason like an owner. For indeed this science is one of the mathematical sciences, all of which are founded on true and certain rules, and are of the first degree of certainty. [52]

---

50. Zarlino, *Istitvtioni*, 279 (III. 71): Boethius' work was imperfect, he wrote, and once Gaffurio and Lefèvre d'Etaples were excluded as simply his commentators, Fogliano was alone in discovering 'le vere Proportioni de gli interualli Musicali', as author of a Latin work 'per mostrare con ogni verità le vere Proportioni delli nominati interualli'.

51. Palisca, *Humanism*, 245.

52. Tigrini, *Compendio*, 1:

Errano grandemente coloro, che sono di parere, che'l comporre della Musica non sia altro, che vna certa prattica; & che le Consonanze si misurino con l'vdito solamente; Percioche se bene pare, che tutto'l principio di questa Scienza consista nel senso dell'vdito: conciosia che, come dice Boetio, se non fusse l'vdito, in nessun modo si potria disputare delle voci; Nondimeno tutto il resto della perfettione, &

Such a series of claims about the relation between sense and reason, particularity and certainty, matter and understanding, individual perception and general rule further helped underline reason's singularity and universality, on which others would now elaborate, stressing even more its mathematico-logical ground. In 1585 Giovanni Battista Benedetti thus repeated Fogliano's analysis of sound and airwaves. But beyond assuming sound to be transmitted by airwaves, he now also supposed pitch to be caused by periodic vibrations and frequency of vibration to be inversely proportional to string length. It has been argued that Isaac Beeckman, Descartes' friend and addressee of his *Compendium*, was the discoverer of this last law. [53] The point is not to detract from the Dutch scholar's achievement, but to note how important technical mathematical research had become to the understanding of expressive effect. The emphasis now returned to music: with poetry inevitably part of any effect being explored there. The physics of sound might be separable from verbal *meaning* as such, but it was essential to any understanding of its actual effect (which was the point of Monteverdi's and others' innovations) – and therefore of what might be comprehended as beautiful, ugly or indifferent, and *known* to have a ruled impact on social 'justice' and individual affections – to think again of Dupleix and Cureau. A developed natural–philosophical logic had found its place.

la forza della cognitione consiste nella ragione; la quale fondandosi nelle vere, & certe regole, non può in alcun modo errare; il che non auiene così de i sensi, non essendo data à tutti vna medesima forza d'intendere, nè ritrouandosi quella nell'huomo sempre eguale. Et per ciò Aristosseno accostandosi solo al senso, & negando la ragione, commesse molti errori: onde i Pitagorici prefero la via del mezo [*sic*]: perche non diedero tutto'l giudicio alle orecchie; nè anco senza quelle furono da essi molte cose ritrouate. Per la qual cosa se bene le consonanze si misurano con l'vdito: con tutto ciò, di quali distanze siano tra loro differenti, questo non già all'orecchie, il giudicio delle quali è offuscato, ma alle regole, & alla ragione si permette; & così il Senso viene à essere, come seruo, & la ragione, come Padrona. Et se bene per essere questa Scienza l'vna delle matematiche, le quali tutte sono fondate nelle vere, & certe regole, & sono nel primo grado di certezza.

(I thank Daniel Javitch for verifying my translation.)
53. For Benedetti, see Palisca, *Humanism*, 258–65; for Beeckman, Buzon, 'Présentation' of Descartes, *Abrégé*, 14. Compare Buzon's 'Descartes' and 'Science'.

In the 1610s the French architect, engineer, musician and scholar
Salomon de Caus was organizing the marvels of Heidelberg Castle for
Frederick and Elizabeth Palatine, future parents of that Princess
Elisabeth who a generation later was to be so important for Descartes'
thinking. By 1621 Caus had to leave the Palatinate, subject now to
destruction by the very army of which Descartes had been a part in
1619/20. Caus eventually ended up at the court of France. Descartes
was to spend many years near and as a frequenter of the Palatine court
in exile at The Hague. These overlaps are especially intriguing because
of another. In 1615, just three years before Descartes wrote the
Compendium, Caus issued his *Institution harmonique*.

This work simply took for granted the various elements we have
explored: 'Music is a science by which low and high sounds, proportional to one another and divided by just intervals, are so disposed that
sense and reason are satisfied.'[1] This definition was preceded by a brief
history, as in Zarlino, and followed by an exploration of the intervals
and proportions in question, as well as their composition. To define
music thus as a theoretical science dealing with the organization of
sounds so as to satisfy 'sense and reason' obviously owed everything
to Zarlino and the tradition culminating in his work. But sense and
reason can both be satisfied only by the practice that Caus did not
mention at this point, and the definition makes sense only if we
remember everything put forward up to this point (especially through
our examination of Zarlino).

For Caus, as for those many others, music was 'the chief of the
sciences based on number', as Frances Yates puts it.[2] Caus was clearly
not just writing of acoustics. But his definition simply assumed practice. Music as a mathematically oriented science was validated by its

---

1. Caus, *Institution*, 2 v: 'Musique, est une science, par laquelle se fait une disposition
   de sons graves, & aigus, proportionables entreux, & separez par iustes interualles,
   dont le sens, & la raison sont satisfaits.'
2. Yates, *Rosicrucian*, 39.

satisfaction of sense and reason. Contrariwise, the reason for such satisfaction was explained by the mathematical logic that was musical
science, the mathematical order embedding it, and that was in
some profound way *like* the effects it produced – 'proportional' to them
and 'explanatory' of them. It was no longer necessary to *say* this.
Everyone took it for granted of music as of its companion arts:
'what else is painting, that we call the Princess of the Arts, than a
pure practice of this science [of mathematical optics]? such that there
has never been a good painter who was not learned in it'. So wrote
Jean-François Nicéron in 1638. [3] Descartes' *Compendium* embodied
the same rationalist claim. It – and Descartes' work as a whole – did
not originate the claim, as we have been seeing. But it did, in a real
way, 'certify' its reliability for future assumptions about the relation
between 'mathematical' reason and imagination, between, too, that
reason and the claims of discovery. His work focused and generalized
such assumptions.

To go so far as to assert the *Compendium* to be simply 'Zarlino,
more geometrico', is probably unjust. [4] Yet Nicolas Poisson was not
misguided when he replaced the *Géométrie* with the *Compendium* in
his 1668 edition of the *Discours*: its rationalist and methodical claim
matched that of the other *Essais* at least in intention. It is certainly
quite wrong to argue originality for his application of quantitative
measure in a hitherto qualitative domain. [5] Painting, music and poetry
had all now seen variously effective attempts to apply some sort of
mathematical analysis to their practice and effects, some far more
precise than others. But in terms of historical effect Descartes marks
an end of the 'passage' from trivium to quadrivium we have been
following, and the 'final' (these things never are) inception of
something new. That is why I shall more or less end this story with
him.

As we recall that Descartes, like Zarlino, Cardano and so many
others, made it a first point to insist that the objective of music – art
– was to please, we must recall, too, how the pleasure in question was

---

3. Nicéron, *Perspective*, préface [unpaginated ii]: 'la peinture, que nous appellons la
   Princesse des Arts, qu'est-ce autre chose qu'vne pure practique de cette science? en
   sorte que iamais il ne s'est veu bon peintre, qui n'y fut sçauant'. In another interesting overlap with Caus, Descartes may have spent some time in 1614/15 in
   Saint-Germain-en-Laye (according to his biographer Adrien Baillet). The Royal
   Gardens there were famous for their automata, many of which Caus depicted in his
   1615 *Raisons*, dedicated to Louis XIII.
4. Cohen, *Quantifying*, 163. Gaukroger comes close to the same assertion in his
   Descartes, 74–80.
5. Augst, 'Descartes' Compendium', 122.

both rational and moral. It retuned the passions. The well-tempered soul would act in accord with prudence, justice, temperance and wisdom, as Le Caron, Tyard and Dupleix held. Descartes was equally taken by these antique virtues. That is surely why he, like Alberti and others, referred first to the effects achieved by 'authors of elegies and tragedies', and why, like contemporaries after him, he insisted that 'proportionality' eased the effect of art. For even as musical and artistic explanation generally came to lay less emphasis on mathematics, it set more, one may say, on a rationalism whose foundations, if not mathematical in any precise sense, were nonetheless wistfully attached to the kind of certainty mathematics was held to enjoy: most notably its progressive steps of analysis. Sounds, like the things seen in the material world or in paintings that suscitate images in the mind, were signs operating according to certain and explicable rule, susceptible of Leonardo's mathematical demonstration, of Zarlino's and Tigrini's rational laws, of Beeckman's micro-mechanical ones. [6]

On the other hand, in music, a particular rationalization *was* being sought through these years (and beyond) that did indeed involve mathematical 'certainty'. I refer to the issue of tuning. And here I can do no better than summarize elements drawn from Michael Chanan. The ancient Greeks did not use the now-familiar European system of scales, but one of *modes*. Pythagoras had 'calculated the numerical ratios of the principal consonances by stopping a taut string along different fractions of its length. Division halfway produced the octave, by a third (3:2) gave the fifth, by three-quarters (4:3) gave the fourth'. This discovery 'served to institutionalize particular musical relations; specifically those we call diatonic'. 'Pythagoras also observed the division of the octave by a fifth, which produces the measure of the diatonic interval.' Above and below the divide, this gives two different intervals: 'the fifth below and the fourth above, the fifth being the larger of the two. The difference between them is critical: Pythagoras calculated it as the ratio 9:8, and it is this interval which constitutes the whole tone.' It was now found that dividing this into the octave gave a fourth, a tone, and another fourth. The fourth itself comprised two tones and a semitone.

This well suited 'the stringing arrangement known as the tetrachord ... : two tetrachords arranged so that the lower string of the top pair sounds a tone higher than the top string of the lower two, produce a scale with the pattern tone-tone-semitone, tone, tone-tone-semitone.

---

6. The comparison to visual images is in Descartes, *Dioptrique*, in *Oeuvres* I. 684–5 (AT VI. 112–13).

This is the equivalent of the scale of C major.' In the tetrachord, however, arrangement of intervals is variable. Further, the two tetrachords need not be the same, and they may also be joined in different ways. One thereby produces 'a series of scales, each beginning on the successive notes of the [original] scale of C, and each with a different shape'. [7] These are the Greek modes. In each of them the precise value of the pitches varies minutely – which is what gave the separate modes their particular affective shape and power, each reputed to have different effects on the listener's affections. Playing in a modal system you are in one or other mode (one can certainly move between them, but they stay distinct). In a tonal harmonic system of scales, you can modulate from one key to another: 'an implicit relation to other keys remains present in the background, and at certain moments you can be in two keys at the same time'. But the possibilities of modulation were limited by the discrepancies of pitch whose mathematical solution was complicated – and not solved until the late eighteenth-century method of 'equal temperament, a form of tuning where the distance between each of the semitones of the chromatic scale is rendered equal and unvarying'. [8]

Greek and medieval 'just temperament' produced 'octaves and fifths [that] are true and perfect', but two different semitones and 'perceptible differences in other intervals'. The fifteenth-century trend towards consorts, grouping instruments of the same kind, and 'emergence of diatonic harmony, which is constructed on the principal of the equivalence of the keys erected on each of the semitones which make up the chromatic scale', posed problems. In this system the 'same chord in a different key has the same structural value because the internal relations are identical' and it was 'theoretically possible to move by modulation from one key to another by changing the component notes of a chord'. Just-tuned instruments could not do this. 'Just intonation was thus replaced by mean-tone temperament, in which thirds were adjusted to enable the system to function for related keys.' Difficulties remained for instruments with notes of fixed value: keyboards. 'In the end, to allow the use of any and every key, it turns out to be necessary to make an adjustment to *every* interval, except the octave itself. This is equal temperament, where adjustments are made which ... render every semitone exactly the same.' It was accomplished in the eighteenth century, hard on the heels of the replacement of mean by

---

7. Chanan, *Musica*, 175–6. A very fine short technical discussion of Greek music theory can be found in Comotti, *Music*, 76–98.
8. Chanan, *Musica*, 177.

well temperament, in which pitch values were adjusted 'to reduce the discrepancies and render the results more tolerable to the ear'. [9]

We should not, though, believe that these developments were the regulated progress of some Whiggish musical history. Chanan argues that they were chiefly due to various external pressures and choices. Schoenberg suggests that they may have resulted no less from tensions internal to the artistic 'system' itself – a combination of factors similar to what we have been following in allied areas of practice. Schoenberg proposes that the eventual dominance of final major chords in church modes may have removed the distinctiveness that we noted as one major characteristic of Greek (and church) modes, so that major and minor distinctions alone remained. He then further proposes that an analogous factor may have affected the harmonic system ruled by well temperament, inasmuch as modulation let the properties of one key be introduced into almost any other, no matter how 'distant': thus in practice doing away with a process that assumed specific keys to have specific tonality. Both systems were created by 'laws established by custom', which must 'eventually be disestablished'. And they are disestablished, among other reasons, because certain of their parts eventually 'do not conform' to the system's principles, and so press 'toward dissolution of the ... system'. [10]

My argument assumes that such rational 'systems' (whether in 'art', 'science', 'philosophy' or whatever) correspond not simply to real human practices, but also to structures of feeling and felt suppositions about the human organism and its relation to a natural and social environment that change over time and place. So it is worth countering Chanan's comment about musical 'results being more tolerable to the ear'. For it might be taken to imply that there exists an absolute standard of, say, ease of relation between reason, physiology of hearing and natural sound (then qualified as 'beautiful'?), and that Western music's progress has been gradually working towards achieving it. But the 'toleration' in question is itself in a symbiotic relation with these systems and practices, all of which have to do less with absolutes than with 'common usage', as Schoenberg puts it. The very judgment of what notes 'are' dissonant has, for instance, changed over time. Indeed, dissonance and consonance are false terms if taken as absolutes. It 'all simply depends', remarks Schoenberg again, 'on the growing ability of the analyzing ear to familiarize itself with the remote overtones, thereby expanding the conception of what is euphonious, suitable

9. Ibid., 181–2, 215.
10. Schoenberg, *Theory*, 28–9. For more comment on modes, 95–6; for precision on modulation, 150–74.

for art, so that it embraces the whole natural phenomenon'. Consonance then simply describes 'the closer, simpler relations to the fundamental tones, dissonances ... those that are more remote'. Not only hearing shapes itself to systemic changes: the very 'scope', for example, 'of that which is singable' also changes. [11]

Chanan notes that conversion to equal temperament has other 'critical implications, because it is a system which falsifies every interval except the octave itself'. He remarks, indeed, how Joseph Needham has shown that the Chinese had calculated it a bit earlier than the Europeans, but 'rejected it, on the grounds that it interfered with the moral order of the universe'. [12] That, of course, is also to make assumptions about certain absolutes. To the point is Schoenberg's remark that the well-tempered system should be seen as 'a compromise between the natural intervals and our inability to use them – that compromise .. which amounts to an indefinitely extended truce'. [13] But it is just one possible such 'compromise', corresponding to the felt needs of a particular time and place. It was a rationalization whose goal, in the case of music as in that of the other arts, at least initially, was to facilitate reception for the production of certain effects.

So, wrote Descartes, musical beat is indicated by the use of bars so that 'we can more easily perceive all the parts of a composition and be pleased by the "proportions" that must be in them. Such proportion is used so very often in the parts of a composition to help our *apprehension* in such a way that when we hear the end, we remember at that very time what was at the start and in the rest of the composition.' This occurs because *nostra imaginatio* easily combines the simple successive proportions marked by bars. [14] Likewise, tones between consonances make the passage between such consonances easier on the listener, for too great a disproportion 'would tire auditors and singers': a comment that may not be foreign to what we have just seen in respect of tuning, for while Descartes seems to be speaking of 'dissonant' tones, he may also have modulation in mind. [15] Again, it was the *simplicity* of the mathematical rule that was 'like' its effect – indeed, its *affect*.

This need to ease the recipient's internalizing of the artwork explains Jean Mairet's and others' demand that theatre not strain imagination

---

11. Ibid., 11, 21, 45.
12. Chanan, *Musica*, 177, 182. The reference to Needham is to his *Science and Civilization in China* IV. 1 (Cambridge: Cambridge University Press, 1962), 214 ff.
13. Schoenberg, *Theory*, 25.
14. Descartes, *Abrégé/Compendium*, 55, 61.
15. Ibid., 91, 97.

and memory by jumping spatial and temporal barriers or by not using the three rules of unity. [16] It explains John Denham's demand, apostrophizing the Thames, that form not obstruct idea: 'O could I flow like thee, and make thy stream / My great example, as it is my theme! / Though deep, yet clear, though gentle, yet not dull, / Strong without rage, without ore-flowing full.' Depth with clarity, variety without confusion, interest with pleasure – so many themes we have seen before, and that have long been familiar, although their sources have not. These lines were written in 1655. Forty years later John Dryden, dedicating the *Aeneid*, made them a 'test of poetic insight'. [17] The need not to impede emotional effect by overworking memory and imagination explains Dominique Bouhours' belief in clarity and 'transparency' of language ('Fine [*beau*] language resembles a pure, clean water without taste') and like views held by almost all. [18] Such clarity, transparency, simplicity and regularity had laws as exact as those of geometry – as all also endlessly iterated. Rules of temperament were among such laws, we just saw, whether mean, as they were now, or equal, as they would become. All were taken to have some direct, nonmetaphorical relation to moral order, whether in the psychological or the social realm.

The aim of such rule, then, in regard of products of the fictive imagination, Boileau's colleague René Rapin pointed out in 1674, was to 'shake the soul with such natural and such human motions [that] all the impressions it receives please it'. [19] Descartes said nothing else. A slow beat roused 'slow' passions – 'languor, sadness, fear, pride and such' – , a fast beat roused fast passions, such as joy. 'A more precise treatise on the matter', he added, 'depends on an exquisite knowledge of the motions of the soul', for which this was not the place; as he insisted again a bit later, noting that he was only writing a 'summary' and that such an exploration exceeded its limits. [20] He might not yet have explored the passions, but knowledge of them was wholly necessary to a full understanding and production of musical effects. When he insisted, too, that the simpler the melody the greater the effect, he was again echoing the view of many before him that clarity of mathematical proportion most moved and tuned the affections.

---

16. Jean Mairet, preface to *Sylvanire*, 16–17.
17. Denham, *Poetical Works*, 77: Last quotation is on 54.
18. Bouhours, *Entretiens* [1671], 37, 34.
19. Rapin, *Reflexions*, 173–4.
20. Descartes, *Abrégé/Compendium*, 63, 89. We may note, however, that when he did write the *Passions de l'âme* thirty years later, music was never once mentioned.

He drew precisely on this when analyzing Jean-Louis Guez de Balzac's letters in 1628. 'Purity of language', he said, was like 'health in the human body'. Language was 'the more excellent as it leaves no impression on the senses'. The beauty of the writing was not in any one case, but 'in the harmony and tempering of the whole [in omnium tali consensu & temperamento]'. What mattered were elegance and variety, 'dignity' of phrase and match between thought and form, an origin 'in zeal for truth and wealth of sense and meaning [ex zelo veritatis & sensûs abundantiâ]'. [21] In letters to Mersenne of December 1629 and the early months of 1630, Descartes returned to music – with language. Both, he wrote, could satisfy the demand that they be universal, both held the possibility, at least, of an emotive and imaginative response in accordance with specifiable rule. These were the years when he had been writing the *Regulae* and was beginning the *Géometrie*. Yet these letters seemed to express doubt: taste depended on individuals and could not be gauged; consonances had no qualities commensurable with the passions; the beautiful might have no common measure since it depended on individual taste, itself related to particular experience and memory. [22]

All this appears diametrically opposed to the *Compendium* and the letter on Balzac, as it seems to echo some views of Cardano, Patrizi or Fracastoro. I think, rather, that it shows deepening of debate. The comprehension of beauty was indeterminable in the case of any given individual: although one might *call* 'the most beautiful' what pleased most people. This was not as radically subjectivist as some have argued. On the contrary, it sought to adjust rule and passion, particular experience and universal humanity. Universal rules were no good, that is to say, unless they enabled 'one's understanding to show the will the choice it must make'. [23] This was the distinction Tigrini had made between the difference and variability of hearing and the certainty of harmonic rule, the clarity of mathematical reason. It was Piero's variable barrels, whose volume was analyzable by universally applicable algebraic rules; or the mathematical demonstrability of the common optical truths underlying Leonardo's paintings. It was also the difference, in music, between true (and irrational) pitch and the successive rationalizations of mean, well and equal temperament (to which one became adapted). To be able to 'adjust' one to the other

---

21. Descartes, *Correspondance*, I. 31–4.
22. Ibid., I. 111 (to Mersenne, January 1630), 123 and 127–8 (to Mersenne, 18 March 1630).
23. Descartes, Regula 1, *Oeuvres*, I. 79. The reference to 'the most beautiful' is to *Correspondance*, I. 128.

was, one might sum up in a vocabulary familiar to the age, to make history proportionate to (and by) geometrical method. It was also to begin to perceive that the universe did, after all, follow a moral order, and that persons and societies could 'fit' with it.

Just like Zarlino and Tigrini (not to mention now nearly two centuries of debate), Descartes' friends Johannes Albertus Bannius and Constantijn Huyghens thought that 'the Beautiful in general and musical art in particular, rested on fixed and immutable laws'. [24] They were far from alone. Such rules bridged understanding and action, imagination and practice. They were simple, and had to show us how and why (*modus* and *ratio*) a given object is 'measurable'. [25] The impress of the earlier work still seems clear. I am indeed tempted to argue that much of the work on the *Regulae* and the later research of the *Passions de l'âme*, whatever particular goals they may have had, responded to this early search to balance rule against experience, to explain the effects of art, to understand how aesthetic pleasure operated, and what it was that one might call the beautiful, the good or the true. In this sense, it corresponded *exactly* to Descartes' search (after Beeckman) for mathematically ruled micro-mechanical explanations for macroscopic phenomena, to explain endlessly variable perceived events by universal rule. [26]

As they concern 'aesthetics' and aspects of the imagination, these issues, and even more these ways of approaching them, have generally been thought to predominate very much later indeed. But it seems clear that the hope (in the sixteenth century) for what one may call 'a quantification of mimesis and catharsis', led directly into explorations in music and painting especially, but also in poetry (where later they became even stronger), that we can readily now recognize as at the root of later aesthetic inquiry. When Rymer and Dennis, Boileau and Rapin, Racine and La Fontaine, Fontenelle and Addison, Lessing and endless others call for artistic rules as trustworthy as Euclid's *Geometry*, enabling us to understand art whose sole purpose, nonetheless, was to please, it is now easy to recognize the source. That is what Edward Gibbon meant when he remarked in 1761: 'Descartes was not a man of letters, but literature is under deep obligation to him'. With

---

24. Huygens, *Correspondance*, xlii–xliii.
25. Regula 14, *Oeuvres*, I. 178. Joachim Burmeister had made an analogous move in an opposite direction. Where Descartes (and so many others) sought to apply rules drawn from mathematical musical studies to writing (rather in the 'Bembo' tradition), Burmeister, in his *Musical Poetics* of 1606, sought to analyze music in 'rhetorical' terms. Perhaps the latter idea corresponds to *ordo*, the former to *methodus*?
26. Gaukroger, *Descartes*, especially 70.

'his ['geometrical'] method of reasoning' true philosophers and critics had already 'thoroughly investigated the true principles of criticism' and given people 'a better acquaintance with the value of the [artistic] treasures in their possession'. [27]

In many ways, the aesthetic rationalization achieved was radically reductionist, as one might suppose it would have to be, to tune 'affection' to 'mathematics'. In music itself, harmonic rationalization worked to repress all expressive elements that failed to fit its particular notion of calculable intervals. The view was exemplified in Jean-Philippe Rameau's 1722 *Traité de l'harmonie*, whose second sentence asserted that 'the [triadic] chord was the basic element of musical discourse, and that melody was therefore based on harmony'. [28] Chanan maintains that Jean-Jacques Rousseau was unique in objecting (in his 'Essay on the Origin of Languages') that such a calculus rejected expressive subleties 'of inflection. Harmony, he wrote "can bring about unification through binding the succession of sounds according to the laws of modulation ... But in the process it also shackles melody ... It eliminates many sounds or intervals which do not fit its system".' Western theory thus had come to consider other cultural assumptions about what music was, those, say, of ancient Greeks or American Indians, as being false. [29] At about the same time, Gibbon made the same point about literature and Europeans' need for a more generous and comprehensive attention, reaching beyond the rationalization now introduced:

An Iriquois work, even were it full of absurdities, would be an invaluable treasure; it would offer an unique specimen of the workings of the human mind, when placed in circumstances which we have never experienced, and influenced by manners and religious opinions entirely contrary to our own. We should be sometimes astonished and instructed by the contrariety of ideas thus produced; we should investigate the causes of their existence; and should trace the progress of the mind from one error to another. Sometimes, also, we should be delighted at recognizing our own principles recurring, but discovered in other ways, and almost always modified and altered. We should there learn not only to own, but also to feel the power of prejudices, not to be astonished at what appears most absurd, and often to distrust what seems best established. [30]

We can of course take this as simply patronizing. But Gibbon knew

---

27. Gibbon, *Essay*, 633. For the previous names, see for example Reiss, *Meaning*, 165–80, 305–7.
28. The paraphrase is from Chanan, *Musica*, 62. The reference is to Rameau, *Treatise*, 3.
29. Chanan, *Musica*, 79, quoting Rousseau.
30. Gibbon, *Essay*, 654. This passage is used to slightly different effect in Reiss, 'Mapping', 670–1.

well that 'error', 'prejudice' and 'modification' could be taken two ways. Perhaps, even, 'modification' and 'alteration' contained something of musical modulation, itself corresponding to 'no natural law . . . eternally valid', but simply being one way 'for producing musical form'. Gibbon was assuredly not making as radical a claim as this of Schoenberg, who would also write of art as simply a system 'by which a body of material is coherently organized and lucidly classified, . . . derived from principles which will assure an unbroken logic' – although such a process is never detachable from the overall cultural context that gives it life (and vice versa) and so is by no means ever arbitrary.[31] Yet, as regards 'literature', at least, Gibbon left space for such thinking: not 'relativism', but awareness of how all claim about absolutes must *first* engage the massive complexities of whole cultures. Less emphatically than Rousseau, he was nonetheless stretching outside the simply aesthetic. Others may well have done as much. To do so was to acknowledge cultural creativity, while not necessarily inhibiting universalist argument (as it did here in Rousseau).

For the aesthetic was not, never had been, alone. We have seen all along how the public sphere had always been at issue, and had become imbued with that rationalization of which the aesthetic offered but one case – component, too, of the public sphere. In ethics, politics, economics, epistemology, just the same rationalization held sway. Like Rousseau and Gibbon, Hobbes thus also used an image of 'the savage people in many places of *America*' subject to the 'brutish manner' of constant pre-covenant war to denote the unruly 'other' of Western culture. Locke and endless others followed his lead. Gibbon's and Rousseau's views do indeed prove a rule, then, and not just in the realm of the fictive imagination.[32] For that 'other' could readily be seen as 'elsewhere' and 'before', outside or to be superseded by the effects of Progress, benign motion of universal reason. In the artistic domain, pleasing was necessarily ruled, aesthetic effect necessarily corresponded to general human emotional possibility. For those very reasons, such ruled art also had moral effect, had an end in ethical public action. Delight and utility coincided.

At least in the West, the ideal of such unity has nowadays so weakened that a contemporary like Charles Taylor (very much 'rationalized' here) allows himself baffled by views of a figure so central to his tradition as Shaftesbury, for whom, in 1711, it was 'as absurd to say that virtue and vice, honour and dishonour, could be a matter of arbitrary

---

31. Schoenberg, *Theory*, 9–10. Compare 413–14.
32. Hobbes, *Leviathan*, 89 (I. 13). I thank Patricia J. Penn Hilden for reminding me of Hobbes' remark.

decree, as 'that the measure or rule of harmony was caprice or will, humour or fashion'. [33] The earl, Taylor wonders,

recurs again and again to this analogy with music – and with architecture and painting. . . . Right and wrong are just as fixed to standards in nature as are harmony or dissonance. Something like a harmony or proportion of numbers is to be found in all these fields. In *Advice [to an Author]*, the true artist is said to be one who is not 'at a loss in those numbers which make the harmony of a mind. For knavery is mere dissonance and disproportion.' He has to have an eye or ear 'for these interior numbers'. And 'the real honest man . . . instead of outward forms or symmetries, is struck with that of inward character, the harmony and numbers of the heart and beauty of the affections [which form the manners and conduct of a truly social life]'.

What, Taylor puzzles, 'did Shaftesbury mean in using these as terms of moral description? It's not entirely clear to us, and perhaps it wasn't so fully to him.' [34]

All the aforegoing would suggest, on the contrary, not only that it was clear to Shaftesbury, but that it was so as well to his contemporaries. Indeed, I have argued elsewhere, such a view was standard beyond John Keats at least well into the nineteenth century. [35] So I see no reason why it may not be clear to us too. This 'harmony', 'numbered' or 'mathematical' order, marked not just the system of the *material* world, but one's perception of it and one's *rational attunement* to it. It was what made reasonable analysis and understanding, ethical behaviour, *and* political and social stability possible at all. It was a thoroughly optimistic view, and that it may now strike 'us' as largely incomprehensible or false is not because 'we' do not credit its grounding premises (as Taylor observes), but because we are at a loss to know how to square them, not with injustices to 'others', with which we mostly have little difficulty, but with horrors committed upon ourselves. [36]

These were not yet a concern of eighteenth- or nineteenth-century thinkers, however. In 1741, Yves-Marie André insisted that 'essential beauty' depended on a 'natural geometry' of symmetry, order, regularity and proportion, the whole dependent on 'unity' but characterized too by 'brilliance' and 'diversity'. It worked both on the 'order of ideas in our minds', and on the 'order of feelings in our hearts' (read

33. Taylor, *Sources*: quoting Shaftesbury, *Characteristics*, I. 227.
34. Taylor, *Sources*, 253–4. The three *Characteristics* citations are from 1.136, 1.216, 2.177. Other examples noted by Taylor include I. 214, 251–2, 314; II. 129, 227–8.
35. Reiss, *Meaning*, 175–9.
36. *This* distinction may indeed suggest that if not 'false' (the adjective is surely misused of historically bound forms of mental life and social action, since it assumes a 'view from nowhere'), the premises have at least always been thought one-sidedly and exclusively of other cultural understandings of operative truth.

'souls'). [37] In 1757, John Brown, an immediate source of later British political economic thought, drew much on Shaftesbury to bemoan, like many others, a lowering of musical standards as immediately correlated with the collapse of polity and social order. [38] Such claims were far from aberrant and by no means dependent on a Shaftesbury (for example). Behind them were some 200 years of debate – more, if we recall Bruni's already optimistic alignment of music and republican order. They indicate how long-lasting were the effects of the explorations we have been examining and how entrenched they had become in Enlightenment thinking. They take us forward to Kant and way beyond. They imply the complex continuance of the change from trivial to quadrivial claim. They suggest, as I proposed in the introduction, that faith in the 'mathematical discovery' of sources, effects and purpose of beauty and moral action did not only signal an end to earlier European analyses of human action, but continued as an aspect of beliefs and an instance of more embracing 'operational ideals' with which, in the West at least, we mostly still live.

By the mid-eighteenth century, I daresay (if not earlier), the idea of mathematical rule in art (music, painting and poetry to be sure, but all others as well) had gradually become as much a matter of metaphor as of anything more literal – although such a claim certainly needs putting to the proof. Yet even if this were so, it would not be an 'empty' metaphor (whatever that could mean in any case). Even as such, the 'metaphor' would show the tail-end of a deeply felt and vehemently maintained belief in a *new* idea and real practice of rational understanding and mathematical discovery. Its origin lay in the erosion of the trivium's ability to pursue truth, and in the turn to once-quadrivial disciplines to create new mathematical sciences able to produce sure new knowledge. While from the trivium, rhetoric especially perhaps, came a particular practice of the arts (one of which modern Europeans have called 'literature'), from the quadrivium came, among other 'scientific' instruments, a critical explanation and identification of aesthetic judgment: one, now principal, area of discovery held to be distinguished (though not separated) from communicative practice. It was also one that typified the *aesthetic rationalism* now fundamental to western analysis and understanding of perhaps the entire spectrum its praxis and activities.

---

37. André, *Essai*, 5–6, 29.
38. P. N. Miller, *Defining*, 108. Among other examples, Miller offers Bolingbroke's remark that 'noble, manly music' was required for firm manners and social order, 'not the 'soft Italian music [which] relaxes and unnerves the soul, and sinks it into weakness' ['On Luxury', *Works*, 4 vols. (London, 1844; rpt. New York: Kelley, 1967) 1.476].

Bibliography

PRIMARY SOURCES

Aaron, Pietro. *Thoscanello de la musica.* Facsimile rpt. of Venice 1523 edn. New York: Broude, 1969.

Agricola, Rodolphus. *De inventione dialectica libri omnes et integri & recogniti . . . per Alardum Amstelredami accuratius emendati. . . .* [Coloniae: Ioannes Gymnicus, 1539.] Facsimile rpt. Frankfurt on Main: Minerva, 1967.

Alberti, Leon Battista. *Della pittura* [1436]. Ed. Luigi Mallè. Florence: Sansoni, 1950.

—— *On Painting and Sculpture. The Latin Texts of De pictura and De statua.* Ed. with trans., introduction, and notes Cecil Grayson. London: Phaidon, 1972.

—— *On the Art of Building in Ten Books.* Trans. J. Rykwert, N. Leach, and R. Tavernor. Cambridge, MA and London: MIT Press, 1988.

—— *La prima grammatica della lingua volgare: La grammatichetta vaticana, Cod. Vat. Reg. Lat. 1370.* Ed. Cecil Grayson. Bologna: Commissione per i Testi di Lingua, 1964.

Alstedius, Iohannes Henricus. *Clavis artis lullianae, et verae logices duos in libellos tributa . . . .* Argentorati [Strasbourg]: Sumptibus Lazari Zetzneri, 1609.

—— *Compendium logicae harmoniae, exhibens universum bene disserendi modum juxta principia Peripateticorum & Rameorum celebriorum . . . .* Herbornae Nassaviorum: n.p., 1615.

—— *Encyclopaedia universa in quatuor tomos divisa.* 2 vols. Lyon: Ioannis Antonii Huguetan filius and Marcus Antonius Ravaud, 1649.

—— *Methodus admirandorum mathematicorum novem libris exhibens universam mathesin.* 3rd edn. Corrected and enlarged. Herbornae Nassaviorum: n.p., 1641.

Andeli, Henri d'. *The Battle of the Seven Arts: a French Poem by Henri d'Andeli, Trouvère of the Thirteenth Century.* Ed. and trans., with introduction and notes Louis John Paetow. Memoirs of the University of California 4.1, History 1.1. Berkeley: University of California Press, 1914.

André, Yves-Marie. *Essai sur le beau.* In *Oeuvres philosophiques.* Ed. Victor Cousin. 1843; rpt. Geneva: Slatkine, 1969. 1–190.

[Anonymous.] *L'art et science de rhétorique (1524–25).* In Langlois, ed. *Recueil.* 265–426.

Les regles de la seconde rhétorique. In Langlois, ed. *Recueil.* 11–103.

Aristides Quintilianus. *The De musica.* In Barker, ed. II. 392–535.

Aristotle. *The Complete Works.* Revised Oxford Translation. Ed. Jonathan Barnes. 2 vols. Princeton: Princeton University Press, 1984.

Bacon, Roger. *The Opus Majus.* Trans. Robert Belle Burke. 2 vols. 1928; rpt. New York: Russell & Russell, 1962.

[Badius Ascensius, Jodocus.] *Josse Bade, dit Badius (1462–1535): Préfaces de Josse Bade (1462–1535). Humaniste, éditeur-imprimeur et préfacier.* Trans., introduction, notes and index by Maurice Lebel. Louvain: Peeters, 1988.

Barker, Andrew D., ed. *Greek Musical Writings.* 2 vols. Cambridge: Cambridge University Press, 1984–89.

Beeckman, Isaac. *Journal . . . de 1604 à 1634.* Ed. Cornélis de Waard. 4 vols. The Hague: Martinus Nijhoff, 1939–53.

Bembo, Pietro. *Prose della volgar lingua.* In *Prose e rima.* Ed. Carlo Dionisotti. 1960; rpt. Turin: Unione Tipografico-Editrice Torinese, 1966.

Boethius, Anicius Manlius Severinus. *Boethian Number Theory: a Translation of the* De institutione arithmetica. With introduction and notes Michael Masi. Amsterdam: Rodopi, 1983.

   Fundamentals of Music [De institutione musica]. Trans. and introduction Calvin M. Bower. Ed. Claude Palisca. New Haven and London: Yale University Press, 1989.

Boissière, Claude de. *L'art d'arythmetique contenant toute dimention, tres-singulier et commode, tant pour l'art militaire que autres calculations.* Paris: Annet Briere, 1554.

   'Autre art poetique reduit en bonne methode [1554]'. In Sebillet. *Art poétique françois,* 1573. 263–305.

Bouhours, Dominique. *Les entretiens d'Ariste et d'Eugène* [1671]. Ed. Ferdinand Brunot. Paris: Colin, 1962.

Bovelles, Charles de. *L'art des opposés.* Text and trans. Pierre Magnard. Précédé d'un essai 'Soleil noir'. Paris: Vrin, 1984.

   De animae immortalitate, dialogus unus; De resurrectione, dialogi duo; De mundi excidio, dialogus unus. Parisiis: Ex officia Reginaldi Calderij, 1551.

   Geometricum opus, duobus libris comprehensum. Paris: Michaelis Vascosanus, 1557.

   In artem oppositorum introductio. Paris: Wolfgang Hopyl, 1501.

   Liber de differentia vulgarium linguarum, & Gallici sermonis varietate . . . ; Que voces apud Gallos sint factitiae & arbitrariae, vel barbariae . . . ; De hallucinatione Gallicanorum nominum. Paris: Robertus Stephanus, 1533.

   Le livre du néant. Text and trans. Pierre Magnard. Précédé d'un essai 'L'étoile matutine'. Paris: Vrin, 1983.

   Le livre du sage. Text and trans. Pierre Magnard. Précédé d'un essai 'L'homme délivré de son ombre'. Paris: Vrin, 1982.

   Livre singulier et utile, touchant l'art et practique de geometrie, composée nouuellement en Françoys. Paris: Simon de Colines, 1542.

   Sur les langues vulgaires et la variété de la langue française / Liber de differentia vulgarium linguarum et Gallici sermonis varietate (1533). Text, trans. and notes Colette Dumont-Demaizière. Paris: Klincksieck, 1973.

Bradwardine, Thomas. *Geometria speculativa*. Latin text and English trans., with introduction and commentary George Molland. Stuttgart: Steiner, 1989.

Burmeister, Joachim. *Musical Poetics*. Trans., introduction and notes Benito V. Rivera. New Haven and London: Yale University Press, 1993.

Cardanus, Hieronymus [Girolamo Cardano]. *Writings on Music*. Trans. and ed. Clement A. Miller. N.p.: American Institute of Musicology, 1973.

Cassiodorus Senator, Flavius Magnus Aurelius. *An Introduction to Divine and Human Readings*. Trans. and introduction Leslie Webber Jones. 1946; rpt. New York: Norton, 1969.

Castiglione, Baldesar, *The Book of the Courtier*. Trans. and introduction George Bull. Harmondsworth: Penguin, 1967.

Caus, Salomon de. *Institution harmonique diuisée en deux parties. En la premiere sont monstrées les proportions des interualles harmoniques, Et en la deuxiesme les compositions dicelles . . . .* Frankfurt: Ian Norton, 1615.

Les raisons des forces mouvantes. Avec diverses machines tant utiles que plaisantes aus quelles sont adioints plusieurs desseings de grotes et fontaines . . . . Frankfurt: Ian Norton, 1615.

Charron, Pierre. *De la sagesse [1601, 1604]*. Ed. Barbara Negroni. Paris: Fayard, 1986.

Christine de Pisan. *The Epistle of Othea*. Trans. Stephen Scrope. Ed. Curt F. Büchler. Early English Text Society 264. Oxford: Oxford University Press, 1970.

Chuquet, Nicolas. *La géométrie. Première géométrie algébrique en langue française (1484)*. Ed. Hervé l'Huillier. Paris: Vrin, 1979.

See also under Secondary Sources: Flegg, Graham, Cynthia Hay, and Barbara Moss, eds.

Cicero, Marcus Tullius. *De finibus bonorum et malorum*. Ed. and trans. H. Rackham. London: Heinemann; Cambridge, MA: Harvard University Press, 1951.

De officiis. Ed. and trans. Walter Miller. London: Heinemann; New York: Macmillan, 1921.

De oratore. Trans. E. W. Sutton. Trans. completed and ed. H. Rackham. 2 vols. 1942; rpt. Cambridge, MA: Harvard University Press; London: Heinemann, 1967–68.

De re publica; De legibus. Trans. Clinton Walker Keyes. 1928; rpt. Cambridge, MA: Harvard University Press; London: Heinemann, 1988.

Cureau de la Chambre, Marin. *Nouvelles pensees sur les causes de la lumiere, du desbordement du Nil, et d'amour d'inclination*. Paris: Pierre Rocolet, 1634.

Denham, Sir John. *The Poetical Works*. Ed. Theodore Howard Banks. 2nd edn. New Haven: Yale University Press, 1969.

Descartes, René. *Abrégé de musique/Compendium musicae*. Ed. and trans. Frédéric de Buzon. Paris: Presses Universitaires de France, 1987.

Abrégé de musique, suivi des Éclaircissements physiques sur la musique de Descartes du R. P. Nicolas Poisson. Trans. and ed. Pascal Dumont. Paris: Méridiens Klincksieck, 1990.

Correspondance. Ed. Charles Adam and Gaston Milhaud, 8 vols. Paris: Alcan, 1936–63.

'La licence en droit de Descartes: un placard inédit de 1616'. Ed., trans. and commentary Jean-Robert Armogathe, Vincent Carraud and Robert Feenstra. *Nouvelles de la République des Lettres* (1988–II): 123–45.

Oeuvres philosophiques. Ed. Ferdinand Alquié. 3 vols. Paris: Garnier, 1963–73.

Deschamps, Eustache. *L'art de dictier et de fere chançons*. In *Oeuvres complètes*. Ed. Gaston Renaud and Queux de Saint-Hilaire. 11 vols. Paris: Didot, 1878–1903. VII. 266–92.

Du Bellay, Joachim. *La deffence et illustration de la langue françoyse* [1548]. Ed. Henri Chamard. 1946; rpt. Paris: Didier, 1970.

Dupleix, Scipion. *L'éthique ou philosophie morale*. Rouen: Manassez de Preaulx, 1626.

Dürer, Albrecht. *The Painter's Manual: a Manual of Measurement of Lines, Areas, and Solids by Means of Compass and Ruler Assembled by Albrecht Dürer for the Use of All Lovers of Art with Appropriate Illustrations Arranged to be Printed in the Year MDXXV*. Trans. with commentary Walter L. Strauss. New York: Abaris, 1977.

The Writings. Trans. and ed. William Martin Conway. Introduction Alfred Werner. New York: Philosophical Library, 1958.

Erasmus, Desiderius. *Ciceronianus or, A Dialogue on the Best Style of Speaking*. In Scott, *Controversies*, pt. 2. 19–130.

The Colloquies [1518–33]. Trans. Craig R. Thompson. Chicago and London: University of Chicago Press, 1965.

On Copia of Words and Ideas (De utraque verborum ac rerum copia). Trans. and Introduction Donald B. King and H. David Rix. Milwaukee: Marquette University Press, 1963.

Estienne, Henri. *Apologie pour Hérodote, ou traité de la conformité des merveilles anciennes avec les modernes* [1566]. Ed. P. Ristelhuber. 2 vols. Paris: Liseux, 1879.

Conformité du langage françois avec le grec [1562]. Ed. Léon Feugère. Paris: Delalain, 1853.

Deux dialogues du nouveau langage françois italianizé et autrement desguizé, principalement entre les courtisans de ce temps [1578]. Ed. P. Ristelhuber. 2 vols. Paris: Lemerre, 1885.

Discours merveilleux de la vie, actions & deportemens de Catherine de Medicis royne mere. Auquel sont recitez les moyens qu'elle a tenus pour vsurper le gouuernement du royaume de France, & ruiner l'estat d'iceluy. [Geneva: n.p.,] 1575. [Probably written by Estienne with Innocent Gentillet.]

La précellence du langage françois [1579]. Ed. Edmond Huguet. Préface L. Petit de Julleville. Paris: Colin, 1896.

Traité de la conformité du langage françois avec le grec (1565), suivi de *De latinitate falso suspecta (1576)*, suivi de *Projet du livre intitulé: De la precellence du langage françois (1579)*. Geneva: Slatkine, 1972.

Estienne, Robert. *Les déclinaisons des noms et verbes . . . .* Paris: Robert Estienne, 1583.

Dictionnaire françoislatin, autrement dit les mots françois, avec les manieres duser diceulx, tournez en latin. Corrigé et augmenté. Paris: Robert Estienne, 1549.

Dictionarium, seu latinae linguae thesaurus, non singulas modo dictiones continens, sed integras quoque latine & loquendi, & scribendi formulas . . . . Paris: Robertus Stephanus, 1531.

Traicté de la grammaire françoise. Paris: Robert Estienne, 1569.

Fabri, Pierre. *Le grant et vray art de pleine rhetorique*. Ed. A. Héron. Rouen: Lestringant, 1890.

Fauvel, John, and Jeremy Gray, eds. *The History of Mathematics: a Reader*. 1987; rpt. Basingstoke: Macmillan; Milton Keynes: Open University Press, 1990.

Ficino, Marsilio. *Three Books on Life [De triplici vita]*. Text ed. and trans. Carol V. Kaske and John R. Clark. Binghamton, NY: Medieval and Renaissance Texts and Studies, 1989.

Finaeus, Orontius. *Protomathesis: opus uarium, ac scitu non minus utile quàm iucundum* . . . . Parisiis: [Impensis Gerardi Morrhij et Ioannis Petri,] 1532.

Fogliano, Lodovico. *Musica theorica*. Facsimile rpt. of Venice 1529 edn. New York: Broude, 1969.

Fouquelin, Antoine. *La rhétorique françoise* . . . . Paris: André Wechel, 1577.

Freig, Johannes Thomas. *Paedagogus 1582: the Chapter on Music*. Trans. and ed. Jeremy Yudkin. Stuttgart: American Institute of Musicology, 1983.

Gaffurio, Franchino. *De harmonia musicorum instrumentorum opus*. Introduction and trans. Clement A. Miller. Neuhausen-Stuttgart: American Institute of Musicology/Hänssler, 1977.

Practica mvsice. Facsimile rpt. of Milan 1496 edn. Introduction Giuseppe Vecchi. Bologna: Forni, 1972.

The Practica musicae of Franchinus Gafurius. Trans. and ed. Irwin Young. Madison and London: University of Wisconsin Press, 1969.

Theorica musice. Facsimile rpt. of Milan 1492 edn. Introduction Giuseppe Vecchi. Bologna: Forni, 1969.

The Theory of Music. Trans. with introduction and notes Walter Kurt Kreyszig. Ed. Claude V. Palisca. New Haven and London: Yale University Press, 1993.

Galilei, Galileo. *Dialogue Concerning the Two Chief World Systems – Ptolemaic and Copernican*. Trans. Stillman Drake. 2nd edn. Berkeley and Los Angeles: University of California Press, 1967.

Le opere. Edizione nazionale. Ed. Antonio Favaro [*et al.*]. 20 vols. Florence: G. Barbèra, 1897–1909.

Galilei, Vincenzo. *Dialogo della musica antica et moderna*. Facsimile rpt. of Florence 1581 edn. Introduction Fabio Fano. Rome: Reale Accademia d'Italia, 1934.

Gibbon, Edward. *An Essay on the Study of Literature. The Miscellaneous Works* . . . . [Ed.] John, Lord Sheffield . . . . London: B. Blake, 1837. 631–70.

Gori, Dionigi. *See under* secondary sources: Franci, Raffaela, and Laura Toti Rigatelli.

Goveanus, Antonius. *Pro Aristotele responsio adversus Petri Rami calumnias*.

Opera iuridica, philologica, philosophica . . . . Ed. Iacobus van Vaassen. Roterodami: Apud Henricum Beman, 1766. 785–815.

Harvey, Gabriel. *Ciceronianus.* Introduction and notes Harold S. Wilson. Trans. Clarence A. Forbes. University of Nebraska Studies, November 1945: Studies in the Humanities 4. Lincoln: University of Nebraska Press, 1945.

Hobbes, Thomas. *Leviathan.* Ed. Richard Tuck. Cambridge: Cambridge University Press, 1991.

Huet, Pierre-Daniel. *Censura philosophiae cartesianae.* Campis: Typis Caspari Cotii, 1690.

Huygens, Constantijn. *Correspondence et oeuvres musicales.* Ed. W. J. A. Jonckbloet and P. P. N. Land. Leiden: E. J. Brill, 1882.

[Isidore of Seville.] *Isidori Hispalensis episcopi Etymologiarum sive originum libri xx.* Ed. W. M. Lindsay. 2 vols. 1911; rpt. Oxford: Clarendon, 1989.

Kretzmann, Norman, and Eleonore Stump, eds. *The Cambridge Translations of Medieval Philosophical Texts.* Volume One: *Logic and the Philosophy of Language.* Cambridge: Cambridge University Press, 1988.

Langlois, Ernest, ed. *Recueil d'arts de seconde rhétorique.* Paris: Imprimerie Nationale, 1902.

La Roche, Estienne de. *L'arismethique nouuellement composee par* . . . . [Lyon:] Constantin Fradin [, 1520].

Launoy, Jean de. *De varia Aristotelis fortuna in Academia Parisiensi* . . . [1653]. *Opera omnia* . . . . 5 tomes in 10 vols. Coloniae Allobrogum [Geneva]: Fabri and Barillot and Marci-Michaelis Bousquet, 1731–32. IV. 1.

Le Caron, Louis. *Dialogues.* Ed. Joan A. Buhlmann and Donald Gilman. Geneva: Droz, 1986.

Lefèvre d'Etaples, Jacques. *The Prefatory Epistles, and Related Texts.* Ed. Eugene F. Rice, Jr. New York and London: Columbia University Press, 1972.

Lemaire de Belges, Jean. *La concorde des deux langages.* Ed. Jean Frappier. Paris: Droz, 1947.

   Oeuvres. Ed. August Jean Steicher. 4 vols. Geneva: Slatkine, 1969.

Le Moyne, Pierre. *Les peintures morales, où les passions sont representees par Tableaux, par Characteres, & par Questions nouuelles & curieuses.* Paris: Sebastien Cramoisy, 1640.

Leonardo da Vinci. *Treatise on Painting (Codex Urbinas Latinus 1270).* Trans. and ed. A. P. McMahon. 2 vols. Princeton: Princeton University Press, 1956.

l'Infortuné. *Le jardin de plaisance et fleur de rhetorique.* Reproduction en facsimile de l'édition publiée par Antoine Vérard vers 1501. Paris: Didot, 1910.

Lipsius, Justus. *Six Bookes of Politickes or Civil Doctrine, written in Latine by Iustus Lipsius: which doe especially concerne Principalitie.* Trans. William Jones. London, 1594. [Facsimile rpt.] The English Experience, 287. Amsterdam: Theatrum Orbis Terrarum; New York: Da Capo, 1970.

Llull, Ramon. *Selected Works.* Ed. and trans. Anthony Bonner. 2 vols. Princeton: Princeton University Press, 1985.

Macrobius Ambrosius Theodosius. *Commentary on the Dream of Scipio*. Trans. and ed. William Harris Stahl. New York: Columbia University Press, 1952.

Mairet, Jean. *Sylvanire*. Ed. Richard Otto. Bamberg: Buchner, 1890.

Martianus Minneius Felix Capella. *The Marriage of Philology and Mercury*. Trans. William Harris Stahl and Richard Johnson with E. L. Burge. Vol. 2 of *Martianus Capella and the Seven Liberal Arts*. 2 vols. New York and London: Columbia University Press, 1971–9.

Mei, Girolamo. *Letters on Ancient and Modern Music to Vincenzo Galilei and Giovanni Bardi: a Study with Annotated Texts*. By Claude V. Palisca. N.p.: American Institute of Musicology, 1960.

Meigret, Louis. *Traité touchant le commun usage de l'escriture françoise* . . . . Paris: Jehan Longis, Vincent Sertenas and Denis Ianot, 1542.

Le tretté de la grammaire françoeze [1550]. Ed. Wendelin Foerster. Sammlung Französischer Neudrucke 7. Heilbronn: Henninger, 1888.

Mersenne, Marin. *Correspondence*. Ed. Cornélis de Waard, Bernard Rochot and Armand Beaulieu. 17 vols. Paris: PUF and CNRS, 1945–88.

Molinet, Jean. *L'art de rhétorique*. In Langlois, ed. *Recueil*. 214–52.

Nebrija, Elio Antonio. *Gramática de la lengua castellana*. Ed. Antonio Quilis. Madrid: Editora Nacional, 1980.

Nicéron, Jean-François. *La perspective cvrievse ov Magie artificielle des effets merveilevx* . . . . Paris: Pierre Billaine, 1638.

Ogier, François. *Apologie pour Monsieur de Balzac*. Paris: Pierre Rocolet, 1628.

Palisca, Claude V., ed. *The Florentine Camerata: Documentary Studies and Translations*. New Haven: Yale University Press, 1989.

Palsgrave, John. *The Comedy of Acolastus*. Trans. from the Latin of Fullonius by John Palsgrave. Ed. P. L. Carver. London: Humphrey Milford, Oxford University Press, 1937.

L'eclaircissement de la langue française . . . . Ed. F. Genin. Paris: Imprimerie Nationale, 1852.

Peletier du Mans, Jacques. *L'algebre* . . . . Lyon: Ian de Tournes, 1554.

L'aritmetique . . . . Poitiers: Ian de Marnef, 1552.

L'art poëtique (1555). Ed. André Boulanger. Paris: Belles Lettres, 1930.

De l'usage de la geometrie . . . . Paris: Gilles Gourbin, 1573.

Dialogue de l'ortografe e pronunciation françoese . . . . Poitiers: Ian e Enguilbert de Marnef, 1550.

Peter of Spain (Petrus Hispanus Portugalensis). *Tractatus* called afterwards *Summule logicales*. First critical edition from the manuscripts with an introduction by Lambertus Marie de Rijk. Assen: Van Gorcum, 1972.

Language in Dispute. An English translation of Peter of Spain's *Tractatus*, called afterwards *Summulae logicales*, on the basis of the critical edition established by L. M. de Rijk. Trans. Francis P. Dinneen, SJ. Amsterdam and Philadelphia: John Benjamins, 1990.

Pico della Mirandola, Giovanni. *De hominis dignitate; Lettera a Ermolao Barbaro*. [With trans. Giovanni Semprini.] Seguito da: *La filosofia di Pico della Mirandola*. Rome: Atanòr, 1986.

On the Dignity of Man. Trans. Charles Glenn Wallis. *On Being and the One.* Trans. Paul J. W. Miller. *Heptaplus.* Trans. Douglas Carmichael. Introduction Paul J. W. Miller. 1965; rpt. New York: Macmillan, 1985.

Piero della Francesca. *De prospectiva pingendi.* Ed. G. Nicco-Fasola. Essays by E. Battista and F. Ghione. Bibliography by E. Battista and R. Pacciani. Florence: Le Lettere, 1984.

    Trattato d'abaco. Dal codice Ashburnhamiano 280 (359*–291*) della Biblioteca Medicea Laurenziana di Firenze. Ed. Gino Arrighi. Pisa: Domus Galilaeana, 1970.

Ptolemy [Claudius Ptolemaeus]. *The Harmonics.* In Barker, ed. II. 270–391.

Quintilianus, Marcus Fabius. *Institutio oratoria.* Ed. and trans. H. E. Butler. 4 vols. 1920; rpt. London: Heinemann; Cambridge, MA: Harvard University Press, 1963.

Rameau, Jean-Philippe. *Treatise on Harmony.* Trans. and ed. Philip Gossett. New York: Dover, 1971.

Ramus, Peter. *Arguments in Rhetoric Against Quintilian.* Trans. and text of Peter Ramus' *Rhetoricae distinctiones in Quintilianum (1549).* Trans. Carole Newlands and James J. Murphy. DeKalb, IL: Northern Illinois University Press, 1986.

    Aristotelicae animadversiones. In Goveanus, *Opera.* 749–84.

    Arithmeticae libri tres .... Paris: Andreas Wechelus, 1555.

    Attack on Cicero. Text and translation of Ramus' *Brutinae quaestiones.* Ed. and introduction James J. Murphy. Trans. Carole Newlands. Davis, CA: Hermagoras, 1992.

    Dialecticae institutiones, ad celeberrimam, et illustrissimam Lutetiae Parisiorvm Academiam. In Goveanus, *Opera.* 721–48.

    Dialecticae libri duo, Audomari Talaei praelectionibus illustrati. Paris: Andreas Wechelus, 1566.

    Dialectica institutiones ... ; Aristotelicae Animaduersiones .... Basel: Sebastianus Henricpetri [,1575].

    Dialectique (1555). Ed. Michel Dassonville. Geneva: Droz, 1964.

    Gramere .... Paris: André Wechel, 1562.

    Grammaire. Paris: André Wechel, 1572.

    Institutionum dialecticarum libri tres .... Paris: Ludouicus Grandinus, 1554.

    Liber de militia C. Julii Caesaris, cum praefatione Joannis Thomae Freigii . ... Basileae: per S. Henricpetri [, 1574].

    The Logike .... Trans. Roland MacIlmaine (1574). Ed. Catherine M. Dunn. Northridge, CA: San Fernando Valley State College, 1969.

    Rudimenta grammaticae .... Paris: Andreas Wechelus, 1559.

    Scholae grammaticae. Paris: Andreas Wechelus, 1559.

    Scholae in liberales artes [1569]. Introduction Walter J. Ong, SJ. Hildesheim and New York: Georg Olms, 1970.

    Scholarum mathematicarum, libri vnvs et triginta. Basileae: per Evsebivm Episcopivm, and Nicolai fratris haeredes, 1569.

    Traitté des meurs et facons des anciens gavloys. Traduit du latin ... par Michel de Castelnau .... Paris: Denys du Val, 1581. [Rpt. of 1559 translation, published the same year as the Latin original.]

and Omer Talon. *Collectaneae: praefationes, epistolae, orationes* [1577, 1599].
   Introduction Walter J. Ong, SJ. Hildesheim: Georg Olms, 1969.
   See also: Talon, Omer.

Rapin, René. *Reflexions sur la poetique d'Aristote, et sur les ouvrages des poetes
   anciens et modernes*. Paris: François Muguet, 1674.

Salutati, Coluccio. 'Letter to Giovanni Dominici'. In *Humanism and Tyranny:
   Studies in the Italian Trecento*. 1925; rpt. Gloucester, MA: Peter Smith,
   1964. 346–77.

Sanchez de las Brozas, Francisco [Sanctius]. *Minerva (1562)*. Introduction and
   ed. Eduardo del Estad Fuentes. Salamanca: University of Salamanca,
   1975.

[Scaliger, Joseph Justus.] *Scaligerana ou bon mots, remarques agreables, et
   remarques judicieuses & sçavantes de J. Scaliger*. Avec les notes de Mr
   Le Fevre, and Mr de Colomies. . . . nlle. ed. A Cologne: Chez ***
   [Amsterdam: Huguetans], 1695.

Scaliger, Julius Caesar. *De causis linguae latinae libri tredecim* . . . [1540]. N.p.:
   Petrus Santandreanus, 1583. [1st edn. 1540.]

Poetices libri septem . . . . Editio secunda. [Geneva:] Petrus Santandreanus,
   1581. [1st edn. 1561.]

Sebillet, Thomas. *Art poétique françois. Pour l'instruction des ieunes studieux,
   & encor' peu auancez en la poésie françoise. Auec le Quiintil Horatian* . . . . Paris: Veufue Jean Ruelle, 1573.

Art poétique françoys (1548). Ed. Félix Gaiffe. Paris: Cornély, 1910.

Shaftesbury, Anthony Ashley Cooper, 3rd earl of. *Characteristics of Men,
   Manners, Opinions, Times*. Ed. John M. Robertson. Introduction
   Stanley Green. 2 vols. [in 1.] Indianapolis and New York: Bobbs-Merrill,
   1964.

Strunk, Oliver, ed. *Source Readings in Music History: Antiquity and the Middle
   Ages*. 1950; rpt. New York: Norton, 1965.

Source Readings in Music History: the Renaissance. 1950; rpt. New York:
   Norton, 1965.

Source Readings in Music History: the Baroque. 1950: rpt. New York: Norton,
   1965.

Suárez, Francisco, SJ. *Metaphysicarum disputationum, in quibus et universa
   naturalis theologiae ordinate traditur, & quaestiones ad omnes duodecim
   Aristotelis libros pertinentes, accuratè disputantur, tomi duo* . . . . Coloniae:
   Franciscus Helvidius, 1614. [1st edn. 1597.]

Opera omnia. 20 vols. in 16. Mainz: for Hermann Mylius Birckmann by
   Balthasar Lippius, 1616–30.

*Selections from Three Works: De legibus, ac deo legislatore, 1612; Defensio
   fidei catholicae, et apostolicae adversus anglicanae sectae errores, 1613;
   De triplici virtute theologica, fide, spe, et charitate, 1621*. Ed. James Brown
   Scott. Trans. Gladys L. Williams, Ammi Brown, and John Waldron, with
   Henry Davis, SJ. 2 vols, Oxford: Clarendon; London: Humphrey Milford,
   1944.

Talon, Omer. *Dialecticae commentarii tres* . . . . Paris: Ludovicus Grandinus,
   1546. [Actually by Ramus.]

Institutiones Oratoriae . . . . Paris: Jacobus Bogardus, 1545.

Rhetorica . . . . Paris: Andreas Wechelus, 1562.

Rhetorica, e P. Rami regii professoris praelectionibus observata. Paris: Andreas Wechelus, 1572.

Tartaglia, Niccolò. *L'arithmetique* . . . . Collected and trans. Guillaume Gosselin. Paris: Adrian Perier, 1613.

Euclide Megarensi acvtissimo philosopho, solo introdvttore delle scientie mathematice. Diligentemente rassettato, et al la integrità ridotto . . . . Venetia: Giouanni Bariletto, 1569.

La noua scientia . . . con una gionta al terzo libro. Venetia: Nicolo de Bascarini, 1550. [Dedicated to Francescomaria della Rovere, 1537.]

Qvesiti et inventioni diverse de Nicolo Tartaglia, di novo restampati con vna gionta al sesto libro, nella quale si mostra duoi modi di reduo une Città inespugnabile. . . . N.p.: Appresso de l'avttore, 1554.

Thomas of Erfurt, *Grammatica speculativa.* Ed., trans., and commentary Geoffrey L. Bursill-Hall. London: Longman, 1972.

Tigrini, Orazio. *Il compendio della mvsica nel qvale brevemente si tratta Dell'Arte del Contrapunto, diviso in qvatro libri* . . . . Venice: Ricciardo Amadino, 1558. Facsimile rpt. New York: Broude, 1966.

Toletus, Franciscus, SJ. *Commentaria . . . in octo libros Aristotelis de physica auscultatione.* [7th edn. revised] Venetiis: Iuntas, 1616. [1st edn. 1573.]

Tory, Geofroy. *Champ fleury ou l'art et science de la proportion des lettres.* Ed. Gustave Cohen. Paris: Bosse, 1931. [Rpt. Geneva: Slatkine, 1973, with additional preface by Kurt Reichenberger and Theodor Berchem.]

Geoffroy Tory and Catherine de Medici. An Unpublished Manuscript of Geoffroy Tory of the Genealogy of the Counts of Boulogne Concerning the French Ancestry of Catherine de Medici, Queen of France. Ed. Gustave Cohen. Trans. Samuel A. Ives. New York: Kraus, 1944.

Tyard, Pontus de. *Solitaire second.* Ed. Cathy M. Yandell. Geneva: Droz, 1980.

Vega Carpio, Félix Lope de. *Arcadia.* Ed. Edwin S. Morby. Madrid: Castalia, 1975.

Vincentino, Nicola. *L'antica musica ridotta alla moderna prattica.* Facsimile of 1555 Rome ed. Postface Edward E. Lowinsky. Kassel, Basel, London and New York: Bärenreiter, 1959.

Vives, Juan Luis. *Against the Pseudodialecticians: A Humanist Attack on Medieval Logic.* Texts, trans., introduction, and notes Rita Guerlac. Synthese Historical Library 18. Dordrecht, Boston and London: Reidel, 1979.

Wilson, Thomas. *The Rule of Reason Conteynyng the Arte of Logique.* Ed. Richard S. Sprague. Northridge, CA: San Fernando Valley State College, 1972.

Wotton, Sir Henry. *Reliquiae Wottoniae. Or, A Collection of Lives, Letters, Poems; with Characters of Sundry Personages: And other Incomparable Pieces of Language and Art.* London: Thomas Maxey, for R. Marriot, G. Bedel and T. Gathwait, 1651.

Zabarella, Jacobus. *De rebus naturalibus libri XXX* . . . . Francofurti: Lazarus Zetznerus, 1607. [1st edn. 1590.]

In Aristotelis libros physicarum, commentaria . . . . Basiliae: Petrus Borgnatius, 1622. [1st edns. 1601, 1602.]

Opera logica . . . . Francofurti: Lazarus Zetznerus, 1608. [1st edn. 1578, but here with 1586 *Apologia de doctrinae ordine* added.]

Zarlino, Gioseffo. *Le istitvtioni harmoniche* . . . *Nelle quali; oltra le materie appartenenti alla mvsica; si trouano dichiarati moltri luoghi di Poeti, d'Historici, & di Filosofi* . . . . Facsimile rpt. of Venice 1558 edn. New York: Broude, 1965.

The Art of Counterpoint: Part Three of Le istitutioni harmoniche, *1558*. Trans. Guy A. Marco and Claude V. Palisca. New Haven and London: Yale University Press, 1968.

Zumthor, Paul, ed. *Anthologie des grands rhétoriqueurs*. Paris: 10/18, 1978.

SECONDARY SOURCES

Ackerman, James. 'The Involvement of Artists in Renaissance Science'. In Shirley and Hoeniger, eds. 94–129.

Adams, John Charles. 'Gabriel Harvey's *Ciceronianus* and the Place of Peter Ramus' *Dialecticae libri duo* in the Curriculum'. *Renaissance Quarterly* 43 (1990): 551–69.

Amsler, Mark. *Etymology and Grammatical Discourse in Late Antiquity and the Early Middle Ages*. Amsterdam and Philadelphia: John Benjamins, 1989.

Apel, Karl-Otto. *L'idea di lingua nella tradizione dell'umanismo da Dante a Vico*. Trans. Luciano Tosti. Bologna: il Mulino, 1975.

Aristotelismo veneto e scienza moderna. See Olivieri, Luigi, ed.

Arts libéraux et philosophie au moyen âge. Actes du Quatriéme Congrès International de Philosophie Médiévale, Université de Montréal, 27 août–2 septembre 1967. Montreal: Institut d'Etudes Médiévales; Paris: Vrin, 1969.

Ashworth, Earline J. 'The Eclipse of Medieval Logic'. In Kretzmann *et al.*, eds. 787–96.

Language and Logic in the Post-Medieval Period. Dordrecht and Boston: Reidel, 1974.

'Traditional Logic'. In Schmitt and Skinner, eds. 143–72.

The Tradition of Medieval Logic and Speculative Grammar from Anselm to the End of the Seventeenth Century: a Bibliography from 1836 Onwards. Toronto: Pontifical Institute of Mediaeval Studies, 1978.

Augst, Bertrand. 'Descartes's Compendium on Music'. *Journal of the History of Ideas* 26.1 (January–March 1965): 119–32.

Auroux, Sylvain, ed. *Histoire des idées linguistiques*. 2 vols. Liège: Pierre Mardaga, 1989–92.

Barker, Peter, and Roger Ariew, eds. *Revolution and Continuity: Essays in the History and Philosophy of Early Modern Science*. Washington, DC: Catholic University of America Press, 1991.

Barnes, Jonathan. 'Aristotle's Theory of Demonstration'. In *Articles on Aristotle, 1: Science*. Ed. Jonathan Barnes, Malcolm Schofield, and Richard Sorabji. London: Duckworth, 1975. 65–87.

Baron, Hans. *The Crisis of the Early Italian Renaissance: Civic Humanism and Republican Liberty in an Age of Classicism and Tyranny*. 2 vols. Princeton: Princeton University Press, 1955.

The Crisis of the Early Italian Renaissance: Civic Humanism and Republican Liberty in an Age of Classicism and Tyranny. Revised one-volume edn with epilogue. Princeton: Princeton University Press, 1966.

Bataillon, Marcel. *Erasmo y España: Estudios sobre la historia espiritual del siglo xvi*. Trans. Antonio Alatorre. Mexico City: Fondo de Cultura Económica, 1950.

Baxandall, Michael. *Giotto and the Orators: Humanist Observers of Painting in Italy and the Discovery of Pictorial Composition, 1350–1450*. Oxford: Clarendon, 1971.

Painting and Experience in Fifteenth-Century Italy: a Primer in the Social History of Pictorial Style. 2nd edn. Oxford and New York: Oxford University Press, 1988.

Beaujouan, Guy. 'The Place of Nicolas Chuquet in a Typology of Fifteenth-Century French Arithmetics'. In Hay, ed. 73–88.

Bec, Christian. *Les marchands écrivains: Affaires et humanisme à Florence, 1375–1434*. Paris and The Hague: Mouton, 1967.

Bernard, Auguste Joseph. *Geofroy Tory, Painter and Engraver, First Royal Printer, Reformer of Orthography and Typography under François I: an Account of His Life and Works*. Trans. George B. Ives. 1909; rpt. New York: Kraus Reprint, 1969.

Bianconi, Lorenzo. *Music in the Seventeenth Century*. Cambridge: Cambridge University Press, 1987.

Bochenski, I. M. *A History of Formal Logic*. Trans. Ivo Thomas. Notre Dame: University of Notre Dame Press, 1961.

Bonner, Anthony. 'Llull's Influence: the History of Lullism'. In Llull, Ramon. *Selected Works*. I. 71–89.

Bowen, Barbara C. *Words and the Man in French Renaissance Literature*. Lexington, KY: French Forum, 1983.

Brathwaite, Kamau. 'MR'. In *Sisyphus and Eldorado: Magical and Other Realisms in Caribbean Literature*. Ed. Kamau Brathwaite and Timothy J. Reiss. *Annals of Scholarship* 12.1–2 (1996): 1–44.

Breva-Claramonte, Manuel. *Sanctius's Theory of Language: a Contribution to the History of Renaissance Linguistics*. Amsterdam and Philadelphia: John Benjamins, 1983.

Brind'amour, Lucie, and Eugene Vance, eds. *L'archéologie du signe*. Toronto: Pontifical Institute of Mediaeval Studies, 1983.

Bruyère, Nelly. *Méthode et dialectique dans l'oeuvre de La Ramée: Renaissance et âge classique*. Paris: Vrin, 1984.

Bruyne, Edgar de. *Etudes d'esthétique médiévale*. 3 vols. 1946; rpt. Geneva: Slatkine, 1975.

Burckhardt, Jacob. *The Civilization of the Renaissance in Italy*. Trans. S. G. C. Middlemore. 2 vols. New York: Harper & Row, 1958.

Bursill-Hall, Geoffrey L. *Speculative Grammars of the Middle Ages: the Doctrine of Partes Orationis of the Modistae*. The Hague and Paris: Mouton, 1971.

Sten Ebbesen, and E. F. Konrad Koerner, eds. *De ortu grammaticae: Studies in Medieval Grammar and Linguistics in Memory of Jan Pinborg*. Amsterdam and Philadelphia: John Benjamins, 1990.

Buzon, Frédéric de. 'Descartes, Beeckman et l'acoustique'. *Archives de Philosophie* 44.4 (October–December 1981): *Bulletin Cartésien* 10. 1–8.

'Science de la nature et théorie musicale chez Isaac Beeckman (1588–1637)'. *Revue d'Histoire des Sciences* 38.2 (April–June 1985): 97–120.

'Sympathie et antipathie dans le *Compendium musicae*'. *Archives de Philosophie* 46.4 (October–December 1983): 647–53.

Bynon, Theodora, and F. R. Palmer, eds. *Studies in the History of Western Linguistics. In Honour of R. H. Robins*. Cambridge: Cambridge University Press, 1986.

Carpenter, Nan Cooke. *Music in the Medieval and Renaissance Universities*. Norman: University of Oklahoma Press, 1958.

Carroll, Lewis. *The Works*. Ed. Roger Lancelyn Green. Feltham, Mddx.: Spring, 1965.

Carruthers, Mary. *The Book of Memory: a Study of Memory in Medieval Culture*. Cambridge: Cambridge University Press, 1990.

Carvalho, Joaquim Barrados de. *António de Gouvea e o Aristotelismo da Renascença: António de Gouvea e Pedro Ramo. Obra completa, I: Filosofia e história da filosofia, 1916–1934*. Lisbon: Fundação Calouste Gulbenkian, 1978. 1–116.

Cassirer, Ernst. *Das Erkenntnisproblem in der Philosophie und Wissenschaften der neueren Zeit*. 4 vols. Berlin: B. Cassirer; Stuttgart: W. Kohlhammer [vol. 4], 1906–57.

The Individual and the Cosmos in Renaissance Philosophy. Trans. Mario Domandi. 1963; rpt. Philadelphia: University of Pennsylvania Press, 1972.

Cave, Terence. *The Cornucopian Text: Problems of Writing in the French Renaissance*. Oxford: Clarendon, 1979.

Cerquiligni, Bernard. *La parole médiévale: discours, syntaxe, texte*. Paris: Minuit, 1981.

Chanan, Michael. *Musica Practica: the Social Practice of Western Music from Gregorian Chant to Postmodernism*. London and New York: Verso, 1994.

Chevalier, Jean-Claude. *Histoire de la syntaxe: naissance de la notion de complément dans la grammaire française (1530–1750)*. Geneva: Droz, 1968.

Cheyfitz, Eric. *The Poetics of Imperialism: Translation and Colonization from 'The Tempest' to 'Tarzan'*. New York: Oxford University Press, 1991.

Chomarat, Jacques. *Grammaire et rhétorique chez Erasme*. 2 vols. Paris: Belles Lettres, 1981.

'Platon et Aristote à Paris au printemps de 1515'. *Moreana* 41 (March 1974): 48–56.

Chomsky, Noam. *Cartesian Linguistics: a Chapter in the History of Rationalist Thought*. New York: Harper & Row, 1966.

Clément, Louis. *Henri Estienne et son oeuvre française (étude d'histoire littéraire et de philologie)*. 1898; rpt. Geneva: Slatkine, 1967.

Cohen, H. F. *Quantifying Music: the Science of Music at the First Stage of the Scientific Revolution, 1580–1650*. Dordrecht: D. Reidel, 1984.

Colish, Marcia L. *The Mirror of Knowledge: a Study in the Medieval Theory of Knowledge*. 2nd edn. Lincoln, NE and London: University of Nebraska Press, 1983.

Colloque International de Tours (xive stage). *L'humanisme français au début de la Renaissance*. [Ed. André Stegmann.] Paris: Vrin, 1973.

Comotti, Giovanni. *Music in Greek and Roman Culture*. Trans. Rosaria V. Munson. Baltimore and London: Johns Hopkins University Press, 1989.

Covington, Michael A. 'Grammatical Theory in the Middle Ages'. In Bynon and Palmer, eds. 23–42.

Crapulli, Giovanni. *Mathesis universalis: Genesi di un'idea nel xvi secolo*. Rome: Edizioni dell'Ateneo, 1969.

Crescini, Angelo. *Le origini del metodo analitico: il Cinquecento*. Udine: Del Bianco, 1965.

Croll, Morris W. *Style, Rhetoric, and Rhythm: Essays*. Ed. J. Max Patrick and Robert O. Evans, with John M. Wallace and R. J. Schoeck. Princeton: Princeton University Press, 1966.

Crombie, Alistair C. 'Experimental Science and the Rational Artist in Early Modern Europe'. *Daedalus* 115.3 (Summer 1986): 49–74.

'Mathematics and Platonism in the Sixteenth-Century Italian Universities and in Jesuit Educational Policy'. In *ΠΡΙΣΜΑΤΑ: Naturwissenschaftsgeschichtliche Studien: Festschrift für Willy Hartner*. Ed. Yasukatsu Maeyama and Walter Gabriel Saltzer. Wiesbaden: Franz Steiner, 1977. 63–94.

Science, Optics and Music in Medieval and Early Modern Thought. London and Ronceverte, WV: Hambledon, 1990.

Dainville, François Oudot de, SJ. 'L'enseignement des mathématiques dans les Collèges jésuites de France du xvie au xviiie siècle'. *Revue d'Histoire des Sciences* 7.1 (1954): 6–21, 109–23.

Damisch, Hubert. *L'origine de la perspective*. New ed. Paris: Flammarion, 1993.

Dassonville, Michel. 'La "Dialectique" de Pierre de La Ramée, première oeuvre philosophique originale de langue française'. *Revue de l'Université Laval* 7.7 (March 1953): 608–16.

Davis, Margaret Daly. *Piero della Francesca's Mathematical Treatises: The 'Trattato d'abaco' and 'Libellus de quinque corporibus regularibus'*. Ravenna: Longo, 1977.

Davis, Natalie Zemon. 'Sixteenth-Century French Arithmetics on the Business Life'. *Journal of the History of Ideas* 21 (1960): 18–48.

Dear, Peter. *Discipline and Experience: the Mathematical Way in the Scientific Revolution*. Chicago and London: University of Chicago Press, 1995.

Mersenne and the Learning of the Schools. Ithaca and London: Cornell University Press, 1988.

De Grazia, Margreta. 'The Secularization of Language in the Seventeenth Century'. *Journal of the History of Ideas* 41.2 (April–June 1980): 319–29.

De Morgan, Augustus. *Arithmetical Books from the Invention of Printing to the Present Time*. London: Taylor & Walton, 1847.

Desan, Philippe. *Naissance de la méthode (Machiavel, La Ramée, Bodin, Montaigne, Descartes)*. Paris: Nizet, 1987.

Dod, Bernard G. 'Aristoteles latinus'. In Kretzmann *et al.*, eds. 45–79.

Duhem, Pierre. *Medieval Cosmology*. Ed. and trans. Roger Ariew. Chicago and London: University of Chicago Press, 1985.

Le système du monde: Histoire des doctrines cosmologiques de Platon à Copernic. 10 vols. Paris: Hermann, 1913–59.

To Save the Phenomena: an Essay on the Idea of Physical Theory from Plato to Galileo. Trans. Edmund Dolan and Chaninah Maschler. Chicago: University of Chicago Press, 1969.

Edgerton, Samuel Y. *The Heritage of Giotto's Geometry: Art and Science on the Eve of the Scientific Revolution*. Ithaca and London: Cornell University Press, 1991.

The Renaissance Rediscovery of Linear Perspective. New York: Basic Books, 1975.

Edwards, William F. 'Jacopo Zabarella: a Renaissance Aristotelian's View of Rhetoric and Poetry and their Relation to Philosophy'. In *Arts libéraux et philosophie* 843–54.

'The Logic of Iacopo Zabarella'. Ph.D. dissertation, Columbia University, 1960.

'Paduan Aristotelianism and the Origins of Modern Theories of Method'. In Olivieri, Luigi, ed. 206–20.

Egmond, Warren Van. 'The Commercial Revolution and the Beginnings of Western Mathematics in Renaissance Florence, 1300–1500'. Ph.D. dissertation, Indiana University, 1976.

'How Algebra Came to France'. In Hay, ed. 127–44.

Practical Mathematics in the Italian Renaissance: a Catalogue of Italian Abbacus Manuscripts and Printed Books to 1600. Florence: Istituto e Museo di Storia della Scienza, 1980.

Elliott, John H. *Imperial Spain, 1469–1716*. 1963; rpt. Harmondsworth: Penguin, 1985.

Elsky, Martin. *Authorizing Words: Speech, Writing, and Print in the English Renaissance*. Ithaca and London: Cornell University Press, 1989.

Fenton, James. 'The Cherry Orchard Has to Come Down'. *New York Review of Books* 43.6 (4 April 1996): 16–17.

Ferruolo, Stephen C. *The Origins of the University: The Schools of Paris and Their Critics, 1100–1215*. Stanford: Stanford University Press, 1985.

Field, J. V. 'Perspective and the Mathematicians: Alberti to Desargues'. In Hay, ed. 236–63.

Flegg, Graham, Cynthia Hay, and Barbara Moss, eds. *Nicolas Chuquet, Renaissance Mathematician: a Study with Extensive Translation of Chuquet's Mathematical Manuscript Completed in 1484*. Dordrecht, Boston, Lancaster: Reidel, 1985.

Foucault, Michel. *Les mots et les choses: une archéologie des sciences humaines*. Paris: Gallimard, 1966.

Franci, Raffaela, and Laura Toti Rigatelli. 'Fourteenth-Century Italian Algebra'. In Hay, ed. 11–29.

Introduzione all'aritmetica mercantile del Medioevo e del Rinascimento: Realizzata attraverso un'antologia degli scritti di Dionigi Gori (sec. xvi). Siena: Quattro Venti, 1982.

French, Roger. *Ancient Natural History: Histories of Nature*. London and New York: Routledge, 1994.

Fumaroli, Marc. *L'âge de l'éloquence: Rhétorique et 'res litteraria' de la Renaissance au seuil de l'époque classique*. Geneva: Droz, 1980.

Gallo, F. Alberto. *Music in the Castle: Troubadours, Books, and Orators in Italian Courts of the Thirteenth, Fourteenth and Fifteenth Centuries*. Trans. Anne Herklotz and Kathryn Krug. Chicago and London: University of Chicago Press, 1995.

Gandillac, Maurice de. 'Lefèvre d'Etaples et Charles de Bovelles: Lecteurs de Nicolas de Cues'. In Colloque International de Tours. 155–71.

Gaukroger, Stephen. *Cartesian Logic: an Essay on Descartes's Conception of Inference*. Oxford: Clarendon, 1989.

    Descartes: an Intellectual Biography. Oxford: Clarendon, 1995.

    Explanatory Structures: a Study of Concepts of Explanation in Early Physics and Philosophy. Atlantic Highlands, NJ: Humanities, 1978.

Gayá, J. 'Algunos temas lulianos en los escritos de Charles de Bovelles'. *Estudios Lulianos* [Palma] 24 (1980): 71–86.

Gellrich, Jesse. *The Idea of the Book in the Middle Ages: Language Theory, Mythology, and Fiction*. Ithaca and London: Cornell University Press, 1985.

Gerl, Hanna-Barbara. *Rhetorik als Philosophie: Lorenzo Valla*. Munich: Wilhelm Fink, 1974.

Giard, Luce. 'L'aristotélisme padouan: Histoire et historiographie'. *Les Etudes Philosophiques* (1986): 281–307.

    'Du latin médiéval au pluriel des langues, le tournant de la Renaissance'. *Histoire, Epistémologie, Langage* 6.1 (1984): 35–55.

    'La mise en théorie du français au XVIe siècle'. *Schifanoia* 2 (1986): 63–76.

Gilbert, Neal W. 'Galileo and the School of Padua'. *Journal of the History of Philosophy* 1.2 (December 1963): 223–31.

    Renaissance Concepts of Method. New York: Columbia University Press, 1969.

Gioseffi, Decio. *Perspectiva artificialis per la storia della prospettiva spigolature e appunti*. Istituto di storia dell'arte antica e moderna 7. Trieste: Università degli Studi di Trieste, Facoltà di Lettere e Filosofia, 1957.

Goldthwaite, Richard A. 'Schools and Teachers of Commercial Arithmetic in Renaissance Florence'. *Journal of European Economic History* 1 (1972): 418–33.

Gombrich, Ernst H. *Art and Illusion: a Study in the Psychology of Pictorial Representation*. 2nd edn. Princeton: Princeton University Press, 1961.

    'Icon'. *New York Review of Books* 43.3 (15 February 1996): 29–30.

Grafton, Anthony. *Joseph Scaliger. A Study in the History of Classical Scholarship, II: Historical Chronology*. Oxford: Clarendon, 1993.

    and Lisa Jardine. *From Humanism to the Humanities: Education and the Liberal Arts in Fifteenth- and Sixteenth-Century Europe*. London: Duckworth, 1986.

Graves, Frank Pierrepont. *Peter Ramus and the Educational Reformation of the Sixteenth Century*. New York: Macmillan, 1912.

Grayson, Cecil. 'Leon Battista Alberti and the Beginnings of Italian Grammar'. *Proceedings of the British Academy* 49 (1963): 291–311.

Greene, Thomas M. *The Light in Troy: Imitation and Discovery in Renaissance Poetry*. New Haven and London: Yale University Press, 1982.

The Vulnerable Text: Essays on Renaissance Literature. New York: Columbia University Press, 1986.

Grendler, Paul F. *Schooling in Renaissance Italy: Education and the Liberal Arts in Fifteenth- and Sixteenth-Century Europe*. Baltimore and London: Johns Hopkins University Press, 1989.

Groethuysen, Bernard. *Anthropologie philosophique*. Paris: Gallimard, 1980. [1st German edn 1928–31.]

Hanke, Lewis. *Aristotle and the American Indians: a Study in Race Prejudice in the Modern World*. 1959; rpt. Bloomington & London: Indiana University Press, 1970.

Harvey, Jonathan. 'Keller's Question'. *Times Literary Supplement* 4824, 15 September 1995: 12–13.

Hay, Cynthia, ed. *Mathematics from Manuscript to Print, 1300–1600*. Oxford: Clarendon, 1988.

Heidegger, Martin. 'The Age of the World Picture'. *The Question of Technology and Other Essays*. Trans. and ed. William Lovitt. New York: Harper & Row, 1977. 115–54.

Heninger, S. K., Jr. 'Oronce Finé [*sic*] and English Textbooks for the Mathematical Sciences'. In *Studies in the Continental Background of English Renaissance Literature: Essays Presented to John L. Lievsay*. Ed. Dale B. J. Randall and George Walton Williams. Durham, NC: Duke University Press, 1977. 171–85.

Hooykaas, Rejner. *Humanisme, science et réforme: Pierre de La Ramée, 1515–1572*. Leiden: J. Brill, 1958.

Howell, Wilbur Samuel. *Logic and Rhetoric in England, 1500–1700*. Princeton: Princeton University Press, 1956.

Hudson, Nicholas. *Writing in European Thought, 1600–1830*. Cambridge: Cambridge University Press, 1994.

Husserl, Edmund. *The Crisis of European Sciences and Transcendental Phenomenology*. Trans. and ed. David Carr. Evanston: Northwestern University Press, 1970.

Irvine, Martin. *The Making of Textual Culture: 'Grammatica' and Literary Theory, 350–1100*. Cambridge: Cambridge University Press, 1994.

Jardine, Lisa A. *Erasmus, Man of Letters: the Construction of Charisma in Print*. Princeton: Princeton University Press, 1993.

Francis Bacon: Discovery and the Art of Discourse. Cambridge: Cambridge University Press, 1974.

'Humanism and Dialectic in Sixteenth-Century Cambridge: a Preliminary Investigation'. In *Classical Influences on European Culture, A.D. 1500–1700*. Ed. R. R. Bolgar. Cambridge: Cambridge University Press, 1976. 141–54.

'Humanism and the Sixteenth-Century Arts Course'. *History of Education* 4 (1975): 16–31.

'Humanism and the Teaching of Logic'. In Kretzmann *et al.*, eds. 796–807.

'Humanistic Logic'. In Schmitt and Skinner, eds. 173–98.

'Lorenzo Valla: Academic Skepticism and the New Humanist Dialectic'. In *The Skeptical Tradition*. Ed. Myles Burnyeat. Berkeley, Los Angeles and London: University of California Press, 1983. 253–86.

'Lorenzo Valla and the Origins of Humanist Dialectic'. *Journal of the History of Philosophy* 15.2 (April 1977): 143–64.

'The Place of Dialectic Teaching in Sixteenth-Century Cambridge'. *Studies in the Renaissance* 21 (1974): 31–62.

See also: Grafton, Anthony.

Jardine, Nicholas. *The Birth of History and Philosophy of Science: Kepler's* A Defence of Tycho against Ursus *with Essays on Its Provenance and Significance*. 1984; rpt. Cambridge: Cambridge University Press, 1988.

'Epistemology of the Sciences'. In Schmitt and Skinner, eds. 687–711.

'The Forging of Modern Realism: Clavius and Kepler against the Sceptics'. *Studies in History and Philosophy of Science* 10 (1979): 141–73.

'Galileo's Road to Truth and the Demonstrative Regress'. *Studies in History and Philosophy of Science* 7 (1976): 277–318.

Jarrott, C. A. L. 'Erasmus' "In Principio Erat Sermo": a Controversial Translation'. *Studies in Philology* 61 (1964): 35–40.

Javitch, Daniel. 'On the Assimilation of the *Poetics* in Sixteenth-Century Italy'. In *The Cambridge History of Literary Criticism*. Volume III: *The Renaissance*. Ed. Glyn P. Norton. Cambridge: Cambridge University Press, 1997.

Poetry and Courtliness in Renaissance England. Princeton: Princeton University Press, 1978.

Jayawardene, S. A. 'Renaissance Mathematics (and Astronomy) in Baldassare Boncompagni's *Bollettino di Bibliografia e di Storia delle Scienze Matematiche e Fisiche* (1868–87)'. In Hay, ed. 190–4.

Jensen, Kristian. *Rhetorical Philosophy and Philosophical Grammar: Julius Caesar Scaliger's Theory of Language*. Munich: Wilhelm Fink, 1990.

Jeppersen, Knud. *Counterpoint: the Polyphonic Vocal Style of the Sixteenth Century*. Trans. Glen Haydon. New foreword Alfred Mann. New York: Dover, 1992.

Jung, Marc-René. *Hercule dans la littérature française du xvie siècle: De l'Hercule courtois à l'Hercule baroque*. Travaux d'humanisme et renaissance 79. Geneva: Droz, 1966.

Kassler, Jamie Croy. 'Music as a Model in Early Science'. *History of Science* 20 (1982): 103–39.

Kessler, Eckhard. 'De significatione verborum: Spätscholastische Sprachtheorie und humanistische Grammatik'. *Res Publica Litterarum* 4 (1981): 285–313.

Kibbee, Douglas A. *For to Speke French Trewely: the French Language in England, 1000–1600: its Status, Description and Instruction*. Amsterdam and Philadelphia: John Benjamins, 1991.

'John Palsgrave's "Lesclaircissement de la langue françoyse" (1530)'. *Historiographia Linguistica* 12. 1–2 (1985): 27–62.

Kipling, Gordon. 'Henry VII and the Origins of Tudor Patronage'. In Lytle and Orgel, eds. 117–64.

Kline, Morris. *Mathematical Thought from Ancient to Modern Times*. 3 vols. 1972; rpt. New York and Oxford: Oxford University Press, 1990.

Mathematics in Western Culture. 1953; rpt. London: Oxford University Press, 1972.

Koerner, E. F. Konrad, Hans-Josef Niederehe, and Robert Henry Robins, eds. *Studies in Medieval Linguistic Thought, Dedicated to Geoffrey L. Bursill-Hall on the Occasion of His Sixtieth Birthday on 15 May 1980.* Amsterdam: John Benjamins, 1980.

Krantz, Émile. *Essai sur l'esthétique de Descartes: Rapports de la doctrine cartésienne avec la littérature classique française au xviie siècle.* 2nd edn. 1898; facsimile rpt. New York: Burt Franklin, 1974.

Kretzmann, Norman, Anthony Kenny, and Jan Pinborg, with Eleonore Stump, eds. *The Cambridge History of Later Medieval Philosophy: from the Rediscovery of Aristotle to the Disintegration of Scholasticism, 1100–1600.* Cambridge: Cambridge University Press, 1982.

Kristeller, Paul Oskar. *Die italienischen Universitäten der Renaissance.* Krefeld: Scherpe [, 1953].

Medieval Aspects of Renaissance Learning: Three Essays. 2nd edn. New York: Columbia University Press, 1992.

Renaissance Thought II: Papers on Humanism and the Arts. New York: Harper & Row, 1965.

Law, Vivian. 'Originality in the Medieval Normative Tradition'. In Bynon and Palmer, eds. 43–55.

Leake, Roy E., Jr. 'The Relationship of Two Ramist Rhetorics: Omer Talon's *Rhetorica* and Antoine Fouquelin's *Rhetorique françoise*'. *Bibliothèque d'Humanisme et Renaissance* 30 (1968): 85–108.

Liaño Pacheco, Jesús María. *Sanctius el Brocense.* Salamanca: Université de Salamanca, 1971.

Llinarès, Armand. 'Le lullisme de Lefèvre d'Étaples et de ses amis humanistes'. In Colloque International de Tours. 127–36.

Logan, Marie-Rose. 'Bovillus on Language'. In *Acta conventus neo-latini amstelodamensis. Proceedings of the Second International Congress of Neo-Latin Studies, Amsterdam, 19–24 August 1973.* Ed. P. Tuynman, G. C. Kuiper, and E. Kessler. Munich: Wilhelm Fink, 1979. 657–66.

Lohr, Charles H. 'The Medieval Interpretation of Aristotle'. In Kretzmann *et al.*, eds. 80–98.

Lubac, Henri de, SJ. *Exégèse médiévale: Les quatre sens de l'écriture.* 2 pts. in 4 vols. Paris: Aubier, 1959–64.

Lusignan, Serge. *Parler vulgairement: Les intellectuels et la langue française aux xiiie et xive siècles.* Paris: Vrin; Montreal: Presses de l'Université de Montréal, 1986.

Lytle, Guy Fitch, and Stephen Orgel, eds. *Patronage in the Renaissance.* Princeton: Princeton University Press, 1981.

Maclean, Ian. *Interpretation and Meaning in the Renaissance: the Case of Law.* Cambridge: Cambridge University Press, 1992.

Maniates, Maria Rika. *Mannerism in Italian Music and Culture, 1530–1630.* Chapel Hill: University of North Carolina Press, 1979.

Margolin, Jean-Claude. 'L'enseignement des mathématiques en France (1540–70): Charles de Bovelles, Fine, Peletier, Ramus'. In *French Renaissance Studies, 1540–70: Humanism and the Encyclopedia.* Ed. Peter Sharratt. Edinburgh: Edinburgh University Press, 1976. 109–55.

'La fonction pragmatique et l'influence culturelle de la *Cornucopiae* de Niccolò Perotti'. *Res Publica Litterarum* 4 (1981): 123–71.

'Mathias Ringmann's *Grammatica figurata*, or, Grammar as a Card Game'. *Yale French Studies* 47 (1972): 33–46.

Masi, Michael, ed. *Boethius and the Liberal Arts: a Collection of Essays*. Berne: Peter Lang, 1981.

Meerhoff, Kees. *Rhétorique et poétique au xvie siècle en France: Du Bellay, Ramus et les autres*. Leiden: E. J. Brill, 1986.

Michelet, Jules. *La Renaissance*. Ed. Robert Casanova. *Oeuvres complètes*. Ed. Paul Viallaneix. Paris: Flammarion, 1978. 7.47–259.

Mikkeli, Heikki. *An Aristotelian Response to Renaissance Humanism: Jacopo Zabarella on the Nature of Arts and Sciences*. Helsinki: SHS, 1992.

Miller, Perry. *The New England Mind: the Seventeenth Century*. Cambridge, MA: Harvard University Press, 1956.

Miller, Peter N. *Defining the Common Good: Empire, Religion and Philosophy in Eighteenth-Century Britain*. Cambridge: Cambridge University Press, 1994.

Minnis, A. J. *Medieval Theory of Authorship: Scholastic Literary Attitudes in the Later Middle Ages*. London: Scolar, 1984.

Monfasani, John. 'Humanism and Rhetoric'. In Rabil, Albert, Jr., ed. 3.171–235.

'Is Valla an Ordinary Language Philosopher?' *Journal of the History of Ideas* 50 (1989): 309–23.

Moyer, Ann E. *Musica Scientia: Musical Scholarship in the Italian Renaissance*. Ithaca and London: Cornell University Press, 1992.

Murdoch, John E. '*Mathesis in philosophiam scholasticam introducta*: the Rise and Development of the Application of Mathematics in Fourteenth-Century Philosophy and Theology'. In *Arts libéraux et philosophie*. 215–54.

Murphy, James J. *Rhetoric in the Middle Ages: a History of Rhetorical Theory from Saint Augustine to the Renaissance*. Berkeley, Los Angeles and London: University of California Press, 1974.

ed. *Renaissance Eloquence: Studies in the Theory and Practice of Renaissance Rhetoric*. Berkeley, Los Angeles and London: University of California Press, 1983.

Murray, Alexander. *Reason and Society in the Middle Ages*. 1978; rpt. Oxford: Clarendon, 1990.

Musial, Stanislas, SJ. 'Dates de naissance et de mort de Charles de Bovelles'. In *Actes du colloque international tenu à Noyon les 14–15–16 septembre 1979: Charles de Bovelles en son cinquième centenaire, 1479–1979*. [Ed. Jean-Claude Margolin (and Marguerite Laporte).] Paris: Guy Trédaniel, 1982. 31–57.

Nelson, Norman E. *Peter Ramus and the Confusion of Logic, Rhetoric, and Poetry*. University of Michigan Contributions in Modern Philology 2. Ann Arbor: University of Michigan Press, 1947.

Olivieri, Luigi, ed. *Aristotelismo veneto e scienza moderna. Atti del 25° anno accademico del Centro per la storia della tradizione aristotelica nel Veneto*. 2 vols. Saggi e testi 17/18. Padua: Antenore, 1983.

Ong, Walter J., SJ. *Ramus and Talon Inventory: a Short Title Inventory of the*

Published Works of Peter Ramus (1515–1572) and of Omer Talon (ca. 1510–1562) . . . . Cambridge, MA: Harvard University Press, 1958.

Ramus, Method, and the Decay of Dialogue: From the Art of Discourse to the Art of Reason. Cambridge, MA: Harvard University Press, 1958.

'Fouquelin's French Rhetoric and the Ramist Vernacular Tradition'. *Studies in Philology* 51 (1954): 127–42.

Padley, G. Arthur. *Grammatical Theory in Western Europe 1500–1700: the Latin Tradition.* Cambridge: Cambridge University Press, 1976.

Grammatical Theory in Western Europe, 1500–1700: Trends in Vernacular Grammar. 2 vols. Cambridge: Cambridge University Press, 1985–88.

Paetow, Louis J. *The Arts Course at Medieval Universities with Special Reference to Grammar and Rhetoric.* University Studies of the University of Illinois 3.7. Champaign: University of Illinois Press, 1910.

Palisca, Claude V. *Humanism in Italian Renaissance Musical Thought.* New Haven and London: Yale University Press, 1985.

'The Science of Sound and Musical Practice'. In Shirley and Hoeniger, eds. *Science and the Arts in the Renaissance.* 59–73.

Panofsky, Erwin. *Perspective as Symbolic Form.* Trans. Christopher S. Wood. New York: Zone, 1991.

Papuli, Giovanni. 'La teoria del *Regressus* come metodo scientifico negli autori della scuola di Padova'. In Olivieri, ed. 221–77.

Parker, Patricia A. *Inescapable Romance: Studies in the Poetics of a Mode.* Princeton and London: Princeton University Press, 1979.

Pater, Walter. *The Renaissance: Studies in Art and Poetry.* Ed. Louis Kronenberger. New York: New American Library, 1959.

Percival, W. Keith. 'Changes in the Approach to Language'. In Kretzmann *et al.*, eds. 808–17.

'The Grammatical Tradition and the Rise of the Vernaculars'. In *Current Trends in Linguistics XIII.* Ed. Thomas A. Sebeok. The Hague and Paris: Mouton, 1975. 231–75.

'The Place of the *Rudimenta grammatica* in the History of Latin Grammar.' *Res Publica Litterarum* 4 (1981): 233–64.

'Renaissance Grammar'. In Rabil, Albert, Jr., ed. *Renaissance Humanism.* 3.67–83.

'Renaissance Grammar: Rebellion or Evolution?' In *Interrogativi dell'umanismo.* Ed. Giovannangiola Tarugi. 3 vols. Florence: L. S. Olshki, 1976. 3.73–90.

Pérez-Ramos, Antonio. *Francis Bacon's Idea of Science and the Maker's Knowledge Tradition.* Oxford: Clarendon, 1988.

Perreiah, Allan. 'Humanist Critiques of Scholastic Dialectic'. *Sixteenth Century Journal* 13.3 (Fall 1982): 3–22.

Pinborg, Jan. *Die Entwicklung der Sprachtheorie im Mittelalter. Beiträge zur Geschichte der Philosophie und Theologie des Mittelalters.* Texte und Untersuchungen 42.2. Münster and Westfalen: Aschendorff; Copenhagen: Frost-Hansen, 1967.

Logik und Semantik im Mittelalter: Ein Überblick. Stuttgart and Bad Canstatt: Frommann-Holzboog, 1972.

Pirro, André. *Descartes et la musique.* 1907; rpt. Geneva: Minkoff, 1973.

Pirrotta, Nino. *Music and Culture in Italy from the Middle Ages to the Baroque: a Collection of Essays*. Cambridge, MA and London: Harvard University Press, 1984.

Poppi, Antonino. *La dottrina della scienza in Giacomo Zabarella*. Padua: Antenore, 1972.

   Introduzione all'aristotelismo padovano. Padua: Antenore, 1970.

Prantl, Carl von. *Geschichte der Logik im Abendlande*. 4 vols. Leipzig: S. Hirzel, 1855–70.

Rabil, Albert, Jr., ed. *Renaissance Humanism: Foundations, Forms, and Legacy*. 3 vols. Philadelphia: University of Pennsylvania Press, 1988.

Randall, John Herman, Jr. 'The Development of Scientific Method in the School of Padua'. In *Renaissance Essays: From the Journal of the History of Ideas*. Ed. Paul Oskar Kristeller and Philip P. Wiener. New York and Evanston: Harper & Row, 1968. 217–51.

Rashdall, Hastings. *The Universities of Europe in the Middle Ages*. Ed. F. M. Powicke and A. B. Emden. 3 vols. 1895, 1936; rpt. Oxford: Clarendon; New York: Oxford University Press, 1987.

Reif, sister Patricia. 'The Textbook Tradition in Natural Philosophy'. *Journal of the History of Ideas* 30 (1969): 17–32.

Reiss, Timothy J. 'Autonomy, Nostalgia, and Writing for the Aesthetic: Notes on Cultures and Exchange'. *Centennial Review* 39.3 (Fall 1995): 513–36.

   'The *concevoir* Motif in Descartes'. In *La cohérence intérieure: Etudes sur la littérature française du xviie siècle, offertes à J.-D. Hubert*. Ed. Jacqueline Van Baelen and David Lee Rubin. Paris: Jean-Michel Place, 1977. 203–22.

   The Discourse of Modernism. Ithaca and London: Cornell University Press, 1982.

   'Du système de la critique classique'. *XVIIe Siècle* 116 (1977): 3–16.

   'The Idea of Meaning and Practice of Method in Pierre de La Ramée, Henri Estienne and Others'. In *Humanism in Crisis: the Decline of the French Renaissance*. Ed. Philippe Desan. Ann Arbor: University of Michigan Press, 1991. 125–51.

   'Mapping Identities: Literature, Nationalism, Colonialism'. *American Literary History* 4.4 (Fall 1992): 649–77.

   The Meaning of Literature. Ithaca and London: Cornell University Press, 1992.

   'Montaigne and the Subject of Polity'. Trans. Timothy Hampton. In *Literary Theory/Renaissance Texts*. Ed. Patricia A. Parker and David Quint. Baltimore and London: Johns Hopkins University Press, 1986. 115–49.

   'Neoaristotle and Method: From Zabarella to Descartes'. Forthcoming.

   'Renaissance Theatre and the Theory of Tragedy'. In *The Cambridge History of Literary Criticism*. Volume III: *The Renaissance*. Ed. Glyn P. Norton. Cambridge: Cambridge University Press, 1997.

   Review essay of Ann E. Moyer, *Musica Scientia*, *Canadian Review of Comparative Literature* 20.3–4 (1993): 513–19.

   '1640, The Jesuit Pedagogue Pierre Le Moyne Publishes *Les Peintures morales*: Problems in Logic and Rhetoric'. In *A New History of French Literature*. General ed. Denis Hollier. Cambridge, MA and London: Harvard University Press, 1989. 258–62.

Tragedy and Truth: Studies in the Development of a Renaissance and Neoclassical Discourse. New Haven and London: Yale University Press, 1980.

'Towards the Early Modern Separation of Disciplines: from Philology to Science and History – Joseph Justus Scaliger'. *Comparative Literature* 48.2 (Spring 1996): 172–9.

The Uncertainty of Analysis: Problems in Truth, Meaning, and Culture. Ithaca and London: Cornell University Press, 1988.

See also: Brathwaite, Kamau.

Renaudet, Augustin. *Préréforme et humanisme à Paris pendant les premières guerres de l'Italie (1494–1517).* 2nd edn. Paris: Librairie d'Argences, 1953.

Rice, Eugene F., Jr. *The Renaissance Idea of Wisdom.* Cambridge, MA: Harvard University Press, 1958.

Rijk, Lambertus Marie de. *Logica modernorum: a Contribution to the History of Early Terminist Logic.* 3 vols. Assen: Van Gorcum, 1962–7.

Risse, Wilhelm. 'La dottrina del metodo di Zabarella'. In Olivieri, ed. 173–86.

Die Logik der Neuzeit, I: 1500–1640. Stuttgart-Bad Canstatt: Friedrich Frommans, 1964.

Robins, Robert Henry. *Ancient and Mediaeval Grammatical Theory in Europe.* London: Bell, 1951.

A Short History of Linguistics. 1967; rpt. London: Longman, 1976.

Rose, Paul Lawrence. *The Italian Renaissance of Mathematics: Studies on Humanists and Mathematicians from Petrarch to Galileo.* Geneva: Droz, 1975.

Rosen, Karl. 'On the Publication of the *Rudimenta grammatica* in France'. *Res Publica Litterarum* 4 (1981): 265–71.

Rosier, Irène. *La grammaire spéculative des Modistes.* Lille: Presses Universitaires de Lille, 1983.

Schabert, Ina. 'Die Trennung von naturwissenschaftlicher und dichterischer Wahrheit im England des 17. Jahrhunderts'. In *Res Publica Litteraria: die Institutionen der Gelehrsamkeit in der frühen Neuzeit.* 2 vols. Wolfenbütteler Arbeiten zur Barockforschung 14. Wiesbaden: Otto Harrassowitz, 1987. 349–64.

Schmitt, Charles Bernard. *The Aristotelian Tradition and Renaissance Universities.* London: Variorum, 1984.

Aristotle and the Renaissance. Cambridge, MA: Harvard University Press, 1983.

Studies in Renaissance Philosophy and Science. London: Variorum, 1981.

and Quentin Skinner, [et al.], eds. *The Cambridge History of Renaissance Philosophy.* Cambridge: Cambridge University Press, 1988.

Schoenberg, Arnold. *Theory of Harmony.* Trans. Roy E. Carter. 1978; rpt. Berkeley and Los Angeles: University of California Press, 1983.

Schüling, Hermann. *Die Geschichte der axiomatischen Methode in 16. und beginnenden 17. Jahrhundert (Wandlung der Wissenschaftauffassung).* Hildesheim and New York: G. Olms, 1969.

Schuster, John Andrew. 'Descartes and the Scientific Revolution, 1618–1634: an Interpretation'. 2 vols. Ph.D. dissertation, Princeton University, 1977.

Scott, Izora. *Controversies over the Imitation of Cicero in the Renaissance.* With translations of letters between Pietro Bembo and Gianfrancesco Pico *On Imitation* and a translation of Desiderius Erasmus, *The Ciceronian (Ciceronianus)*. 1910; rpt. Davis, CA: Hermagoras, 1991.

Seigel, Jerrold E. *Rhetoric and Philosophy in Renaissance Humanism: The Union of Eloquence and Wisdom, Petrarch to Valla*. Princeton: Princeton University Press, 1968.

Sharratt, Peter. 'La Ramée's Early Mathematical Teaching'. *Bibliothèque d'Humanisme et Renaissance* 28 (1966): 605–14.

'Peter Ramus and the Reform of the University: the Divorce of Philosophy and Eloquence?' In *French Renaissance Studies, 1540–70: Humanism and the Encyclopedia*. Ed. Peter Sharratt. Edinburgh: Edinburgh University Press, 1976. 4–20.

Shelby, Lon R. 'Geometry'. In Wagner, ed. *The Seven Liberal Arts*. 196–217.

Shirley, John W., and F. David Hoeniger, eds. *Science and the Arts in the Renaissance*. Washington: Folger Shakespeare Library; London and Toronto: AUP, 1985.

Sinfield, Alan. *Faultlines: Cultural Materialism and the Politics of Dissident Reading*. Berkeley, Los Angeles and Oxford: University of California Press, 1992.

Skulsky, Harold. 'Paduan Epistemology and the Doctrine of the One Mind'. *Journal of the History of Philosophy* 6.4 (October 1968): 341–61.

Stegmann, André. 'La politique de Lefèvre d'Etaples'. In Colloque International de Tours. 303–12.

Stock, Brian. *The Implications of Literacy: Written Language and Models of Interpretation in the Eleventh and Twelfth Centuries*. Princeton: Princeton University Press, 1983.

Listening for the Text: on the Uses of the Past. Baltimore and London: Johns Hopkins University Press, 1990.

Strong, Edward W. *Procedures and Metaphysics: a Study in the Philosophy of Mathematical-Physical Sciences in the Sixteenth and Seventeenth Centuries*. Berkeley: University of California Press, 1936.

Sullivan, Margaret A. *Bruegel's Peasants: Art and Audience in the Northern Renaissance*. Cambridge: Cambridge University Press, 1994.

Swetz, Frank J. *Capitalism and Arithmetic: the New Math of the Fifteenth Century*. Including the Full Text of the *Treviso Arithmetic*. Trans. David Eugene Smith. La Salle, IL: Open Court, 1987.

Taylor, Charles. *Sources of the Self: The Making of the Modern Identity*. Cambridge, MA and London: Harvard University Press, 1989.

Tobin, Richard. 'Ancient Perspective and Euclid's *Optics*'. *Journal of the Warburg and Courtauld Institutes* 53 (1990): 14–41.

Tomlinson, Gary. *Monteverdi and the End of the Renaissance*. 1987; rpt. Berkeley and Los Angeles: University of California Press, 1990.

Music in Renaissance Magic: Toward a Historiography of Others. Chicago: University of Chicago Press, 1993.

Treitler, Leo. *Music and the Historical Imagination*. Cambridge, MA and London: Harvard University Press, 1989.

Tuck, Richard. 'Hobbes and Descartes'. In *Perspectives on Thomas Hobbes*. Ed. G. A. J. Rogers and Alan Ryan. Oxford: Clarendon, 1988. 11–41.

Vance, Eugene. *Mervelous Signals: Poetics and Sign Theory in the Middle Ages.* Lincoln, NE and London: University of Nebraska Press, 1986.
    See also: Brind'amour, Lucie.
Vasoli, Cesare. *La dialettica e la retorica dell'Umanesimo: 'Invenzione' e 'Metodo' nella cultura del xv e xvi secolo.* Milan: Feltrinelli, 1968.
    'Introduction'. In Jacobi Zabarellae. *De methodis libri quatuor; Liber de regressu.* Ed. Cesare Vasoli. Bologna: CLUEB, 1985. xi–xxviii.
Verdonk, Johannes Jacobus. *Petrus Ramus en de Wiskunde.* Assen: Van Gorcum, 1966.
Vickers, Brian. *In Defence of Rhetoric.* 1988; rpt. Oxford: Clarendon, 1990.
Victor, Joseph M. *Charles de Bovelles, 1479–1553: an Intellectual Biography.* Geneva: Droz, 1978.
    'Charles de Bovelles and Nicholas de Pax: Two Sixteenth-Century Biographies of Ramon Lull'. *Traditio* 32 (1976): 313–45.
    'The Revival of Lullism at Paris, 1499–1516'. *Renaissance Quarterly* 28.4 (Winter 1975): 504–34.
Waddington, Charles Tzaunt. *Ramus (Pierre de La Ramée): Sa vie, ses écrits et ses opinions.* Paris: Ch. Meyrueis, 1855.
Wagner, David Leslie, ed. *The Seven Liberal Arts in the Middle Ages.* Bloomington: Indiana University Press, 1983.
Walker, Daniel Pickering. *Music, Spirit and Language in the Renaissance.* Ed. Penelope Gouk. London: Variorum, 1985.
    Studies in Musical Science in the Late Renaissance. London: Warburg Institute; Leiden: Brill, 1978.
Wallace, William A., OP. 'Aristotelian Science and Rhetoric in Transition: the Middle Ages and the Renaissance'. *Rhetorica* 7.1 (1989): 7–21.
    Galileo and His Sources: the Heritage of the Collegio Romano in Galileo's Science. Princeton and London: Princeton University Press, 1984.
    Galileo, the Jesuits and the Medieval Aristotle. London: Variorum, 1981.
    Prelude to Galileo: Essays on Medieval and Sixteenth-Century Sources of Galileo's Thought. Dordrecht, Boston and London: Reidel, 1981.
Waswo, Richard. *Language and Meaning in the Renaissance.* Princeton: Princeton University Press, 1987.
    'Motives of Misreading'. *Journal of the History of Ideas* 50 (1989): 324–32.
Weimann, Robert. *Authority and Representation in Early Modern Discourse.* Ed. David Hillman. Baltimore and London: Johns Hopkins University Press, 1996.
White, John. *The Birth and Rebirth of Pictorial Space*, 3rd edn. Cambridge, MA: Harvard University Press, 1987.
Whitrow, G. J. 'Why Did Mathematics Begin to Take Off in the Sixteenth Century?' In Hay, ed. *Mathematics from Manuscript to Print.* 264–9.
Woolf, Virginia. *To the Lighthouse.* 1927; rpt. New York: Modern Library, 1937.
Yates, Frances Amelia. *The French Academies of the Sixteenth Century.* Studies of the Warburg Institute XV. 1947; rpt. Nendeln, Liechtenstein: Kraus, 1968.
    The Rosicrucian Enlightenment. 1972; rpt. St. Albans: Paladin, 1975.

Zedelmaier, Helmut. *Bibliotheca universalis und Bibiotheca selecta: Das
 Problem der Ordnung des gelehrten Wissens in der frühen Neuzeit.*
 Cologne, Weimar and Vienna: Böhlau Verlag, 1992.
Zumthor, Paul. *Essai de poétique médiévale.* Paris: Seuil, 1972.
 Le masque et la lumière: la poétique des grands rhétoriqueurs. Paris: Seuil,
 1978.

Index

Dates are given for people born before 1800. Moderns are indexed only if named for other than a simple bibliographical reference.

CAMBRIDGE STUDIES IN RENAISSANCE LITERATURE AND CULTURE

General Editor
STEPHEN ORGEL
Jackson Eli Reynolds Professor of Humanities, Stanford University

DATE DUE

APR 1 6 1998	
APR 1 3 2000	

UPI 261-2505 G   PRINTED IN U.S.A.